"十三五"江苏省高等学校重点教材（编号：2020-2-258）

A Crash Course on Keylearning
and Keywriting for Chinese

# 汉字键学与键写简明教程

季一木　主编

哈尔滨工业大学出版社

## Abstract

This textbook is a concise tutorial written for those foreigners who are in the early stage of learning Chinese language, teaching the integrated solution of "Chinese character keylearning" and "Chinese character keywriting". It has two purposes: First, it is convenient for the foreign Chinese beginners who are familiar with the most basic knowledge of Chinese Pinyin and Chinese characters to easily code Chinese characters, so that they can look up and learn a new Chinese character that is not known by them how to read it and what its meaning is on the dictionary APP at anytime and anywhere; The second is to improve the efficiency and accuracy of foreigners' character input in paperless Chinese office, so as to give play to their keyboard writing skills that can be typed blindly. In authors' opinion, the tool introduced in this tutorial belong to the category of informatization infrastructure for TCFL.

## 内容简介

本书是为初学汉语的外国人编写的、教授"汉字键学"与"汉字键写"一体化解决方案的简明教程。其目的有二：一是方便那些已经熟悉汉语拼音和汉字最基本知识的外国汉语初学者对汉字进行编码，以便随时随地可以在字典APP上查阅、学习不知道读音和意思的汉语生字；二是提高外国人中文无纸化办公的文字输入效率和正确率，以便发挥他们可以盲打的键盘写作技能。在我们看来，本书所述工具属于对外汉语教学信息化基础设施的范畴。

### 图书在版编目(CIP)数据

汉字键学与键写简明教程＝A Crash Course on Keylearning and Keywriting for Chinese：汉、英/季一木主编. —哈尔滨：哈尔滨工业大学出版社，2023.1

ISBN 978-7-5767-0527-0

Ⅰ.①汉… Ⅱ.①季… Ⅲ.①汉语-对外汉语教学-教材 Ⅳ.①H195.4

中国版本图书馆 CIP 数据核字(2023)第 016278 号

责任编辑　丁桂焱
封面设计　刘　乐
出版发行　哈尔滨工业大学出版社
社　　址　哈尔滨市南岗区复华四道街10号　邮编150006
传　　真　0451-86414749
网　　址　http://hitpress.hit.edu.cn
印　　刷　黑龙江艺德印刷有限责任公司
开　　本　787 mm×1092 mm　1/16　印张13　字数309千字
版　　次　2023年1月第1版　2023年1月第1次印刷
书　　号　ISBN 978-7-5767-0527-0
定　　价　39.80元

(如因印装质量问题影响阅读,我社负责调换)

# Foreword
# 前　言

The two main characters of the cartoon *Tom & Jerry* often came into our conversations since we planned to write this book. Just like Tom and Jerry trying to teach each other his ∕ her own language, it is obviously very difficult to teach a foreign language to someone who is lack of the target language environment. Such is the case with teaching Chinese as a foreign language. More unfortunately, most of the foreigners studying Chinese all over the world are learning Chinese without a Chinese environment. So, this book was written for them.

自从我们打算撰写本书之日起,卡通片《猫和老鼠》的两位主角就时常出现在我们的交谈之中。外语教学,就像 Tom 和 Jerry 各自想要教会对方掌握自己的语言一样,在对方欠缺语言环境的情况下,这显然是一件苦差事。汉语对外教学就是如此。更令人遗憾的是,在全球学习汉语的外国人当中,大多数都是在没有中文环境的情况下学习汉语的。所以,本书就是为他们而写的。

In fact, the Easy Chinese Code™ (ECCode™ for short) introduced in this book is an entirely new and effective patent way of lifelong learning Chinese characters for Chinese learners, especially for the beginners without a Chinese environment while wanting to know how to read a new character, what its meanings, etc. Meanwhile, with higher speed and lower error rate, i.e., with more efficiency and better quality, ECCode™ is the best method for those foreign people who use Chinese as a working language to KEYWRITE Chinese characters especially in the paperless office environment.

事实上,对于汉语学习者来说,本书所介绍的"汉易码™"(英文简称 ECCode™)是一种全新有效的、帮助汉语学习者终身学习汉字的专利方法。尤其是对那些没有汉语环境而想知道汉语生字怎么读、是什么意思……的初学者而言,这个方法更加有效。同时,对于那些把汉语当作工作语言的外国人来说,"汉易码™"是他们键写汉字的最好方法。尤其是在无纸化办公的要求下,这个方法具有更高的打字速度、更低的打错字比率,亦即打字效率更高、打字质量更好。

As a reader, if you have been familiar with Chinese Pinyin which can help you know how to read a Chinese character after you have found it out in an e-dictionary, you can skip the 3.2 "Pronunciation of the Chinese character (Chinese Pinyin)" and directly read other contents. Of course, we wish you to do the exercises seriously in each section which can help you understand the content of each section better.

作为读者,如果大家已经十分熟悉那些可以帮助认读在电子词典中查到的汉语拼音的话,那么就可以跳过 3.2 节"汉字发音(汉语拼音)"这一节,直接阅读其他章节内容。

当然，我们希望读者能够认真地做一下各章所附的练习题，这些练习题将有助于加深读者对各章节所教授内容的理解。

Here, we would like to express our heartfelt thanks to Mr. Ma Hong, the inventor of the ECCode™. Thanks to him for giving us a detailed introduction to the design ideas and principles of the ECCode™, which is very helpful for us to formulate the architecture of this book. At the same time, we would also like to thank Mr. Ma Wei for his help in creating many Chinese character deconstruction pictures and his good suggestions on the layout of the book. Finally, thank Nanjing Chengyou Information Technology Co., Ltd. for its support.

在此，我们要对"汉易码™"的发明人马洪先生表示衷心的感谢。感谢他给我们详细地介绍了"汉易码™"的设计思想和设计原则，这对于我们构思本书的架构十分有益。同时，我们还要感谢马玮先生帮助制作了不少汉字拆解图片，并对全书的篇章布局提供了很多很好的建议。最后，感谢南京承邮信息科技有限公司的支持。

If you have any questions or suggestions about this book, please do not hesitate to contact us directly by using the following contact methods:

关于本书，如果大家有什么疑问或建议，请不要犹豫，可使用下面的联系方法直接跟我们联系：

E-mail(邮箱):jiym@njupt.edu.cn; lsd@njupt.edu.cn; mawei@fingerchinese.com

WeChat ID(微信账号): kaijikaoti

WeChat QR Code(微信二维码):

扫一扫上面的二维码图案，加我为朋友

Yimu Ji(季一木)

Oct. 31, 2021(2021 年 10 月 31 日)

# Chart Indices
# 图索引

Figure 2.1 NEW PRACTICAL CHINESE READER(BOOK 1)
图 2.1《新实用汉语读本》(第一册) ·················································· 14

Figure 3.1 Knowledge framework of the computer Chinese character theory of ECCode™
图 3.1 "汉易码™"计算机汉字知识框架 ············································ 17

Figure 3.2 Constituent classification of a Chinese character
图 3.2 汉字组分示例 ·································································· 18

Figure 3.3 Illustration of initial, final and syllable in Chinese Pinyin
图 3.3 汉字声母、韵母和音节示例 ·················································· 20

Figure 3.4 The syllable of the Chinese character "永"
图 3.4 汉字"永"的音节示例 ························································· 45

Figure 3.5 Chinese vowel illustration adapted from Google images
图 3.5 改编自谷歌的汉语元音舌位图 ··············································· 54

Figure 3.6 Examples of a Chinese character with a different meaning because of a different tone
图 3.6 相同音节不同声调表示不同汉字的例字 ································· 55

Figure 3.7 Graph of the sound value of Tone 1 and its feature of pronunciation flatness
图 3.7 第一声的音高值及其发音平滑度示例 ····································· 57

Figure 3.8 Graph of the sound value of Tone 2 and its feature of pronunciation flatness
图 3.8 第二声音高值及其发音平滑度示例 ········································ 57

Figure 3.9 Graph of the sound value of Tone 3 and its feature of pronunciation flatness
图 3.9 第三声音高值及其发音平滑度示例 ········································ 57

Figure 3.10 The tone of a character with Tone 3 changes with the subsequent character with other tones
图 3.10 后面跟其他声调的第三声汉字的音调变化示例 ······················· 58

Figure 3.11 The tone of a character with Tone 3 changes because of the subsequent Tone 3 character
图 3.11 后面跟第三声汉字的第一个第三声汉字的声调变化示例 ··········· 58

Figure 3.12 Graph of the sound value of Tone 4 and its feature of pronunciation flatness
图 3.12 第四声音高值及其发音平滑度示例 ······································ 59

Figure 3.13 Graphic explanation of the sound value of light tone or neutral tone
图 3.13 中性声调音高值图示 ······················································· 60

Figure 3.14 Comparison of the sound interval and volume of the four tones and the light tone
图 3.14 四个声调以及轻声的音程及其音高值变化比较图示 ················· 60

Figure 3.15 Illustration of the complete composition of Pinyin

图 3.15 汉字拼音的完整构成 ·················································· 61
Figure 3.16 The disassembly map of the Chinese character "赢"
图 3.16 汉字"赢"的拆解示例 ·················································· 64
Figure 3.17 Illustrating dictionary lookup method by the ECCode™
图 3.17 图解"汉易码™"查字典方法 ·········································· 67
Figure 3.18 One situation of learning Chinese characters anywhere and anytime
图 3.18 随时随地学习汉语的一种场景示例 ·································· 68
Figure 3.19 Character with the combination of its last two strokes
图 3.19 汉字最后两笔画组合的例字 ··········································· 81
Figure 3.20 Two characters with the stroke combination (丿、)
图 3.20 笔画组合为(丿、)的两个汉字字例 ································· 81
Figure 3.21 A character with the stroke combination (一 乛)
图 3.21 笔画组合为(一 乛)的字例 ············································ 82
Figure 3.22 A character with the stroke combination (丿 乛)
图 3.22 笔画组合为(丿 乛)的字例 ············································ 82
Figure 3.23 A character with the combination (、一) as its first two strokes
图 3.23 前两笔画组合为(、一)的字例 ······································· 83
Figure 3.24 The combination of the first or last two strokes of the character "象"
图 3.24 "象"字前两个笔画组合与最后两个笔画组合 ······················ 83
Figure 3.25 The combination of the first or last two strokes of the character "赢"
图 3.25 "赢"字的前两个笔画和最后两个笔画的组合图示 ················ 83
Figure 3.26 Inclusion relationship between constituents and radicals of Chinese characters
图 3.26 汉字组分与字根之间的包含关系 ····································· 84
Figure 3.27 Classification of shape constituents (letters) of the Chinese character
图 3.27 汉字字形组分(字母)构成分类示例 ································· 86
Figure 3.28 Left-right structure
图 3.28 左右结构汉字 ···························································· 104
Figure 3.29 Two-upper-and-one-lower structure
图 3.29 "上二下一"结构示例 ··················································· 104
Figure 3.30 One-upper-and-two-lower structure
图 3.30 "上一下二"结构示例 ··················································· 105
Figure 3.31 The Chinese Character "哭"
图 3.31 汉字"哭" ································································· 106
Figure 4.1 Graphic explanations of the constituents of a computer Chinese character code
图 4.1 计算机汉字代码的构成组分图解 ······································ 112
Figure 4.2 Illustration of the macro stroke order of the character "品"
图 4.2 汉字"品"宏观笔顺示例 ················································· 117

Figure 4.3 biáng biáng miàn, the name of a kind of Chinese noodles

图 4.3 biáng biáng 面,一种中国面条的名称 ·················· 122

Figure 4.4 The encoding formula of ECCode™

图 4.4 "汉易码™"编码公式 ························· 126

Figure 4.5 The encoding flow chart of the Mixed Chinese Character

图 4.5 杂合体字编码流程图 ························· 153

Figure 4.6 A nonfigurative expression of an MCC

图 4.6 杂合体字的抽象图示法 ······················· 155

Figure 4.7 Character display box

图 4.7 汉字显示框示例 ··························· 178

Figure 4.8 Illustration of a display box with more than one question mark key "?" while inputting a character

图 4.8 多个问号键"?"情况下的输入显示框示例 ············ 179

Figure 4.9 Illustration of the code for a phrase including two characters

图 4.9 双字词编码举例 ··························· 181

Figure 4.10 Illustration of the code for a phrase including three characters

图 4.10 三字词编码举例 ·························· 182

Figure 4.11 Illustration of the code for a phrase including four characters

图 4.11 四字词编码举例 ·························· 183

Figure 4.12 Illustration of the code for a phrase including more than four characters

图 4.12 四个字以上词组编码举例 ···················· 183

# Table Indices
# 表索引

Table 1.1 The basic similarities and differences between Chinese characters and English words
表1.1 中英文字的基本异同点对比表 ·················································· 3
Table 3.1 The initial list and explanation of Chinese Pinyin
表3.1 汉语拼音声母表说明 ·························································· 21
Table 3.2 The final list and explanation of Chinese Pinyin
表3.2 汉语拼音韵母表说明 ·························································· 31
Table 3.3 Individual explanations
表3.3 特别说明 ········································································ 45
Table 3.4 Chinese Pinyin initial and final spelling chart
表3.4 汉语拼音声母韵母拼读表 ···················································· 47
Table 3.5 Examples of "light tone"
表3.5 "轻声"汉字音节举例 ························································· 60
Table 3.6 Illustration of adjacent/noncontact relation between two strokes
表3.6 笔画位置之分离关系举例 ···················································· 64
Table 3.7 Illustration of intersection relation between two strokes
表3.7 笔画位置之交叉关系举例 ···················································· 64
Table 3.8 Illustration of connecting relation between two strokes
表3.8 笔画位置之相连关系举例 ···················································· 65
Table 3.9 Various shapes of brush strokes in Chinese characters
表3.9 汉字各种形状毛笔笔画表 ···················································· 66
Table 3.10 Table of 5 basic strokes which cover respectively its same type stroke of itself
表3.10 5个基本笔画所代表的同类笔画示例 ····································· 70
Table 3.11 The combinations of two strokes out of the five basic strokes
表3.11 5个基本笔画中挑出2个笔画的组合 ····································· 80
Table 3.12 Simplication of Table 3.11 for two-stroke combinations
表3.12 两笔画组合简化表 ··························································· 80
Table 3.13 Examples of characters including the radical "亻"
表3.13 含有"亻"的汉字举例 ······················································· 85
Table 3.14 The key mapping table of shape constituents (letters) of Chinese characters in EC-Code™
表3.14 "汉易码™"汉字字形键位(字母)表 ···································· 87
Table 3.15 The radicals with the property of phonetic similarity
表3.15 具有音相似属性的字根表 ·················································· 89
Table 3.16 The radicals with the property of shape similarity

1

表 3.16 形相似字根表 ·················································································· 96
Table 3.17 The radical and its code-element which need to be remembered on purpose
表 3.17 一个需要费心记忆的字根及其码元 ························································ 98
Table 3.18 Ten combinations of two different strokes, five combinations of one stroke and itself and their code-elements
表 3.18 10 个不同笔画组合以及 5 个基本笔画与自身的组合及其码元 ················· 99
Table 3.19 Classification of Detached Chinese Characters
表 3.19 分体字分类表 ··············································································· 100
Table 3.20 Abstract graphic expression of Mixed Chinese Characters
表 3.20 杂合体字的抽象表达方式 ································································ 101
Table 3.21 General rules of stroke order
表 3.21 笔顺的一般规则 ············································································ 102
Table 4.1 The computer code of "百"
表 4.1 汉字"百"的计算机代码 ···································································· 118
Table 4.2 The computer code of "米"
表 4.2 汉字"米"的计算机代码 ···································································· 119
Table 4.3 The computer code of "秦"
表 4.3 汉字"秦"的计算机代码 ···································································· 120
Table 4.4 The computer code of traditional Chinese character "東"
表 4.4 繁体字"東"的计算机代码 ·································································· 121
Table 4.5 The general site ($S_x$) for each encoding constituent of the Detached Chinese Character
表 4.5 分体字中每个编码组分的大致位置 ····················································· 123
Table 4.6 Nonfigurative sketch for the general site ($S_x$) for each encoding constituent of an MCC
表 4.6 杂合体字中每个编码组分大致位置的抽象示意图 ································· 124
Table 4.7 The demonstrations of supplemental provision 1~4 on DCC
表 4.7 针对分体字的补充规定之字例 ·························································· 128
Table 4.8 The demonstrations of supplemental provision 5 on DCC
表 4.8 分体字补充规则 5 字例 ···································································· 130
Table 4.9 The disassembly of "川" and its coding demon.
表 4.9 汉字"川"的拆解及其编码示例 ·························································· 132
Table 4.10 The disassembly of "坚" and its coding demon.
表 4.10 汉字"坚"的拆解及其编码示例 ························································ 132
Table 4.11 The disassembly of "你" and its coding demon.
表 4.11 汉字"你"的拆解及其编码示例 ························································ 133
Table 4.12 The disassembly of "他" and its coding demon.
表 4.12 汉字"他"的拆解及其编码示例 ························································ 133

Table 4.13 The disassembly of "她" and its coding demon.
表4.13 汉字"她"的拆解及其编码示例 ·················································· 134
Table 4.14 The disassembly of "妈" and its coding demon.
表4.14 汉字"妈"的拆解及其编码示例 ·················································· 134
Table 4.15 The disassembly of "吗" and its coding demon.
表4.15 汉字"吗"的拆解及其编码示例 ·················································· 135
Table 4.16 The disassembly of "码" and its coding demon.
表4.16 汉字"码"的拆解及其编码示例 ·················································· 136
Table 4.17 The disassembly of "印" and its coding demon.
表4.17 汉字"印"的拆解及其编码示例 ·················································· 136
Table 4.18 The disassembly of "朝" and its coding demon.
表4.18 汉字"朝"的拆解及其编码示例 ·················································· 137
Table 4.19 The disassembly of "乱" and its coding demon.
表4.19 汉字"乱"的拆解及其编码示例 ·················································· 138
Table 4.20 The disassembly of "故" and its coding demon.
表4.20 汉字"故"的拆解及其编码示例 ·················································· 138
Table 4.21 The disassembly of "题" and its coding demon.
表4.21 汉字"题"的拆解及其编码示例 ·················································· 139
Table 4.22 The disassembly of "赵" and its coding demon.
表4.22 汉字"赵"的拆解及其编码示例 ·················································· 140
Table 4.23 The disassembly of "毯" and its coding demon.
表4.23 汉字"毯"的拆解及其编码示例 ·················································· 140
Table 4.24 The disassembly of "邀" and its coding demon.
表4.24 汉字"邀"字的拆解及其编码示例 ··············································· 141
Table 4.25 The disassembly of "逛" and its coding demon.
表4.25 汉字"逛"的拆解及其编码示例 ·················································· 142
Table 4.26 The disassembly of "哭" and its coding demon.
表4.26 汉字"哭"的拆解及其编码示例 ·················································· 142
Table 4.27 The disassembly of "器" and its coding demon.
表4.27 汉字"器"的拆解及其编码示例 ·················································· 143
Table 4.28 Part A and Part B of "器"
表4.28 汉字"器"的 A 和 B 两个部分的划分示例 ·································· 143
Table 4.29 The disassembly of "架" and its coding demon.
表4.29 汉字"架"的拆解及其编码示例 ·················································· 144
Table 4.30 The disassembly of "赢" and its coding demon.
表4.30 汉字"赢"的拆解及其编码示例 ·················································· 145
Table 4.31 Part A and Part B of "赢"
表4.31 汉字"赢"的 A 部分和 B 部分划分方法示例 ······························· 145

Table 4.32 The disassembly of "霞" and its coding demon.
表4.32 汉字"霞"的拆解及其编码示例 ················································ 146
Table 4.33 The disassembly of "范" and its coding demon.
表4.33 汉字"范"的拆解及其编码示例 ················································ 147
Table 4.34 The disassembly of "茄" and its coding demon.
表4.34 汉字"茄"的拆解及其编码示例 ················································ 147
Table 4.35 The disassembly of "茫" and its coding demon.
表4.35 汉字"茫"的拆解及其编码示例 ················································ 148
Table 4.36 The disassembly of "准" and its coding demon.
表4.36 汉字"准"的拆解及其编码示例 ················································ 149
Table 4.37 Part A and Part B of "准"
表4.37 像"准"一类左右结构汉字的A部分和B部分的划分方法 ················ 149
Table 4.38 The disassembly of "续" and its coding demon.
表4.38 汉字"续"的拆解及其编码示例 ················································ 150
Table 4.39 The disassembly of "掉" and its coding demon.
表4.39 汉字"掉"的拆解及其编码示例 ················································ 150
Table 4.40 The disassembly of"被" and its coding demon.
表4.40 汉字"被"的拆解及其编码示例 ················································ 151
Table 4.41 The disassembly of the MCC "春" and its coding demon.
表4.41 杂合体字"春"的拆解及其编码示例 ·········································· 157
Table 4.42 The disassembly of the MCC "表" and its coding demon.
表4.42 杂合体字"表"的拆解及其编码示例 ·········································· 159
Table 4.43 The disassembly of the MCC "严" and its coding demon.
表4.43 杂合体字"严"的拆解及其编码示例 ·········································· 161
Table 4.44 The disassembly of the MCC "我" and its coding demon.
表4.44 杂合体字"我"的拆解及其编码示例 ·········································· 162
Table 4.45 The disassembly of the MCC "在" and its coding demon.
表4.45 杂合体字"在"的拆解及其编码示例 ·········································· 164
Table 4.46 The disassembly of the MCC "束" and its coding demon.
表4.46 杂合体字"束"的拆解及其编码示例 ·········································· 165
Table 4.47 The disassembly of the MCC "夹" and its coding demon.
表4.47 杂合体字"夹"的拆解及其编码示例 ·········································· 167
Table 4.48 The disassembly of "第" and its coding demon.
表4.48 杂合体字"第"的拆解及其编码示例 ·········································· 168
Table 4.49 The disassembly of "承" and its coding demon.
表4.49 杂合体字"承"的拆解及其编码示例 ·········································· 168
Table 4.50 The disassembly of "爽" and its coding demon.
表4.50 杂合体字"爽"的拆解及其编码示例 ·········································· 169

Table 4.51 The disassembly of "母" and its coding demon.
表4.51 杂合体字"母"的拆解及其编码示例 ·················· 170
Table 4.52 The disassembly of "壹" and its coding demon.
表4.52 杂合体字"壹"的拆解及其编码示例 ·················· 170
Table 4.53 The disassembly of "聋" and its coding demon.
表4.53 杂合体字"聋"的拆解及其编码示例 ·················· 171
Table 4.54 The disassembly of "病" and its coding demon.
表4.54 杂合体字"病"的拆解及其编码示例 ·················· 172
Table 4.55 The disassembly of "包" and its coding demon.
表4.55 杂合体字"包"的拆解及其编码示例 ·················· 172
Table 4.56 The disassembly of "司" and its coding demon.
表4.56 杂合体字"司"的拆解及其编码示例 ·················· 173
Table 4.57 The disassembly of "国" and its coding demon.
表4.57 杂合体字"国"的拆解及其编码示例 ·················· 174
Table 4.58 The disassembly of "再" and its coding demon.
表4.58 杂合体字"再"的拆解及其编码示例 ·················· 174
Table 4.59 The disassembly of "画" and its coding demon.
表4.59 杂合体字"画"的拆解及其编码示例 ·················· 175
Table 4.60 The disassembly of "笔" and its coding demon.
表4.60 杂合体字"笔"的拆解及其编码示例 ·················· 176
Table 4.61 The disassembly of "戈" and its coding demon.
表4.61 杂合体字"戈"的拆解及其编码示例 ·················· 176
Table 4.62 The disassembly of "必" and its coding demon.
表4.62 杂合体字"必"的拆解及其编码示例 ·················· 177
Table 4.63 Code of the character "浙" while not knowing its pronunciation
表4.63 不知道读音时"浙"字的代码 ························ 178

# Contents
# 目 录

Chapter 1　The similarities and differences between learning Chinese by ECCode™ and learning English 英语学习与使用"汉易码™"学习汉语的异同点 ················· 1

 1.1　The basic similarities and differences between Chinese and English characters 中英文字的基本异同点 ·················································· 1

 1.2　Introduction to "Keylearning Chinese Characters" and "Keywriting Chinese Characters" "汉字键学"与"汉字键写"简介 ··························· 7

 1.3　What problems does the course solve 本教程解决哪些问题 ··············· 9

 Review 1 复习题1 ······························································ 10

Chapter 2　Introduction to Chinese character encoding 汉字编码概述 ············ 11

 2.1　What are a computer Chinese character and its encoding theory 什么是计算机汉字及其编码理论 ···················································· 11

 2.2　Overview of the development of CCCT 计算机汉字理论概述 ············ 11

 2.3　How to evaluate the quality of the Chinese character encoding theory 如何评价一种汉字编码理论的质量 ················································· 13

 Review 2 复习题2 ······························································ 14

Chapter 3　Basic knowledge 基础知识 ············································ 16

 3.1　A constituent of a Chinese character 汉字的构成组分 ···················· 16

 3.2　Pronunciation of the Chinese character (Chinese Pinyin) 汉语拼音 ······ 19

 3.3　Strokes and their position relation 笔画及笔画间的位置关系 ············ 62

 3.4　Five basic strokes and stroke combination 5个基本笔画及笔画组合 ····· 68

 3.5　Differences between shape constituents and radicals of Chinese Characters 汉字的字形组分与字根(偏旁部首)的区别 ······································ 84

 3.6　Structures of Chinese characters in the ECCode™ "汉易码™"定义的汉字结构 ························································································ 99

 3.7　Stroke order and macro stroke order 笔顺与宏观笔顺 ·················· 102

 Review 3 复习题3 ····························································· 105

Chapter 4　How to input a Chinese character without knowing its pronunciation 如何输入不知道读音的汉字 ························································· 111

 4.1　A brief introduction to the encoding theory of the Easy Chinese Code (ECCode™) "汉易码™"编码理论概要 ·········································· 111

 4.2　Probability thinking of Easy Chinese Code and four encoding rules "汉易码™"中的概率思想及四个编码规则 ········································· 113

 4.3　A coding formula of Chinese characters in ECCode™ "汉易码™"编码公式 ······ 121

1

  4.4 Supplemental provision on the structure of Detached Chinese Character 对分体字的补充规定 ·················································································· 127
  4.5 The encoding method and examples of Chinese characters with unknown pronunciation 未知读音汉字的编码方法及其举例 ················································· 177
  4.6 Phrase input method 词组输入方法································································ 180
  Review 4 复习题 4 ····················································································· 183
Appendixes 附录 ······························································································ 189
  Appendix 1 Encoding flow chart of ECCode™ 附录 1　"汉易码™"编码流程图 ······ 189
  Appendix 2 Glossary 附录 2　术语 ······················································· 191
References 参考文献 ························································································ 192

# Chapter 1   The similarities and differences between learning Chinese by ECCode™ and learning English

# 英语学习与使用"汉易码™"学习汉语的异同点

## 1.1   The basic similarities and differences between Chinese and English characters
## 中英文字的基本异同点

Many foreign friends plunge into the "forest" of Chinese characters and are often puzzled by the Chinese characters paralleling "trees" one by one when they just start to learn Chinese. Faced with the Chinese characters completely different from any kind of phonography they are familiar with, they often feel that learning Chinese characters seems like a prohibitively difficult thing.

很多外国朋友学习汉语的时候,一头扎进汉字的"森林"里,往往会被一个个汉字"树木"所困扰——面对完全不同于自己所熟知的表音文字,他们会常常感到学习汉字真的比登天还难。

Therefore, in order to avoid the drawbacks of this learning method of "Can't see the forest for the trees" and ease the fear of learning Chinese, it's given here a comparative table of the characteristics of Chinese characters and alphabetic writing in terms of characters, so that you can macroscopically grasp the similarities and differences between Chinese characters and phonographic writing you are familiar with (see Table 1.1 below). It is hoped that the comparison can help to deepen your perceptual understanding of Chinese characters and then step into the palace of Chinese calmly.

所以,为了避免这种"只见树木,不见森林"的学习方法之弊端,也为了缓解读者对汉语学习的畏难情绪,我们列出了汉语和拼音语言在文字方面的特征对比表(参见表1.1),以便大家能够从宏观上把握汉语与自己所熟悉的表音文字的异同点。借此,我们希望能够帮助大家加深对汉字的感性认识,进而从容地迈进汉语的殿堂。

Of course, since everybody may still "have no clear concept" for Chinese characters now, each one may feel puzzled about some of the noun concepts described in Table 1.1. But it doesn't matter, you just need to know their comparative items (namely their counterparts) in

English and have some impression left. With the continuous deepening of Chinese learning in the future, you will have much time to "chew the cud like a cow" to recall the significance of all the comparative items in Table 1.1, which will be of great help to your Chinese learning.

  当然了,由于大家现在对汉字可能还处于"完全没有概念"的状态,所以表1.1当中有关汉字描述的一些名词概念,大家可能同样也感到莫名其妙。但没有关系,大家只需了解其在英文当中的对比项而留有些许印象即可。随着以后汉语学习的不断深入,大家会有大量的时间反复了解消化表1.1中各项对比的意义之所在,进而对汉语学习产生巨大的助益。

# Chapter 1  The similarities and differences between learning Chinese by ECCode™ and learning English
英语学习与使用"汉易码™"学习汉语的异同点

Table 1.1  The basic similarities and differences between Chinese characters and English words
表 1.1  中英文字的基本异同点对比表

| Comparisons 比较项目 | Language types 语言类型 ||||
|---|---|---|---|---|
| | Various alphabetic writing 各种拼音文字 || Chinese character 汉字 ||
| | Letter 字母 | Opinions & explanations 观点与说明 | Stroke—including two geometrical elements: dot and line 笔画——包含点和线两种几何元素 | Opinions & explanations 观点与说明 |
| The smallest constituent unit of an English word or a Chinese character 字词构成最小单元 | | Letters among a word can be mostly handwritten in succession as a single stroke, making the word appear as a whole 手书时构成单词的字母可以多个字母甚至所有字母连写，从而使得一个单词看上去为一个整体 | | In principle, the vast majority of Chinese characters cannot be handwritten in succession as a single stroke unless some inverted strokes are allowed 原则上来说，除非允许"倒笔画"现象，绝大多数汉字是无法通过单一笔画的连续书写来完成的 |
| Structure: The geometric dimensionality of the writing of words or characters 结构：文字书写的几何维度 | It doesn't emphasize the positioning layout of letters composing a word 不强调构词单词字母的位置布局 | There's no importance of top, bottom, left or right position for the constituted strokes of a letter 对于构成字母的笔画来说，其上下左右的位置概念并不重要 | It is a kind of two-dimensional writing, constrained by the structures of Chinese characters, and emphasizes the positioning layout of strokes composing a character 受制于汉字结构，汉字都是二维书写，强调构字笔画的位置布局 | It pays special attention to the top, bottom, left or right position of strokes in the Chinese character 汉字对笔画的上下左右位置特别重视 |

3

Table 1.1 (Continued) 表 1.1（续）

| Comparisons 比较项目 | Language types 语言类型 | | | |
|---|---|---|---|---|
| | Various alphabetic writing 各种拼音文字 | Opinions & explanations 观点与说明 | Chinese character 汉字 | Opinions & explanations 观点与说明 |
| Shape constituents of a word or a character 字词的字形组分 | Word root or letter 字根或字母 | There're no concepts of top or bottom position 对于构词字根或字母来说，没有上下的位置概念 | Basic structural parts of Chinese characters, RADICALs or strokes 偏旁部首或笔画 | The positions of all of the basic structural parts in a Chinese character, namely the positions of radicals and (／or ) strokes, determine what a character it would be 汉字中偏、旁、部首和笔画的位置决定了这个汉字究竟是哪个字 |
| Phoneme-grapheme relationship 音形关系 | Phoneme and grapheme connect with each other closely 关系紧密，音形相伴 | The spelling of a word can basically be inferred from its pronunciation, and the pronunciation of a word can basically be inferred from its spelling 基本上可以由音知道词的拼写，由拼写知道词的发音 | Phoneme and grapheme separate from each other and there's no obvious relationship between them 字音分离，字音与字形之间没有明显的关系 | Knowing the pronunciation of a Chinese character does not necessarily mean knowing the way it is written. Similarly, knowing its writing does not necessarily mean knowing its pronunciation 知道汉字的读音不一定就知道这个字的写法，知道写法也不一定知道这个字的读法 |

Chapter 1　The similarities and differences between learning Chinese by ECCode™ and learning English
英语学习与使用"汉易码™"学习汉语的异同点

**Table 1.1 (Continued)　表 1.1(续)**

| Comparisons 比较项目 | Language types 语言类型 | | | |
|---|---|---|---|---|
| | Various alphabetic writing 各种拼音文字 | Opinions & explanations 观点与说明 | Chinese character 汉字 | Opinions & explanations 观点与说明 |
| Syllable 音节 | There are monosyllables and polysyllables in alphabetic writings 单音节、多音节均有 | It is one of the features of alphabetic writing 拼音文字的特点 | Normal Chinese characters are monosyllabic characters 传统汉字都是单音节字 | Only among normal Chinese phrases, there are phenomena of multisyllable 传统汉语中,只有词组有多音节现象 |
| Stress 重音 | There is a change of stress in the pronunciation of a word 单词有读音方面的轻重变化 | It is one of the necessary attributes of polysyllabic words 多音节词的必然属性 | There is no stress for a Chinese character 汉字没有轻重音之说 | Normal Chinese characters don't have this necessary polysyllabic attribute of English 传统汉字没有英语那样的多音节属性 |
| Tones 声调 | A word has no tones but in some cases sentences have 单词没有声调的变化,某些情况下句子有声调变化 | This is a phenomenon puzzling a speaker from a country of phonography 这对于来自表音文字国家的汉语学习者来说,是一个令人困惑的现象 | Every Chinese character has its own tone in a sentence 在一个句子当中,每个汉字都有自己的声调 | There are four tones (even five in another classification) in Chinese character which makes a sentence sound with cadence 汉字共有四种声调(亦有五种之说),读起来使句子很有抑扬顿挫之感 |

5

**Table 1.1 (Continued)** 表 1.1（续）

| Comparisons 比较项目 | Language types 语言类型 | | | |
|---|---|---|---|---|
| | Various alphabetic writing 各种拼音文字 | Opinions & explanations 观点与说明 | Chinese character 汉字 | Opinions & explanations 观点与说明 |
| The end sound of a syllable 音节结尾 | Generally, the end sound of a syllable is a consonant 一般辅音结尾 | A feature of a kind of phonography 这是表音文字的一个特点 | The end sound of a syllable is a vowel or a nasal consonant 元音或鼻辅音 | A feature of ideographic characters 这是表意文字的特征 |
| How to distinguish different words or characters 不同字词如何区别 | The alphabetical order and the number of letters in a word determine which word it is 字母排列顺序及字母数量决定了单词之间的区别 | Both the position and the number of letters are key factors for recognizing a word 单词识别受制于字母位置与字母数量这两个因素 | The stroke state, stroke amount, or the relative position between strokes determines which character it is 笔画状态、笔画数量或笔画相对位置决定了汉字之间的区别 | The stroke amount, the stroke state, the relative position between strokes all affect the recognition of a character 笔画数量、笔画状态或笔画相对位置关系都会影响对汉字的确认 |
| Concept of character 字 | There is not such a concept in any kind of phonography 任何表音文字当中都没有这种"字"的概念 | There are only a concept of word in a kind of phonography 表音文字当中只有单词的概念 | There is 汉语当中有"字"这个概念 | There are both characters and phrases (words) 汉语当中有字和词的概念 |

6

# Chapter 1　The similarities and differences between learning Chinese by ECCode™ and learning English
英语学习与使用"汉易码™"学习汉语的异同点

## 1.2　Introduction to "Keylearning Chinese Characters" and "Keywriting Chinese Characters"
## "汉字键学"与"汉字键写"简介

Please look back upon how you learned a new English word with an information device. First, typed in each letter of the word one by one. Second, looked it up in the e-dictionary. Third, learned how to pronounce the word, what its meaning is, how to use the word through various example sentences and so on from the e-dictionary. Finally, after having mastered English, you would use the keyboard to start a paperless office. In short, you use a keyboard not only to learn English, but also to "write" it. Both of the two tasks related to the keyboard are what we call KEYLEARNING and KEYWRITING for English. Correspondingly, their counterparts in Chinese language are respectively called "Chinese Character Keylearning" and "Chinese Character Keywriting".

大家可以回忆一下自己是如何借助于一部信息设备学习英语新单词的。首先,得把单词字母逐个输入信息设备。其次,就是查电子词典。再次,找到目标单词后,了解这个单词如何发音、都有哪些意思、通过各种例句学习如何使用这个单词等。最后,在大家学成英语之后,就会使用键盘进行无纸化办公了。总之,大家既使用键盘学习英语,也使用键盘"书写"英文。这两项任务都与键盘有关,我们称之为"英文键学"和"英文键写"。对应于中文当中,我们则称之为"汉字键学"与"汉字键写"。

So, in this book we wish to teach how to learn Chinese characters in a similar method, by the same steps, and with the same information device. This method is called Easy Chinese Code™ (ECCode™ for short) or 汉易码™ (read as /hàn yì mǎ/ in Chinese). For this purpose, the concept of CONSTITUENT in a Chinese character will be defined that its role is the same as a letter in an English word. In other word, the constituent is also a "letter" of a Chinese character, but the "letter" having or not having a pronunciation does not matter because a Chinese character is one of the phoneme-grapheme separation language symbols. Fortunately, it is assured for beginners that the memory of these Chinese "letters" is regular—it is very easy to master. Talking about how much time it takes to master these Chinese "letters", an Italian student commented, "It is like learning to play a piano. There's a quick way of teaching kids how to read the notes on sheet music that is coloring each nail with different colors. The kids will remember which color represents which note, and that's it. Although it is troublesome to paint nails with different colors, this method leads to the rapid mastery of piano fingering. Similarly, keeping these Chinese 'letters' in mind is helpful to expand the vocabulary of Chinese characters more quickly."

所以,在本书当中,我们希望用相似的方法、相同的步骤,并借助于相同的信息设备,教大家学习汉字。这个方法就叫"汉易码"（中文读作/hàn yì mǎ/，英文简称为ECCode™）。为此，我们定义一个"汉字组分"的概念，其作用就跟英文单词当中的字母一样。换句话说，这个"汉字组分"也是汉字的一种"字母"，但这个"字母"有没有读音倒不重要，因为汉字毕竟是音形分离的一种语言文字。但非常庆幸的是，大家尽可放心，这些中文"字母"的记忆都有规律可循——掌握它们很容易。而就需要花费点时间记住这些中文"字母"一事，一位意大利女学生就评论道："这就像学习弹钢琴。有一种教授孩子们如何阅读乐谱上音符的快捷方法，那就是给每个指甲标记不同的颜色。孩子们只需记住哪个颜色代表哪个音符，就万事大吉了。虽然给指甲涂上不同的颜色有点麻烦，但这有利于孩子们快速掌握钢琴指法。同样的道理，记住这些中文'字母'也有利于快速扩大汉语词汇量。"

Generally, there are two basic differences between learning Chinese by ECCode™ and learning English. Firstly, the Chinese "letter", namely the constituent, is divided into two kinds: one kind is called PHONETIC CONSTITUENT (PC for short) that is related to the attribute of the voice of a Chinese character, the other is called SHAPE CONSTITUENT (SC for short) that is related to the attribute of the geometry shape of a Chinese character. If not knowing how to read a Chinese character, just caring about its SCs will do as well. And through using ECCode™ to input the character into the e-dictionary, a user will learn its pronunciation as well as other information about it. Secondly, unlike an English word that maybe have many letters, a Chinese character represented by ECCode™ has no more than four Chinese "letters", namely, no more than four constituents. I. e., a COMPUTER CHINESE CHARACTER (CCC for short) made of the ECCode™ has one PC which is not essential and no more than three SCs which will be introduced later. Therefore, just need to remember (or see) the SCs in a Chinese character and which English letter key they are respectively situated in. Moreover, SCs in Chinese characters are mostly visible.

一般来说，在使用"汉易码™"学习汉字时，其与英语学习的区别有两点。首先，汉字的"字母"，即汉字组分，被划分成两类：一类叫字音组分（PC）——与汉字的发音有关，另外一类叫字形组分（SC）——与汉字的几何形状有关。如果大家不知道一个汉字该怎么发音，那么只关注字形组分也行。通过使用"汉易码™"把汉字输入电子词典，大家就能够学到这个字怎么发音以及其他一些有关该字的信息了。其次，不像英文单词的字母往往有很多，一个用"汉易码™"表示的汉字代码所拥有的汉字"字母"数量不会超过4个，即汉字代码所含组分不会超过4个。也就是说，一个"汉易码™"计算机汉字（CCC）是由一个并非不可或缺的字音组分和后面将要介绍的不超过3个字形组分所构成。所以，只需记住（或看出）汉字里面的字形组分，并记住这些字形组分分别配置于哪一个英文字母键上就可以了。更何况，汉字的字形组分大部分情况下都是肉眼可见的。

Chapter 1　The similarities and differences between learning Chinese by ECCode™ and learning English
英语学习与使用"汉易码™"学习汉语的异同点

## 1.3　What problems does the course solve
## 本教程解决哪些问题

The crash course focuses on resolving the issues of KEYLEARNING and KEYWRITING for Chinese characters. It's hoped that by solving these two problems, the initiative of Chinese character keylearning could be returned to Chinese language learners so that they could have much more time to learn Chinese characters without the limits of learning place as well as volume of software vocabulary.

这个简明教程所要解决的问题就是"汉字键学"与"汉字键写"这两个问题。希望通过这两个问题的解决,能够把汉字查询的主动权交还给汉语学习者,从而使他们的汉字学习不再受时间和地点的限制,也不再受语言教学软件所含词汇量有限的制约。

In practice, there are a lot of software helping learners to look up a new Chinese character in the e-dictionary, but all with their own advantages and disadvantages. Comparing them with the ECCode™ introduced later in this book, you will find that under most situations, the best method of man-machine conversation is the solution based on the keyboard. Of course, the one-time FIVE-STROKE input method has left many people with nightmares of memory, but the ECCode™ is as simple as you can't imagine—one Ghanaian and one Kazakhstan international students taking a professional course by using English in China understood its basic principle in a lecture for less than 30 minutes.

事实上,现在有很多帮助大家在电子字典中查询一个汉语生字的软件,但是这些软件各有利弊。把这些软件与我们后面将要介绍的"汉易码™"解决方案相比较,大家将会发现,在大多数情况下,最好的人机对话方法就是基于键盘的解决方案。当然,曾经的五笔输入法给许多人留下了记忆的"噩梦",但是"汉易码™"则简单到了大家无法想象的程度——一位在中国用英语上专业课的加纳国际学生和一位与其情况一样的哈萨克斯坦学生都在不到30分钟的讲座之内就听懂了"汉易码™"的基本原理。

For example, There is an e-dictionary of software that allows users to select a constituent as the search information of a Chinese character from many given constituents of Chinese characters and find out the meanings of the target character. The most protuberant problem faced by such a software tool is that it is too inefficient, which uses only one shape information of a Chinese character to look it up in the e-dictionary every time while the ECCode™ could allow users to use several shape information of a character to do that at one time. As everyone knows that the more given information, the higher the search efficiency is. That is to say, this method of looking up a Chinese dictionary is much less efficient than using a keyboard-based one to look up an English dictionary. Furthermore, such a software tool has almost nothing to do with the keyboard which is the most relevant tool to keylearning and keywriting for a language. As a result, it does not integrate keylearning and keywriting for Chinese characters.

举例而言,有一款汉英电子字典软件,这款软件只允许用户在它给定的许多汉字组分当中找出一个组分作为字典查询的检索信息,并据此找出目标汉字。但这样的软件所面临的最突出的问题就是效率太低,此类软件每次只使用一个汉字字形信息来查询字典,而"汉易码™"则可以同时使用多个汉字字形信息进行字典查询。众所周知,已知信息越多,字典查询效率就越高。也就是说,像这样的中文字典比起使用键盘查询英文字典来,在效率方面要低得多。更何况,像这样的软件几乎跟键盘没有什么关系,而键盘则是与语言键学和键写关系最为密切的一种工具。其结果就是,这类软件没有把"汉字键学"与"汉字键写"有机地结合起来。

# Review 1
# 复习题 1

Q1：What are the similarities and the differences between Chinese-learning and English-learning?
思考题 1:汉语学习与英语学习有哪些异同点?

Q2：How many kinds of CONSTITUENTs in a Chinese character are divided into?
思考题 2:汉字组分分为哪几种?

Q3：How many "letters / constituents" are there in a Chinese character at most?
思考题 3:一个汉字中最多有多少个"字母/组分"?

Q4：How many pieces of shape information in a Chinese character does the ECCode™ input method allow users to make use of at most?
思考题 4:"汉易码™"输入法允许用户最多使用一个汉字的几条字形信息?

Q5：To illustrate such a viewpoint by an example that the more information describing something, the better it is for finding it. Is that a strength of the ECCode™ over the software as example?
思考题 5:通过举例说明这样一种观点,即描述事物的信息越多,对找到这个事物就越有好处。这一点是不是"汉易码™"相对于举例的软件的一大优点呢?

# Chapter 2    Introduction to Chinese character encoding

# 汉字编码概述

## 2.1  What are a computer Chinese character and its encoding theory
## 什么是计算机汉字及其编码理论

The CCC, or the Computer Chinese Character Code (CCCC for short), is a keyboard character string that allows information devices to receive Chinese character information based on the keyboard which serves as a man-machine conversation tool. And the theory of how to transform a Chinese character into a keyboard string is called Computer Chinese Character Theory (CCCT for short), sometimes referred to as "Chinese Character Encoding Method (CCEM for short)" "Encoding Theory (ET for short)" or "Encoding Scheme (ES for short)". In some CCCTs, the constituents of a CCCC even include keyboard function keys or/and numeric keys, but most of the CCCTs only use English letters as their constituents of a CCCC.

计算机汉字就是基于键盘这个人机对话的工具而让信息设备接收汉字信息的键盘字符串,这些键盘字符串也叫计算机汉字代码(CCCC)。而研究如何把汉字转变成键盘字符串这种代码的理论就被叫作计算机汉字理论(CCCT)。有时,计算机汉字理论也被称为"汉字编码方法(CCEM)""编码理论(ET)"或"编码方案(ES)"。在一些汉字编码理论当中,其汉字代码的组成成分当中甚至包含键盘功能键或/和数字键,而大多数计算机汉字编码则只使用英文字母作为其汉字代码的组成成分。

## 2.2  Overview of the development of CCCT
## 计算机汉字理论概述

Chinese is a LOGOGRAPHIC LANGUAGE (LL for short) in which one "character" corresponds roughly to one "word" in a phonographic language, or meaning that there are vastly more Chinese characters or glyphs than the keys on a standard computer keyboard.

汉语是一种语标性语言文字(LLL),其中一个字相当于表音文字里面的一个"词";或者说,汉字的数量比计算机标准键盘上的字母数量要多得多。

In order to input Chinese characters with standard keyboards, a variety of keyboard input methods have been designed.

所以,为了使用标准键盘输入汉字,人们就设计了各种各样的汉字键盘输入方法。

# A Crash Course on Keylearning and Keywriting for Chinese
## 汉字键学与键写简明教程

Keyboard input methods can be classified into 3 main types: by encoding, by pronunciation, and by structure of Chinese characters. The following are just some samples of Chinese input methods. Many of those input methods have variations. Simple Pinyin and Double Pinyin are the variations of the Pinyin input method. Besides, the input methods which require the user to select a character from a menu generally have such mature functions as a phrase association function for guessing which next characters the user intends to input based on context.

汉字的键盘输入方法主要可以分为三种类型:编码输入方法、拼音输入方法和汉字结构输入方法。下面所举例子仅仅是众多汉字输入法中的一小部分。这些输入法都有变种。例如,简拼与双拼都是拼音输入法的变种。除此之外,那些要求用户从菜单栏选出一个汉字的方法都有根据上下文猜测用户下面想要输入哪些字的成熟方法,例如,词组联想功能。

Different people prefer different methods and each standard has its strength and weakness. For example, for someone (e.g., a Chinese) who is already familiar with Pinyin, the Pinyin method can be learned most quickly. However, the maximum typing rate with the Pinyin method is limited, and learning the system is meaningless to those who don't know a character's Pinyin or how to read a Chinese character. Though it takes much effort to learn the FIVE-STROKE method, expert typists can input text with the method much faster than the Pinyin method. Because of these factors, people begin to pessimistically think that there is no likelihood of a "normal" input method for Chinese characters to be evolved.

不同的人喜欢不同的汉字输入方法,每种方法的标准都各有利弊。例如,对于那些已经十分熟悉汉语拼音的(中国)人来说,相比其他两种类型的输入方法,能够使其最快掌握的应该就是拼音输入法了。但是,拼音输入法的最大打字速度却极其有限,而且当很多汉字不会读时,学习这种输入方法就没有什么意义了。与之相比,五笔字型输入法虽然能够让专业打字员的文本输入速度远远快于使用拼音输入法的打字速度,但却需要花费很大的精力才能学会这种五笔字型输入法。由于存在着这些因素,人们就开始悲观地认为,各方面都"正常"的汉字输入方法是不可能出现的了。

Other input methods for Chinese characters have not been widely adopted except for the handwriting input method equipped with handwriting recognition software. As one of the most common alternatives, optical character recognition and speech recognition are beginning to be seen as input methods for Chinese characters. All these methods have a high error rate for Chinese character recognition with the same situation as English.

除了配有手写识别软件的手写输入法之外,其他汉字输入方法都没有被广泛地推广开来。作为一种最为常见的替代方案,现在光学字符识别以及语音识别作为一种汉字输入手段,也开始映入人们的眼帘。与英语一样,所有这些方法的汉字识别也都有很高的出错率。

Therefore, the best man-machine conversation tool for Chinese information process is still the keyboard, but this requires people to first create an EVALUATION INDEX SYSTEM(EIS for short) for CCEMs. Then, under the guidance of this EIS, people can have a clear development goal.

所以,中文信息处理方面最好的人机对话工具依然是键盘,但这需要人们首先创建一个汉字编码方法的评价指标体系(EIS)。然后,在这个评价指标体系的指导之下,人们才能有明确的开发目标。

## 2.3 How to evaluate the quality of the Chinese character encoding theory
## 如何评价一种汉字编码理论的质量

The EIS has been constantly improved either with the emergence of various CCEMs. Especially when the EIS takes foreigners learning and using Chinese into consideration, the evaluation indicators become more realistic and challenging. The following set of indicators constitutes such an EIS.

事实上,随着各种汉字编码方法的不断涌现,评价指标体系也在不断得到完善。尤其是把学习和使用汉语的外国人纳入考虑范围的时候,评价指标就更具现实性和挑战性了。下面这组评价指标就构成了这样一种评价指标体系。

- Good learnability (easy to remember—less memory, not easy to forget, suitable for the initial state of Chinese character knowledge of foreign Chinese-learners, such as the knowledge of Chinese characters in the following textbook Volume 1 shown in Figure 2.1 or its first half, or a quick primer on the basic knowledge of Chinese characters in this book).
  易学性好(容易记忆——记忆量少,不容易忘记,适合初学汉语的外国人的汉字知识状态,例如像图2.1所示教材第一册或其上半册汉字知识水平即可,或以本书速成这些汉字基础知识也行)。
- Simple encoding rules (easy to master).
  编码规则简单(容易掌握)。
- Low rate of coincidental code (at least lower than the five-stroke method).
  重码率低(至少低于五笔字型)。

Figure 2.1　*NEW PRACTICAL CHINESE READER*（BOOK 1）
图2.1　《新实用汉语读本》(第一册)

- Good standardization (encoding strictly in accordance with the stroke order, namely consistent with the teaching norms of Chinese character writing).
  规范性好(编码严格按照笔顺进行,即与汉字书写教学规范相一致)。
- High input efficiency (satisfying the requirement of foreigners'"blind typing", low probability of mistyping characters).
  输入效率高(满足外国人盲打的需要,打错字的概率很低)。
- Suitable for the psychological rule of the computer writing after mastering Chinese—while typing, the sound of a Chinese character appearing first in mind then its shape.
  适合学成汉语之后用电脑写作的心理学规律——即在打字时,浮现在脑海中的先是字音后是字形。
- Suitable for foreigners' habit of computer word processing (text input not using keys such as function or number keys other than alphabetic keys).
  适合外国人计算机文字处理的习惯(文本输入不使用功能键或数字键等非字母键)。
- The key position layout of the SCs of Chinese characters conforms to the probability layout of English letter keys.
  汉字字形组分的键位布局符合英文字母键的概率布局。

# Review 2
# 复习题2

　　Q1: When encoding Chinese characters so as to input a Chinese character into a computer, which of the following methods is better:

## Chapter 2  Introduction to Chinese character encoding
### 汉字编码概述

A. The Chinese character code only uses English letters.

B. It contains other non-alphabetic keys, such as function keys or number keys.

思考题1:在对汉字进行计算机编码时,下面哪种方法更好:

A. 汉字代码只使用英文字母。

B. 夹带着使用了其他非字母键,如功能键或数字键。

Q2: What is the most primary shortcoming of the Pinyin Input method?

思考题2:拼音输入方式最主要的缺点是什么?

Q3: Can the Pinyin Input method help Chinese language learners to learn a new Chinese character that is not known how to read it by them?

思考题3:拼音输入法可以帮助汉语学习者学习汉语生字吗?

Q4: Please rank the importance of the indexes in the EIS of Chinese character coding introduced in the text (the index at the top indicates that the index is the most important).

思考题4:请对课文介绍的汉字编码评价指标体系当中的几个指标进行重要性排序(排在最前面的指标表示该指标最重要)。

# Chapter 3　Basic knowledge
# 基础知识

Just as learning English from such basic knowledge as letters is an inevitable step, phonetic symbols and so on, it's essential to begin Chinese learning with some basic knowledge. Furthermore, companying the application space of Chinese characters having marched into the virtual world, the scope of the basic knowledge of Chinese language has also increased. The ECCode™ is a convenient "bridge" and an efficient "transport" for Chinese characters to shuttle between the real world and the virtual world. And the figure below (Figure 3.1) is the knowledge framework of the computer Chinese character theory of the ECCode™ for reference. Thus, a general first impression of it could be left.

就像大家学习英语不得不从字母、音标等基础知识开始学起一样,学习汉语也需要从一些基础知识开始。尤其是随着汉字应用空间已经延伸至虚拟世界,汉字基础知识的范围也扩大了。"汉易码™"就是汉字在现实世界与虚拟世界之间穿梭往来的一座便捷的"桥梁"和一个高效的"交通工具"。图3.1就是"汉易码™"计算机汉字理论的知识框架,大家可以先对其有一个大致的总体印象。

## 3.1　A constituent of a Chinese character
## 3.1　汉字的构成组分

As mentioned above, the constituents of a Chinese character may be illustrated as the following Figure 3.2 in term of the ECCode™.

如上所述,从"汉易码™"的角度来看,汉字的组分如图3.2所示。

# Chapter 3　Basic knowledge
基础知识

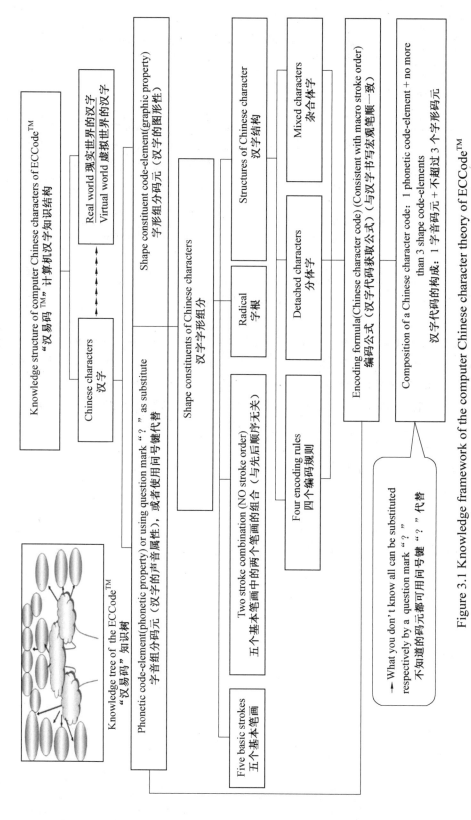

Figure 3.1 Knowledge framework of the computer Chinese character theory of ECCode™

图 3.1 "汉易码"™ 计算机汉字知识框架

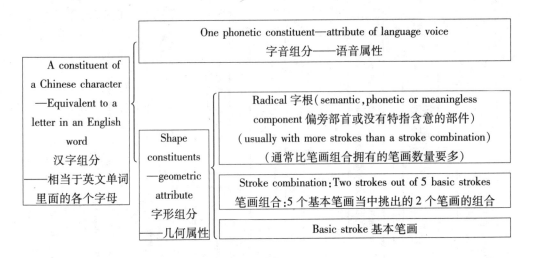

Figure 3.2　Constituent classification of a Chinese character
图 3.2　汉字组分示例

In addition to the statement that a CONSTITUENT in a Chinese character works as the same role of a letter in an English word, the following new concepts appeared in Figure 3.2 above will be introduced in detail respectively in the following chapters or sections.

除了汉字组分的作用与英文单词中字母的作用一样这种说法之外,图 3.2 中出现的以下几个新概念也将会在后面几个章节当中分别加以详细介绍。

- phonetic constituent 字音组分
- shape constituent 字形组分
- stroke 笔画
- basic stroke 基本笔画
- combination of two strokes out of 5 basic strokes 两笔画组合
- radical 字根
- other related concepts 其他相关概念

Chapter 3　Basic knowledge
基础知识

## 3.2　Pronunciation of the Chinese character (Chinese Pinyin)
## 汉语拼音

Although the ECCode™ allows you to look up a Chinese character in the e-dictionary just like checking an English dictionary without knowing how to pronounce it, you still want to know how to read the character after finding it from the e-dictionary to tell you, is that right?

尽管"汉易码™"允许大家在不知道汉字读音的情况下像查英文字典一样地查汉语字典,但大家仍然想在查到某个生字之后让字典告知这个汉字该如何发音,是吧?

So, it's necessary to know the pronunciation system of Chinese characters, also called Chinese Pinyin, which is a kind of phonetic notation of a Chinese character's sound. In fact, it is very easy for a Chinese-learner from the country of alphabetic writing to master it. Of course, the best way for learners to learn Chinese pronunciation is to listen to and mimic the tutor and other Chinese people around.

所以,大家有必要熟悉汉字的发音系统,也叫"汉语拼音",这是一种标记汉字读音的方法。事实上,对于那些来自表音文字国家的汉语学习者而言,掌握"汉语拼音"是很容易的。当然,学习汉语发音的最好方法,就是仔细听并模仿老师和其他恰好出现在大家身边的中国人是如何说中文的。

Now, let me make a brief introduction to Chinese Pinyin.
下面就对汉语拼音做个简单的介绍。

It's maybe known that Chinese is a syllabic language, each normal character consisting of one syllable (such a character as "瓩 [ read as /qiān wǎ/]" is not a normal Chinese character). Generally, apart from individual exceptions, most syllables include three parts (see Figure 3.3), the initial, the final and the tone. And for the sake of convenience, the book will make use of this handy division.

大家可能知道汉语是一种音节性语言,每个正常汉字都是一个音节("瓩"读作"千瓦",就不是一个正常的汉字)。总的来说,除了个别音节之外,大多数汉字音节都包括三个部分(参见图3.3):声母、韵母和声调。出于方便考虑,本书也采用了这种划分方法。

Unlike European languages, clusters of letters—INITIALs (read as /shēngmǔ/) and FINALs(read as /yùnmǔ/) — and not consonant and vowel letters, form the fundamental elements in pinyin (and most other phonetic systems used to describe the Han language). Every Mandarin Chinese (also called Putonghua) syllable can be spelled with exactly one initial followed by one final, except for the special syllable "er" or when a trailing "-r" is considered part of a syllable. The latter case, though a common practice in some sub-dialects, is rarely

19

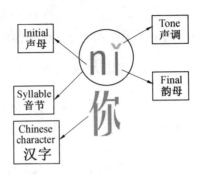

Figure 3.3   Illustration of initial, final and syllable in Chinese Pinyin
图 3.3   汉字声母、韵母和音节示例

used in official publications.

与欧洲语言不同,拼音(以及用于描述汉语言的大多数其他语音系统)的基本元素是由字母组合而成的——即声母和韵母而不是辅音和元音字母组合而成。除了特殊音节"er"(用作韵尾时写成"r")被视为音节的一部分外,普通话音节都可以用一个声母后面紧跟一个韵母拼写而成。而韵尾音"r"虽然在一些方言中很常见,但在普通话当中则很少出现。

### 3.2.1   The initials
声母

Initial refers to the Chinese phonological term, one consonant used before the final, with the final together to form a complete syllable. The initial of Chinese characters determines the position and pronunciation method of the tongue tip (such as z, c, s) and tongue surface (such as j, q, x) or tongue edge (such as I, etc.) during the pronunciation of a Chinese character. The second column of the Table 3.1 below lists all of the Chinese initials in. The ellipsis sign "…" after each initial indicates that there are also omitted finals.

声母是一个汉语音韵学术语,使用在韵母前面的辅音,跟韵母一同构成一个完整的音节。汉字声母决定了汉字发音时舌尖(如 z、c、s)、舌面(如 j、q、x)或舌边(如 i 等)的位置与发音方法。表 3.1 第二列列出了所有的汉字声母。其中每个声母后面的省略号"…"表示后面跟着一个省略了的韵母。

Chapter 3　Basic knowledge
基础知识

**Table 3.1　The initial list and explanation of Chinese Pinyin**
**表 3.1　汉语拼音声母表说明**

| NO.<br>编号 | Initials<br>声母 | Explanations of pronunciation<br>发音说明 |
|---|---|---|
| 1 | [b⋯] | Sounds a bit like "b" in "bay", in Chinese it's a voiceless consonant because the vocal cords don't vibrate while saying it. Unaspirated<br>有点像字母 b 在单词"bay"里面的发音,汉语中是清辅音,发音时声带不震动,不送气<br><br>Pronunciation diagram of the sound "b"<br>[b]发音口型图 |
| 2 | [p⋯] | Sounds a bit like "p" in "pay", a voiceless consonant. Aspirated<br>有点像字母 p 在单词"pay"里面的发音,是一个清辅音,送气音<br><br>Pronunciation diagram of the sound "p"<br>[p]发音口型图 |
| 3 | [m⋯] | Sounds a bit like "m" in "mom", in Chinese it's a voiced consonant because the vocal cords vibrate while saying it<br>有点像字母 m 在单词"mom"里面的发音。在汉语中,由于发这个音时声带震动,所以是一个浊辅音<br><br>Pronunciation diagram of the sound "m"<br>[m]发音口型图 |

21

Table 3.1(Continued)　表3.1(续)

| NO.<br>编号 | Initials<br>声母 | Explanations of pronunciation<br>发音说明 |
|---|---|---|
| 4 | [f…] | Sounds a bit like "f" in "fun", a voiceless consonant<br>有点像字母 f 在单词"fun"里面的发音,是一个清辅音<br><br>Pronunciation diagram of the sound "f"<br>[f]发音口型图 |
| 5 | [d…] | Sounds a bit like "d" in "day", a voiceless consonant. Unaspirated<br>有点像字母 d 在单词"day"里面的发音,是一个清辅音,不送气<br><br>Pronunciation diagram of the sound "d"<br>[d]发音口型图 |
| 6 | [t…] | Sounds a bit like "t" in "top", a voiceless consonant. Aspirated<br>有点像字母 t 在单词"top"里面的发音,是个清辅音,送气音<br><br>Pronunciation diagram of the sound "t"<br>[t]发音口型图 |

Chapter 3　Basic knowledge
基础知识

Table　3.1(Continued)　表3.1(续)

| NO.<br>编号 | Initials<br>声母 | Explanations of pronunciation<br>发音说明 |
|---|---|---|
| 7 | [n…] | Sounds a bit like "n" in "no", a voiced consonant<br>有点像字母 n 在单词"no"里面的发音,是一个浊辅音<br><br>Pronunciation diagram of the sound "n"<br>[n]发音口型图 |
| 8 | [l…] | Sounds a bit like "l" in "love", a voiced consonant<br>有点像字母 l 在单词"love"里面的发音,是一个浊辅音<br><br>Pronunciation diagram of the sound "l"<br>[l]发音口型图 |
| 9 | [g…] | Sounds a bit like "g" in "go", a voiceless consonant. Unaspirated<br>有点像字母 g 在单词"go"里面的发音,是一个清辅音,不送气<br><br>Pronunciation diagram of the sound "g"<br>[g]发音口型图 |

Table 3.1(Continued) 表3.1(续)

| NO. 编号 | Initials 声母 | Explanations of pronunciation 发音说明 |
|---|---|---|
| 10 | [k…] | Sounds a bit like "k" in "kill", a voiceless consonant. Aspirated 有点像字母 k 在单词"kill"里面的发音,是一个清辅音,送气音<br><br>Pronunciation diagram of the sound "k"<br>[k]发音口型图 |
| 11 | [h…] | Sounds a bit like "h" in "high", but a little more guttural, i. e., with a heavier pronunciation, a voiceless consonant 有点像字母 h 在单词"high"里面的发音,但喉音更重一些,是一个清辅音<br><br>Pronunciation diagram of the sound "h"<br>[h]发音口型图 |
| 12 | [y…] = […i]<br>See Table 3.2 | Sounds a bit like "y" in "you", with rounded lips, a voiceless consonant 有点像字母 y 在单词"you"里面的发音,嘴唇呈圆形,是清辅音 |
| 13 | [w…] = […u]<br>See Table 3.2 | Sounds a bit like "w" in "we", a voiceless consonant 有点像字母 w 在单词"we"里面的发音,是一个清辅音 |

Chapter 3　Basic knowledge
基础知识

Table　3.1（Continued）　表3.1（续）

| NO.<br>编号 | Initials<br>声母 | Explanations of pronunciation<br>发音说明 |
|---|---|---|
| 14 | [s…] | Sounds a bit like "s" in "sun", a voiceless consonant<br>有点像字母 s 在单词"sun"里面的发音,是一个清辅音 <br><br>Pronunciation diagram of the sound "s"<br>[s]发音口型图 |
| 15 | [c…] | A "ts" sound, pronounced just like the end of "hats" or "cats", a voiceless consonant. Aspirated<br>发"ts"音,就像单词"hats"或"cats"的尾部发音,是清辅音,送气音 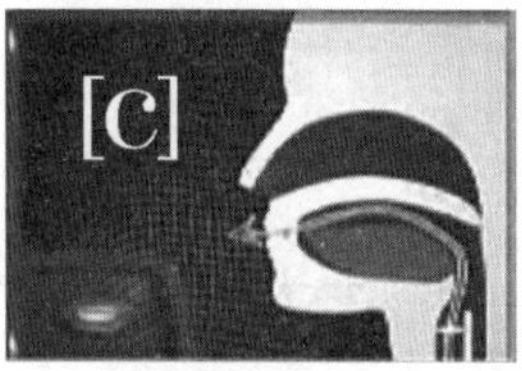<br><br>Pronunciation diagram of the sound "c"<br>[c]发音口型图 |
| 16 | [z…] | A "dz" sound. No English words start with this sound, but it is like the end of many English words, e.g. kids, reads, suds, a voiceless consonant. Unaspirated<br>发"dz"音。英语里面没有哪个单词是由这个音打头的,但是很多英语单词的结尾部分倒是很像这个发音,例如单词 kids、reads 和 suds 尾部的发音就跟这个音很像,是一个清辅音,不送气 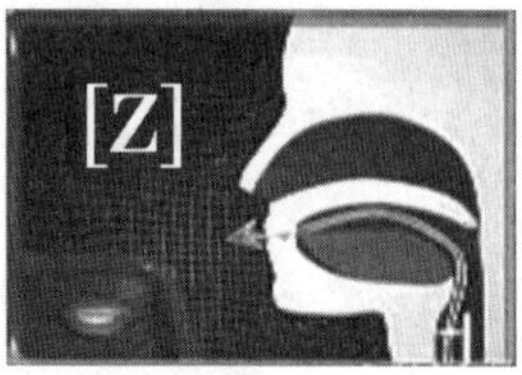<br><br>Pronunciation diagram of the sound "z"<br>[z]发音口型图 |

25

Table 3.1(Continued)　表3.1(续)

| NO.<br>编号 | Initials<br>声母 | Explanations of pronunciation<br>发音说明 |
|---|---|---|
| 17 | [j…] | No equivalent in English. More or less like "j" in "jeep", but with the tongue just a little further forward, i.e., with your tongue tip touching the back of your lower incisors and the middle of your tongue arching upwards, a voiceless consonant. Unaspirated<br>英语当中没有汉语里面的这个发音。汉语的这个发音或多或少有点像字母 j 在单词"jeep"里面的发音,但是舌头略微向前靠一点,也就是说,舌尖要触及下门牙的后部,舌头的中部要向上拱起,是一个清辅音,不送气<br><br>Pronunciation diagram of the sound "j"<br>[j]发音口型图 |
| 18 | [q…] | No equivalent in English. More or less like "ch" in "cheap", but with the tongue just a little further forward, i.e., with your tongue tip touching the back of your lower incisors, the middle of your tongue arching upwards as well as the mouth opening, a voiceless consonant<br>英语当中没有汉语里面的这个发音。汉语的这个发音或多或少有点像字母组合 ch 在单词"cheap"里面的发音,但是舌头略微向前靠一点,也就是说,舌尖要触及下门牙的后部,舌头的中部要向上拱起,同时嘴唇张开,是一个清辅音<br><br>Pronunciation diagram of the sound "q"<br>[q]发音口型图 |

Chapter 3　Basic knowledge
基础知识

Table　3.1(Continued)　表3.1(续)

| NO. 编号 | Initials 声母 | Explanations of pronunciation 发音说明 |
|---|---|---|
| 19 | [x…] | No equivalent in English. More or less like "sh" in "she", but with the tongue just a little further forward, i. e., with your tongue tip touching the back of your lower incisors, the middle of your tongue arching upwards as well as the mouth opening, a voiceless consonant<br>英语当中没有汉语里面的这个发音。汉语的这个发音或多或少有点像字母组合 sh 在单词"she"里面的发音,但是舌头略微向前靠一点,也就是说,舌尖要触及到下门牙的后部,舌头的中部要向上拱起,同时嘴唇张开,是一个清辅音<br><br>Pronunciation diagram of the sound "x"<br>[x]发音口型图 |
| 20 | [zh…] | More or less like "j" in "joke" "jump" or "junk", but with the tongue curled upwards, i. e., with the tip of the tongue a little further back, a voiceless consonant<br>有点跟字母 j 在单词"joke""jump"或"junk"里面的发音相似,只是舌头要向上卷曲,也就是说,舌尖略微往后一点,是一个清辅音<br><br>Pronunciation diagram of the sound "zh"<br>[zh]发音口型图 |

27

Table 3.1(Continued)　表3.1(续)

| NO.<br>编号 | Initials<br>声母 | Explanations of pronunciation<br>发音说明 |
|---|---|---|
| 21 | [ ch… ] | More or less like "ch" in "chin" or "chip", but with the tongue curled upwards, i. e., with the tongue further back, a voiceless consonant<br>有点跟字母组合 ch 在单词"chin"或"chip"中的发音类似,只是舌头要向上卷曲,也就是说,舌头要向后卷曲,是一个清辅音<br><br>Pronunciation diagram of the sound "ch"<br>[ch]发音口型图 |
| 22 | [ sh… ] | More or less like "sh" in "ship" or "shoe", but with the tongue curled upwards, i. e., with the tongue further back; very similar to "marsh" in American English, a voiceless consonant<br>有点跟字母组合 sh 在单词"ship"或"shoe"中的发音相似,只是舌头要向上卷曲,也就是说,舌头要向后卷曲;其实,汉语这个发音有点类似读美式英语单词"marsh"时字母组合 sh 的发音,是清辅音<br><br>Pronunciation diagram of the sound "sh"<br>[sh]发音口型图 |

Chapter 3 Basic knowledge
基础知识

Table 3.1(Continued) 表3.1(续)

| NO. 编号 | Initials 声母 | Explanations of pronunciation 发音说明 |
|---|---|---|
| 23 | [r…] | No equivalent in English. More or less like "r" in "rink", but with the tongue a bit higher to buzz slightly, i. e. , curl the tongue up and make an "r" in "rink", a voiced consonant<br>英语当中没有汉语里面的这个发音。汉语的这个发音或多或少有点类似字母 r 在单词"rink"中的发音,只是发音时舌头稍微高一点,这样才会发出轻微的嗡嗡声,也就是说,把舌头卷起来发出单词"rink"中的字母 r 音,是一个浊辅音<br><br>Pronunciation diagram of the sound "r"<br>[r]发音口型图 |

Among Table 3.1, many speakers from the countries of alphabetic writing often have trouble in distinguishing the two groups of sound such sounds as "j""q""x" and "zh""ch""sh". For instance, to native English speakers, "x" and "sh" sound similar, but to native Chinese speakers, the sounds are completely different with different tongue and lip positions. For "sh", the tip of the tongue should touch the roof of the mouth, but for "x", the tip of the tongue should touch the behind of the lower teeth.

在表3.1中,许多来自表音文字国家的汉语学习者很难区分"j""q""x"与"zh""ch""sh"。例如,对于很多说英文的人来讲,"x"与"sh"听起来很相似,但是,对于说中文的人来说,它们是完全不同的两个音,其发音的舌头和嘴唇的位置完全不同。发"sh"音时,舌尖应该抵住口腔顶部,而发"x"音时舌尖则应该抵住牙齿背面的下部。

In general, some Chinese consonants are rather similar to English consonants, but it's important to hear the differences and get all details as accurate as possible. In this way, a learner can learn Chinese listening and speaking through difference comparison.

一般来说,有些汉语辅音的发音很像英文的辅音发音,但尽可能地听出它们之间的细小区别很重要。这样一来,就可以通过差异比较学习汉语听说了。

The initials in Chinese can be roughly divided into the following categories.
汉语中的声母大致可以分为以下几类。

**Labial**: a sound pronounced by one or both lips, such as "b" "p" "m" "f".
唇音:是指发音时用到上下嘴唇之一或同时用到两个嘴唇的音,例如 b、p、m、f。

**Alveolar(blade-alveolar)**: a sound pronounced with the tip of the tongue against the bony ridge behind the upper incisors, such as "d" "t" "n" "l".
齿槽音(舌尖中音):是指发音时舌尖抵住上门牙骨脊处的音,例如 d、t、n、l。

**Velar**: a sound pronounced with the back of the tongue close to or touching the soft part of the roof of the mouth, such as "g" "k" "h".
软腭音:是指发音时舌后部几乎要贴近或抵到口腔软腭的音,如 g、k、h。

**Palatal**: a sound pronounced with the back and middle of the tongue close to or touching the roof of the mouth, such as "j" "q" "x"。
上腭音:是指发音时舌头中后部贴近或接触到口腔上颚,如 j、q、x。

**Dental sibilant**: a sound pronounced with the tip of the tongue close to or touching the back of the upper incisors, such as "z" "c" "s".
齿擦音:是指发音时舌头贴近或触及上门牙背面的音,如 z、c、s。

**Retroflex**: a sound pronounced with the tongue curled back so that it touches (or almost touches) the hard part of the roof of the mouth, such as "zh" "ch" "sh" "r".
卷舌音:是指发音时舌头后部卷曲以便后部舌面触及或几乎触及口腔顶部硬腭面的音,如 zh、ch、sh、r。

Other initial letters in Mandarin Chinese, such as "w" "y".
普通话当中其他需要注意的声母还有 w、y。

### 3.2.2 The finals
韵母

Final also refers to the term of Chinese phonology, the part of Chinese character sound other than initial and tone. The finals determine the extent to which the mouth opens while speaking Mandarin Chinese. The second column of the Table 3.2 below lists all of the Chinese finals. The ellipsis sign "…" before each final indicates that there are also omitted initials.

韵母也是一个汉语音韵学术语,指汉语字音中除声母和声调以外的部分。说普通话时韵母决定了嘴巴张开的程度。表 3.2 第三列列出了汉语中的所有韵母,其中每个韵母前面的省略号表示有声母省略了。

Chapter 3　Basic knowledge
基础知识

Table **3.2**　The final list and explanation of Chinese Pinyin
表3.2　汉语拼音韵母表说明

| NO.编号 | Finals 韵母 | | Explanations of pronunciation 发音说明 |
|---|---|---|---|
| 1 | Single finals 单韵母 | [⋯ɑ] | Sounds a bit like "a" in "f<u>a</u>ther" (especially like American pronunciation)<br>有点像字母"a"在单词"f<u>a</u>ther"里面的发音(尤其像美式发音)<br><br>Pronunciation diagram of the sound "ɑ"<br>[ɑ]发音口型图 |
| 2 | | [⋯o] | Sounds a bit like "<u>wo</u>". Don't close your mouth as the sound is made. Instead, open the mouth wider<br>有点像字母组合"<u>wo</u>"的发音一样。当发这个音时嘴唇不要闭起来,相反地,要把嘴唇张大一点<br><br>Pronunciation diagram of the sound "o"<br>[o]发音口型图 |
| 3 | | [⋯e] | Sounds a bit like the pronunciation of "<u>uh</u>" in "d<u>uh</u>" or "<u>ur</u>" in "f<u>ur</u>", or similar to "u" in "<u>u</u>nder"<br>有点像字母组合"<u>uh</u>"和"<u>ur</u>"分别在英语单词"d<u>uh</u>"和"f<u>ur</u>"中的发音一样<br><br>Pronunciation diagram of the sound "e"<br>[e]发音口型图 |

Table 3.2(Continued)　表3.2(续)

| NO. 编号 | Finals 韵母 | | Explanations of pronunciation 发音说明 |
|---|---|---|---|
| 4 | Single finals 单韵母 | [⋯i-] | Sounds a bit like "ir" in "shirt", but the "r" sound is lighter<br>有点像字母组合"ir"在单词"shirt"中的发音一样,但是字母"r"的发音要轻一些<br><br>Pronunciation diagram of the sound "i-"<br>[i-]发音口型图 |
| 5 | | [⋯i] | Generally pronounced as a short vowel after "c/s/z" and "ch/sh/zh/r". A bit like "i" in "it", "zit" and "sit"<br>一般紧跟在声母"c/s/z"和声母"ch/sh/zh/r"后面时,这个音发短元音,有点像字母"i"在单词"it""zit"和"sit"中的发音<br><br>Pronunciation diagram of the short final "i"<br>短韵母[i]发音口型图 |
| 6 | | [⋯-i] | Usually pronounced as "ee" in "he" "bee" or "see"<br>通常这个音发成单词"he""bee"和单词"see"中的"ee"的发音<br><br>Pronunciation diagram of the long final "-i"<br>长韵母[-i]发音口型图 |

Chapter 3　Basic knowledge
基础知识

Table 3.2(Continued)　表3.2(续)

| NO.<br>编号 | Finals<br>韵母 | | Explanations of pronunciation<br>发音说明 |
|---|---|---|---|
| 7 | | [⋯u] | Sounds like "u" in fl<u>u</u>te. But pronounced as an umlaut "u" ("ü", another final introduced latter) after "j/q/x" and sometimes "n/l"<br>　　有点像"u"在单词"fl<u>u</u>te"里面的发音一样。但是,紧跟在声母"j/q/x"以及有时候跟在声母"n/l"后面时,"u"的发音要改成发其变音"ü"音了(下面将介绍这个"ü"音) 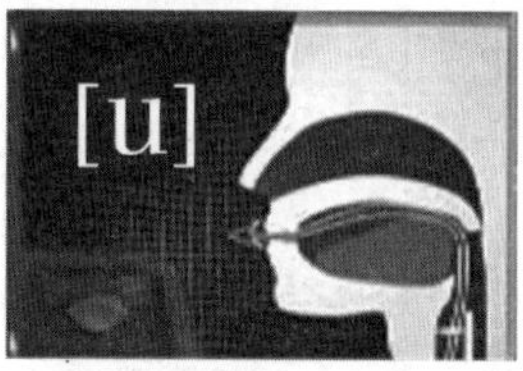<br><br>Pronunciation diagram of the sound "u"<br>[u]发音口型图 |
| 8 | Single finals<br>单韵母 | [⋯ü] | No equivalent in English. Start by saying "cheeeeeeeeeese" and then round out your lips immediately (just like the mouth shape in the figure below). Namely, sounds like the umlaut "u" in German and French, a combination of "<u>eee</u>" and "<u>ooo</u>" (Make an "<u>eee</u>" sound with your jaw, and then round your lips for an "<u>ooo</u>" without moving your jaw)<br>　　在英语当中没有这个发音。要想发这个音,就得以说"cheeeeeeeeeese"开始,但是紧接着就得把嘴唇变成扁圆形(如下面发音口型图所示)。换句话说,就像德语和法语中发变元音"u"一样,类似德语或法语当中的"eee"音与"ooo"音连在一起发音(即把下颌发出"eee"音,然后把嘴唇收为扁圆发出"ooo"音,但上下颌的位置不要发生变化) 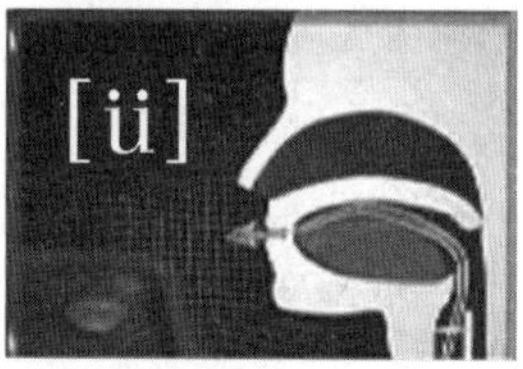<br><br>Pronunciation diagram of the sound "ü"<br>[ü]发音口型图 |

Table 3.2(Continued)　表3.2(续)

| NO. 编号 | Finals 韵母 | | Explanations of pronunciation 发音说明 |
|---|---|---|---|
| 9 | | [···er] | Sounds a bit like "er" in "teache<u>r</u>" of American English, but the mouth opened a little more<br>有点像"teache<u>r</u>"当中字母组合"er"的美式发音,但嘴巴张得稍微大一些<br><br>Pronunciation diagram of the sound "er"<br>[er]发音口型图 |
| 10 | Compound finals 复韵母 | [···ɑi] | Sounds a bit like the pronunciation of "eye", or like "y" in "sky"<br>有点像单词"eye"的发音,或者说像字母"y"在单词"sky"中的发音<br><br>Pronunciation diagram of the sound "ɑi"<br>[ɑi]发音口型图 |
| 11 | | [···ei] | Sounds a bit like "ay" in "bay" "day" or "pay"<br>有点像字母组合"ay"在单词"bay""day"和"pay"中的发音<br><br>Pronunciation diagram of the sound "ei"<br>[ei]发音口型图 |

Chapter 3　Basic knowledge
基础知识

Table 3.2(Continued)　表3.2(续)

| NO. 编号 | Finals 韵母 | | Explanations of pronunciation 发音说明 |
|---|---|---|---|
| 12 | Compound finals 复韵母 | [ ⋯ɑo] | Sounds a bit like "ow" in "cow" "how" or "meow", but the "a" sound is longer<br>有点像字母组合"ow"在单词"cow""how"或"meow"中的发音,但"ɑ"音发得稍微长点<br><br>Pronunciation diagram of the sound "ɑo"<br>[ɑo]发音口型图 |
| 13 | | [ ⋯ou] | Sounds a bit like "o" in "so" "go" of American pronunciation with lips slightly closing at end of the sound<br>有点像字母"o"在单词"so""go"中的美式发音,嘴唇在发音结束时轻轻地闭合起来<br><br>Pronunciation diagram of the sound "ou"<br>[ou]发音口型图 |
| 14 | | [ ⋯iɑ] | Sounds a bit like the "ee" sound combined with the "a" sound in "father"; or like the word "ya" (Swedish for "yes")<br>有点像英文中的"ee"音和字母"a"在单词"father"中的发音连在一起发音;或者说像单词"ya"(瑞典语中"yes"的意思)的发音<br><br>Pronunciation diagram of the sound "iɑ"<br>[iɑ]发音口型图 |

35

Table 3.2(Continued) 表3.2(续)

| NO. 编号 | Finals 韵母 | | Explanations of pronunciation 发音说明 |
|---|---|---|---|
| 15 | Compound finals 复韵母 | [⋯iɑo] | Sounds a bit like the "ee" sound combined with the "ow" sound in "cow", similar to "yow"<br>有点像英文中的"ee"音和字母组合"ow"在单词"cow"中的发音连在一起发音,有点像单词"yow"的发音<br><br>Pronunciation diagram of the sound "iɑo"<br>[iɑo]发音口型图 |
| 16 | | [⋯ie] | Sounds a bit like the "ee" sound combined with the "e" sound in "yet", similar to "ye" in "yet"<br>有点像英文中的"ee"音和字母"e"在单词"yet"当中的发音连在一起发音,听起来有点像字母组合"ye"在单词"yet"当中的发音<br><br>Pronunciation diagram of the sound "ie"<br>[ie]发音口型图 |
| 17 | | [⋯iu]<br>=<br>[⋯iou] | Sounds a bit like "yo". Or sounds like the "ee" sound combined with the "o" sound in "so". This would be easier to remember if it was spelled "io"<br>有点像单词"yo"的发音。或者说,就像英文中的"ee"音和字母"o"在单词"so"当中的发音连在一起发音。当然,如果把这个音写成"io"可能更容易记忆一些<br><br>Pronunciation diagram of the sound "iou"<br>[iou]发音口型图 |

Chapter 3  Basic knowledge
基础知识

Table 3.2(Continued)  表3.2(续)

| NO. 编号 | Finals 韵母 | | Explanations of pronunciation 发音说明 |
|---|---|---|---|
| 18 | Compound finals 复韵母 | [⋯uɑ] | Sounds a bit like "wa" in "water", i.e., similar to the "oo" sound combined with the "a" sound in "father"<br>有点像字母组合"wa"在单词"water"中的发音,也就是有点像英文中的"oo"音与字母"a"在单词"father"中的发音连在一起发音<br><br>Pronunciation diagram of the sound "uɑ"<br>[uɑ]发音口型图 |
| 19 | | [⋯ui]<br>=<br>[⋯uei] | Sounds a bit like the "oo" sound combined with the "ay" sound in "hay" or "pay". The "i" here is pronounced like an "ei" sound. Also sounds like the word "way"<br>有点像英文中的"oo"的音与字母组合"ay"在单词"hay"或单词"pay"中的发音连在一起发音。在这里,这个"i"音有点像英文中的"ei"音。也可以说,这个韵母的发音有点像单词"way"的发音<br><br>Pronunciation diagram of the sound "ui"<br>[ui]发音口型图 |
| 20 | | [⋯uo] | Sounds a bit like the exclamation "woe"<br>有点像感叹词"woe"的发音<br><br>Pronunciation diagram of the sound "uo"<br>[uo]发音口型图 |

37

Table 3.2(Continued)　表3.2(续)

| NO.<br>编号 | Finals<br>韵母 | | Explanations of pronunciation<br>发音说明 |
|---|---|---|---|
| 21 | Compound finals<br>复韵母 | […uɑi] | Sounds a bit like "wi" in "wild", or like the word "why" with no "h", i.e., "oo" sound combined with the word "eye"<br>有点像字母组合"wi"在单词"wild"中的发音,或者像单词"why"中没有"h"时的发音,亦即是英文中的"oo"音和"眼睛"这个单词"eye"的发音连在一起发音一样<br><br>Pronunciation diagram of the sound "uɑi"<br>[uɑi]发音口型图 |
| 22 | | […üe] | Sounds a bit like the final "ü" above combined with "e" in "yet"<br>有点像前面介绍的韵母"ü"的发音与字母"e"在单词"yet"中的发音连在一起发音<br><br>Pronunciation diagram of the sound "üe"<br>[üe]发音口型图 |
| 23 | Nasal finals<br>鼻韵母 | […ɑn] | Sounds a bit like "an" in "pecan" or "Juan"<br>有点像字母组合"an"在单词"pecan"或"Juan"中的发音<br><br>Pronunciation diagram of the sound "ɑn"<br>[ɑn]发音口型图 |

Chapter 3　Basic knowledge
基础知识

Table　3.2(Continued)　表3.2(续)

| NO. 编号 | Finals 韵母 | | Explanations of pronunciation 发音说明 |
|---|---|---|---|
| 24 | | [⋯en] | Sounds like "en" in "taken"; or like "un" in "under" but with the vowel pronounced a little higher and further forward<br>就像字母组合"en"在单词"taken"发音一样;或者说像字母组合"un"在单词"under"中的发音一样,只是这个"under"中元音稍微发得大声一点,并稍微靠前一点发这个元音<br><br>Pronunciation diagram of the sound "en"<br>[en]发音口型图 |
| 25 | Nasal finals 鼻韵母 | [⋯ɑng] | Sounds a bit like "a" in "father" combined with "ng" in "song"<br>有点像字母"a"在单词"father"中的发音和字母组合"ng"在单词"song"中的发音连在一起发音<br><br>Pronunciation diagram of the sound "ɑng"<br>[ɑng]发音口型图 |
| 26 | | [⋯eng] | Sounds a bit like "uh" in "duh" combined with "ng" in "song"; or like "ung" in "hung"<br>有点像字母组合"uh"在单词"duh"中的发音和字母组合"ng"在单词"song"中的发音连在一起发音;或者说像字母组合"ung"在单词"hung"中的发音<br><br>Pronunciation diagram of the sound "eng"<br>[eng]发音口型图 |

39

Table 3.2(Continued)  表3.2(续)

| NO.编号 | Finals 韵母 | | Explanations of pronunciation 发音说明 |
|---|---|---|---|
| 27 | | [⋯ong] | Sounds a bit like "o" in "worn" combined with "ng" in "long". No corresponding sound in English, but not difficult to make<br>有点像字母"o"在单词"worn"里面的发音加上字母组合"ng"在单词"long"里面的发音连在一起发音。实际上,英语中没有对应的发音,但这个音也不难发<br><br>Pronunciation diagram of the sound "ong"<br>[ong]发音口型图 |
| 28 | Nasal finals 鼻韵母 | [⋯ian] | Sounds a bit like the "ee" sound combined with the "an" sound. Sounds like the word "yen"<br>有点像英文中的"ee"音和上面的韵母"an"的发音连在一起发音。听起来就像单词"yen"的发音<br><br>Pronunciation diagram of the sound "ian"<br>[ian]发音口型图 |
| 29 | | [⋯in] | Pronounced about halfway long between "een" in "green" and "in" in "pin". Sounds a bit like "een" in "preen" or "teen"<br>这个音的发音介于单词"green"中"een"的发音与单词"pin"中"in"的发音长度之间,有点像字母组合"een"在单词"preen"或"teen"中的发音<br><br>Pronunciation diagram of the sound "in"<br>[in]发音口型图 |

Table 3.2(Continued) 表3.2(续)

| NO. 编号 | Finals 韵母 | | Explanations of pronunciation 发音说明 |
|---|---|---|---|
| 30 | Nasal finals 鼻韵母 | [⋯iang] | Sounds a bit like "yang". Rhyme with the final "ang" above, i.e., similar to the "ee" sound combined with the final "ang"<br>有点像单词"yang"的发音,与上面的韵母"ang"押韵,即为英文中的"ee"音和韵母"ang"的发音连在一起发音<br><br>Pronunciation diagram of the sound "iang"<br>[iang]发音口型图 |
| 31 | | [⋯ing] | Sounds a bit like "ing" in English but with the first sound a little higher and longer, i.e., similar to the "ee" sound combined with the "ng" sound<br>有点像英语中的字母组合"ing"的发音,但是第一个字母的发音稍微高一点和长一点,就像英文中"ee"音和"ng"的发音连在一起发音<br><br>Pronunciation diagram of the sound "ing"<br>[ing]发音口型图 |
| 32 | | [⋯iong] | Sounds a bit like the final "ong" above but preceded by the "y(i)" sound, i.e., similar to the "ee" sound combined with the "ong" sound<br>有点像前面介绍的韵母"ong"的发音,但在其前面要加上一个"y(i)"音,也就是像英文中的"ee"音和韵母"ong"的发音连在一起发音<br><br>Pronunciation diagram of the sound "iong"<br>[iong]发音口型图 |

Table 3.2(Continued)　表3.2(续)

| NO. 编号 | Finals 韵母 | | Explanations of pronunciation 发音说明 |
|---|---|---|---|
| 33 | Nasal finals 鼻韵母 | […uɑn] | Usually sounds a bit like "uan" in "Juan". But if preceded by the initials "y/j/q/x", it sounds like "en" in "when"<br>这个韵母通常有点像字母组合"uan"在单词"Juan"中的发音。但是,紧跟在声母"y/j/q/x"后面时,这个韵母的发音就像字母组合"en"在单词"when"中的发音了<br><br>Pronunciation diagram of the sound "uan"<br>[uɑn]发音口型图 |
| 34 | | […un], almost equal to sound […uen] 几乎相同于 […uen]音 | Sounds a bit like the "oo" sound combined with "en" in "taken". A bit difficult to pronounce and pronounced like "uen"<br>就像英文中的"oo"音与字母组合"en"在单词"taken"中的发音连在一起发声。这个音发起来有点难度,有点像字母组合"uen"的发音<br><br>Pronunciation diagram of the sound "un"<br>[un]发音口型图 |
| 35 | | […uɑng] | Sounds a bit like "wang". Rhyme with the final "ang" above, i.e., similar to the "oo" sound combined with the final "ang"<br>有点像"wang"的发音,与前面介绍的韵母"ang"的发音押韵,即类似英文中的"oo"音和韵母"ang"的发音连在一起发声<br><br>Pronunciation diagram of the sound "uang"<br>[uɑng]发音口型图 |

Chapter 3 Basic knowledge
基础知识

Table 3.2(Continued) 表3.2(续)

| NO. 编号 | Finals 韵母 | | Explanations of pronunciation 发音说明 |
|---|---|---|---|
| 36 | | [⋯ueng] | Sounds a bit like the "oo" sound combined with the final "eng", i.e., similar to "weng"<br>有点像英文中的"oo"音和韵母"eng"的发音连在一起发音,即类似"weng"的发音<br><br>Pronunciation diagram of the sound "ueng"<br>[ueng]发音口型图 |
| 37 | Nasal finals 鼻韵母 | [⋯üan] | Sounds a bit like the final "ü" combined with "an" in "pecan"<br>有点像韵母"ü"的发音和字母组合"an"在单词"pecan"中的发音连在一起发音<br><br>Pronunciation diagram of the sound "üan"<br>[üan]发音口型图 |
| 38 | | [⋯ün] | Sounds a bit like the final "ü" combined with "en" in "taken". A bit difficult to pronounce and pronounced like "üen"<br>有点像韵母"ü"的发音和字母组合"en"在单词"taken"中的发音连在一起发音。这个发音有点难度,因为这个发音有点像发"üen"音<br><br>Pronunciation diagram of the sound "ün"<br>[ün]发音口型图 |

For the final "ü", there is now a convention that when the finals "ü" "üe" "üan" and "ün" go after the initials "j/q/x/y", the top two dots in the finals of "ü" "üe" "üan" and "ün" are omitted. So, it is written as "yue" and "yuan" in formal written spelling rather than "yüe" or "yüan".

针对韵母"ü",现在有个约定,就是当"ü""üe""üan"和"ün"跟在声母"j/q/x/y"后面时,"ü"上面两个点就被省略掉了。所以,书面拼写时,"yüe"的写法就变成了"yue","yüan"的写法就变成了yuan。

Generally speaking, the final "ü" should be written as the letter "v" when it follows the initial "n" or "l", or written as the letter "u" when it follows other initials.

总的来说,韵母"ü"跟在声母"n"和"l"后面时,就被写成了字母v,跟在其他声母后面时就被写成了字母u。

And you should know that the process ways mentioned above for "ü" are especially beneficial for typing Chinese on the keyboard of English, i. e., keywriting, because there is no letter "ü" in English at all.

同时,大家还得了解到上述针对"ü"的处理方法对于汉字打字而言——即对于汉字键写——特别有好处,因为英文里面没有"ü"这个字母。

### 3.2.3 The Syllable
音节

The syllable is the smallest unit of speech that can be distinguished clearly by hearing. In Chinese, the pronunciation of a normal Chinese character usually contains only one syllable, i. e., one normal Chinese character has only one syllable. Most syllables in Chinese consist of two parts: the initial and the final (see Figure 3.4), however, some few syllables only have the final, which are called "ZERO INITIAL" syllables. When spelling Chinese syllables, there is a characteristic needed to pay attention to that the final sound is louder and the initial sound is lighter.

音节是语音中能够被清楚区别的最小单位。在汉语当中,汉字发音通常只有一个音节,也就是说,一个汉字只有一个音节。汉字中绝大多数音节都由两部分构成:声母和韵母(参见图3.4)。不过,也有个别音节只有韵母而没有声母。这种音节我们称之为"零声母"音节。当拼写音节时,需要注意的一点是,韵母读得洪亮一些,而声母则读得轻一些。

[y]+[ǒng]→a syllable[yǒng]
[y]+[ǒng]→音节(读作/yīnjíe/)

yǒng

always/forever/perpetually

Figure 3.4  The syllable of the Chinese character "永"

图 3.4  汉字"永"的音节示例

For a completed syllable, the finals including "i" "u" or "ü" and finals started with one of them should follow an initial. But the finals including "a" "o" or "e" and finals started with one of them can be independent syllables (namely zero initial syllables).

就一个完整的音节而言,包含 i、u 或"ü"的韵母,以及由这三者打头的韵母都应该跟在声母后面。但是,包含 a、o 或 e 的韵母,或者以这三者打头的韵母则可以独立成为音节,即所谓零声母音节。

In addition, there are several syllables in Chinese Pinyin which need to be explained in Table 3.3 below.

除此之外,汉语中还有一些音节需要说明一下,详情请参见表3.3。

**Table 3.3  Individual explanations**

**表3.3  特别说明**

| No.<br>编号 | Syllables<br>音节 | Explanations of pronunciation<br>发音说明 |
|---|---|---|
| 1 | wu | Sounds like "woo"<br>听起来就像是在发"woo"音 |
| 2 | yi | Sounds like "yee"<br>听起来就像是在发"yee"音 |
| 3 | yu | It is pronounced as the initial "y" combined with the final "ü". E. g., the pronunciation of Chinese character "鱼" is "yü"<br>这是声母"y"音与韵母"ü"合在一起发出的声音。例如,汉字"鱼"就读"yü"音 |

The Table 3.4 below is the "Chinese Pinyin initial and final spelling chart". It basically covers all possible syllable combinations of "initial + final" in Mandarin Chinese, but these syllables have not added the concept of tone that will be introduced later. However, you can try to spell the syllables of each combination of an initial and a final in Table 3.4, so that you can experience the feeling of the syllables in Mandarin Chinese first. In Table 3.4, all initials are listed in the first column, all finals are listed in the first line, and the syllables listed in the second line are respectively the syllables corresponding to the finals in the first line as zero initial syllables (the blanks in the second line indicate that their corresponding finals in the first line do not have corresponding zero initial syllables). The phoneme combination shown in each grid in the Table 3.4 is a Chinese character syllable preceded by an initial and followed by a final, while the blank indicates that there is no such combination of initial and final in Chinese (i.e., there is no such Chinese character).

表3.4是"汉语拼音声母韵母拼音表"。表3.4涵盖了几乎所有的汉语音节,只是表3.4尚未纳入后面将要介绍的声调概念。不过,大家可以尝试着把表3.4中每一个声母与韵母的组合拼读一下,以便先行找找汉语音节的感受。在表3.4当中,所有的声母都列在第一列里面,所有的韵母都列在第一行里面,而第二行每个单元格里面的字母则是其对应第一行里面韵母作为零声母音节时的音节(第二行中的空格表示其对应第一行里面的韵母没有相应的零声母音节)。表3.4当中每个单元格里面的音素组合都是一个汉字音节,其打头的是声母,紧跟其后的是韵母,而空格则表示此处的声母与韵母在汉字中没有相应的汉字发此两者相结合的音节。

Table 3.4  Chinese Pinyin initial and final spelling chart
表 3.4  汉语拼音声母韵母拼读表

| | a | o | e | i | er | ai | ei | ao | ou | an | en | ang | eng | ong | i | ia | iao | ie | iu | ian | in | iang | ing | iong | u | ua | uo | uai | ui | uan | un | uang | ueng | ü | üe | üan | ün |
|---|---|---|---|---|---|---|---|---|---|---|---|---|---|---|---|---|---|---|---|---|---|---|---|---|---|---|---|---|---|---|---|---|---|---|---|---|---|
| | a | o | e | | er | ai | ei | ao | ou | an | en | ang | eng | | yi | ya | yao | ye | you | yan | yin | yang | ying | yong | wu | wa | wo | wai | wei | wan | wen | wang | weng | yu | yue | yuan | yun |
| b | ba | bo | | | | bai | bei | bao | | ban | ben | bang | beng | | bi | | biao | bie | | bian | bin | | bing | | bu | | | | | | | | | | | | |
| p | pa | po | | | | pai | pei | pao | pou | pan | pen | pang | peng | | pi | | piao | pie | | pian | pin | | ping | | pu | | | | | | | | | | | | |
| m | ma | mo | me | | | mai | mei | mao | mou | man | men | mang | meng | | mi | | miao | mie | miu | mian | min | | ming | | mu | | | | | | | | | | | | |
| f | fa | fo | | | | | fei | | fou | fan | fen | fang | feng | | | | | | | | | | | | fu | | | | | | | | | | | | |
| d | da | | de | | | dai | dei | dao | dou | dan | den | dang | deng | dong | di | | diao | die | diu | dian | | | ding | | du | | duo | | dui | duan | dun | | | | | | |
| t | ta | | te | | | tai | | tao | tou | tan | | tang | teng | tong | ti | | tiao | tie | | tian | | | ting | | tu | | tuo | | tui | tuan | tun | | | | | | |
| n | na | | ne | | | nai | nei | nao | nou | nan | nen | nang | neng | nong | ni | | niao | nie | niu | nian | nin | niang | ning | | nu | | nuo | | | nuan | | | | nü | nüe | | |
| l | la | | le | | | lai | lei | lao | lou | lan | | lang | leng | long | li | lia | liao | lie | liu | lian | lin | liang | ling | | lu | | luo | | | luan | lun | | | lü | lüe | | |
| g | ga | | ge | | | gai | gei | gao | gou | gan | gen | gang | geng | gong | | | | | | | | | | | gu | gua | guo | guai | gui | guan | gun | guang | | | | | |
| k | ka | | ke | | | kai | kei | kao | kou | kan | ken | kang | keng | kong | | | | | | | | | | | ku | kua | kuo | kuai | kui | kuan | kun | kuang | | | | | |
| h | ha | | he | | | hai | hei | hao | hou | han | hen | hang | heng | hong | | | | | | | | | | | hu | hua | huo | huai | hui | huan | hun | huang | | | | | |
| y | ya | | ye | | | | | yao | you | yan | | yang | | yong | yi | | | | | | | ying | | | | | | | | | | | | | | |
| w | wa | wo | | | | wai | wei | | | wan | wen | wang | weng | | | | | | | | | | | | | | | | | | | | | | | | |
| z | za | | ze | zi | | zai | zei | zao | zou | zan | zen | zang | zeng | zong | | | | | | | | | | | zu | | zuo | | zui | zuan | zun | | | | | | |

Table 3.4 (Continued) 表 3.4（续）

| | a | e | i | - | ai | ao | ou | an | en | ang | eng | ong | i | ia | iao | ie | iu | ian | in | iang | ing | iong | u | ua | uo | uai | ui | uan | un | uang | ü | üe | üan | ün |
|---|---|---|---|---|---|---|---|---|---|---|---|---|---|---|---|---|---|---|---|---|---|---|---|---|---|---|---|---|---|---|---|---|---|---|
| c | ca | ce | ci | | cai | cao | cou | can | cen | cang | ceng | cong | | | | | | | | | | | cu | | cuo | | cui | cuan | cun | | | | | |
| s | sa | se | si | | sai | sao | sou | san | sen | sang | seng | song | | | | | | | | | | | su | | suo | | sui | suan | sun | | | | | |
| zh | zha | zhe | | zhi | zhai | zhei | zhao | zhou | zhan | zhen | zhang | zheng | zhong | | | | | | | | | | zhu | zhua | zhuo | zhuai | zhui | zhuan | zhun | zhuang | | | | |
| ch | cha | che | | chi | chai | | chao | chou | chan | chen | chang | cheng | chong | | | | | | | | | | chu | chua | chuo | chuai | chui | chuan | chun | chuang | | | | |
| sh | sha | she | | shi | shai | shei | shao | shou | shan | shen | shang | sheng | | | | | | | | | | | shu | shua | shuo | shuai | shui | shuan | shun | shuang | | | | |
| r | | re | | ri | | | rao | rou | ran | ren | rang | reng | rong | | | | | | | | | | ru | rua | ruo | | rui | ruan | run | | | | | |
| j | | | | | | | | | | | | | | ji | jia | jiao | jie | jiu | jian | jin | jiang | jing | jiong | | | | | | | | ju | jue | juan | jun |
| q | | | | | | | | | | | | | | qi | qia | qiao | qie | qiu | qian | qin | qiang | qing | qiong | | | | | | | | qu | que | quan | qun |
| x | | | | | | | | | | | | | | xi | xia | xiao | xie | xiu | xian | xin | xiang | xing | xiong | | | | | | | | xu | xue | xuan | xun |

A Tip: There are many pronunciation resources of initials, finals and syllables in Pinyin on the internet. It's suggested that readers should search and listen to them.

一个提示：互联网上有很多汉语拼音的声母、韵母和音节的发音资源，读者可以自己搜索并跟着听读一下。

# Chapter 3  Basic knowledge
## 基础知识

At last, letus introduce the use of the apostrophe (') in syllables. For example, the corresponding Chinese character to "piǎo" maybe "漂 ( to rinse )" according to the situation or context, but the apostrophe (') between the two syllables of "pí'ǎo" indicates that the corresponding Chinese characters of these two syllables are "皮袄", a title of the leather garment in Chinese. Similarly, the corresponding Chinese character to the syllable of "xiān" maybe "先(first)" according to the situation or context, but when an apostrophe (') separates the two syllables, they mean "西安", a city name of China.

最后,我们介绍一下撇号(')在音节中的应用。例如,在汉语当中,与"piǎo"对应的可能是汉字"漂",但用撇号(')把这个双音节变成了"pí'ǎo"后,其对应的双音节就可能是汉字"皮袄"了——中文里一种皮衣的名称。同样的,音节"xiān"可能是指汉字"先",但加上撇号('),音节写法变成"xi'ān"后,这个双音节就表示两个汉字——即指中国的一个叫"西安"的城市了。

Obviously, you maybe have found that the apostrophe between the two syllables usually appears when the second syllable is the zero initial syllable just starts with "a/o/e", and the two syllables separated by the apostrophe stand for a disyllabic word in Chinese, a word made of two Chinese characters.

显然,大家可能已经发现了,当第二个音节为由"a/o/e"打头的零声母音节时,往往用这个撇号(')把这两个音节分开,以表示汉语中由两个汉字组成的一个双音节词。

### 3.2.4  Difficulties in pronunciation
### 发音难点

As noted above, most of the Chinese Pinyin does not pose serious obstacles to speakers of alphabetic writing. There are, however, a few points that deserve a bit of extra attention.

正如前面所言,绝大多数汉语拼音不会对源自表音文字国家的汉语学习者形成障碍。但仍然有一些发音需要大家特别小心。

1. The retroflex sounds: zh-, ch-, sh-, and r-

卷舌音 zh-、ch-、sh-和 r-

These initials are called "retroflex" sounds because they are all pronounced with the tongue curved back into the back part of the mouth. For the first three of these, there is a corresponding sound that is pronounced with the tongue forward to the front part of the mouth. One key to mastering standard Mandarin Chinese pronunciation is being able to distinguish between the retroflex initial and its corresponding sound that is pronounced with the tongue forward to the front part of the mouth. The pairs are:

这些声母被称为"卷舌音",是因为这些音发音时,舌面都向口腔后半部卷曲。就这四个音的前三个音而言,它们分别都有一个发音时舌面伸向口腔前半部位的音与之对应。掌握汉语标准发音的一个关键就是要能够区分卷舌声母和与之对应的、发音时舌面前伸的声母。这些成对的音素分别是：

- zh- and j-

zh-和 j-

Both "zh-" and "j-" sound like "j" in "jump". But for the initial "zh-" the tip of the tongue is curved back into the back part of the mouth and for "j-" it is forward to the front part of the mouth.

这两者在发音上都有点像字母"j"在单词"jump"当中的发音,但就声母"zh-"而言,发音时其舌尖有点向口腔后半部卷曲,而声母"j-"发音时舌尖则向前伸。

- ch- and q-

ch-和 q-

Both "ch-" and "q-" sound like "ch" in "chip". But for the initial "ch-" the tongue is curved back into the back part of the mouth and for "q-" it is forward to the front part of the mouth.

这两个音都有点像字母组合"ch"在单词"chip"中的发音,但是,就声母"ch-"而言,发音时,舌头向后半部卷曲;而声母"q-"发音时,舌头则要向前伸一些。

- sh- and x-

sh-和 x-

Both "sh-" and "x-" sound like the "sh" in "ship", but for "sh-" the tongue is curved back into the back part of the mouth and for "x-" it is forward to the front part of the mouth.

这两个音都有点像字母组合"sh"在单词"ship"当中的发音。但是,就声母"sh-"而言,其发音时的舌头要向口腔后面卷曲,而声母"x-"发音时,舌头则要向口腔前部伸一些。

Here are two important notes：

这里有两个重要提示:

(1) One way the sounds above are distinguished from each other is by the position of the tongue. However, they are also distinguished as much or more by the fact that "j-" "q-", and "x-" are always followed by a loud front vowel "-i" (an "ee" sound), or "-ü", but "zh-" "ch-", and "sh-" never are. So, even if you pronounce both members of a pair the same way there is little possibility of confusion as long as you get the rest of the characters right.

区分上述三对音素的一种方法就是看舌头的位置。不过,区别它们的一个重要特征就是 j-、q-和 x-后面往往跟着一个发音响亮的前元音"-i"(发"ee"音),或者后面跟着"-ü"音,而 zh-、ch-和 sh-后面则没有这种现象出现。所以,即使以同样的方式发一组音素当中的两个音,只要把其他汉字读音发正确了,别人一般也能理解你所要表达的意思。

## Chapter 3　Basic knowledge
### 基础知识

(2) Retroflex sounds are more typical of northern Chinese speech than that of other parts of China; in fact, in many parts of China people pronounce all these sounds with their tongue forward. Thus, "zh-" is pronounced as "z-", "ch-" as "c-", and "sh-" as "s-". While you should pronounce them in a standard manner, you still need to get used to the Chinese speakers who can't make these distinctions. You may take comfort in the fact that many Chinese find the distinction between these pairs troublesome as you.

卷舌音在中国更具北方特色；事实上，在中国的许多地方，人们在发这些音素时，其舌头都会前伸。结果，声母"zh-"变成了声母"z-"，声母"ch-"变成了声母"c-"，而声母"sh-"则变成了声母"s-"。当你想着发音要尽量发得标准时，你不妨想想那些对此也察觉不出什么区别的中国人。也许，一想到很多中国人跟自己一样发音不准，可能你就会心里好受不少了。

2. Difficult sounds to pronounce
**难发的音**

In addition to the retroflex sounds discussed above, there are a few other sounds in Chinese that are just plain difficult for the speakers of alphabetic writing to make.

除了上面介绍过的卷舌音，对于来自表音文字国家的汉语学习者来说，汉语中还有一些其他的音是比较难发的。

● r-

The most difficult sounds to pronounce must be the retroflex initial "r-". It sounds like "r" in "rink" but with tongue just a bit higher so that it buzzes ever so slightly. (Again, in many areas of China, even Chinese people can't make this sound as standard as Beijing Mandarin, so you will be allowed some latitude in getting this one right.)

最难发的音应该就是卷舌声母"r-"音了。这个音有点像字母"r"在单词"rink"中的发音，但发音时其舌头则要稍微抬高一点，以便发出轻微的"嗡嗡"声。（再说一遍，在中国的许多地方，当发这个音时，当地人甚至也无法像北京人的发音那样准，所以大家发不准也不会引起太多的注意）

● c-

This "ts" sound does exist in English, but never at the beginnings of words. To make it, firstly say "cats" and then eliminate the "ca-" part.

英语里面也有发这个"ts"音的，但是却从来不会在一个单词的开头部分发这个音。为了发这个音，你可以先做着好像要说"cats"的样子，但省略掉"ca-"这个字母组合的音不要发，余下的那部分发音就是声母"c"的发音"ts"了。

● -ü

English does not have this sound (although German and French do). The simplest explanation is that "-ü" is the combination of "ooo" and "eee". To make it, make an "eee" sound with your jaw, and then round your lips for an "ooo" without moving your jaw.

英语中并没有"-ü"这个发音(德语和法语中倒是有这个发音)。最简单的理解可以是这样的,即你可以把"-ü"音看成是英语里面"ooo"音与"eee"音的组合。读者可以用下巴发出"eee"音,然后在不挪动下巴位置的情况下把嘴唇变圆发出"ooo"音,就可以发出"-ü"音了。

3. Difficulties in Spelling
**拼写难点**

On the whole, the Pinyin system is quite logical and far more logical than English spelling. For example, there are a few anomalies even you haven't noticed.

总体而言,汉语拼音极具逻辑性,大多数情况下都远比英语拼写系统更具逻辑性。例如,即使有极个别的例外,读者也许都不曾留意到。

● -i

Usually, "-i" sounds like "ee" in "he". But after the initials "c-/s-/z-" and "ch-/sh-/zh-/r-" it is pronounced as a short vowel, similar to the "i" in "it" and "in". The easiest way to pronounce "-i" is just to remember that the following initials are followed by the short duration tone: ci, si, zi, chi, shi, zhi, and ri.

通常,这个"-i"音被发成英语单词"he"里面的"ee"音,但在声母"c、s、z-"和声母"ch-、sh-、zh-和r-"后面,这个"-i"音就被发成了短元音,有点类似英文单词"it"里面的"i"的发音一样。克服这个发音难点的一个最简单的方法就是记住这么一点,即这些声母后面需要跟着的是短促音:ci、si、zi 和 chi、shi、zhi 和 ri。

● -u

Usually, "-u" sounds like "oo" in "you". But after "y-/j-/q-/x-" it is pronounced as an umlaut "u" ("ü"). Again, the best way to pronounce "-u" is to memorize that the following initials are followed by the final "ü": yu, ju, qu, xu, yun, jun, qun, and xun.

通常,这个音就像单词"you"里面的音"oo"。但是,在声母"y-、j-、q、x-"后面时,这个音就成为了"u"音的异化音了(即 ü 音)。再提示一下,克服这个发音难点的最好方法就是记住,这些声母后面需要紧跟韵母"ü",即其拼写为:yu、ju、qu、xu、yun、jun、qun 和 xun。

Generally speaking, after "n-" and "l-", "-u" is sometimes pronounced as "u" (oo) and sometimes as "ü". (If the sound is the umlaut "ü", it should be marked as "-ü", but Chinese usually know from the context how it should be pronounced so the umlaut marking is sometimes omitted when the character is spelled out in Pinyin.)

总的来说,在声母"n-"和"l-"的后面,"-u"有时读"u(oo)"音,有时则发"ü"音。

(事实上,如果这个音是变音"ü",那么应该标记为"-u";但是,通常中国人能够从上下文当中分辨出来究竟这个音应该怎么发,所以依照汉语拼音的标准,这个变音"ü"上面的两个点就省略不标注了)

- -e

When alone, "-e" sounds like "uh" in English, similar to "u" in "under". But in the following combinations it is pronounced as follows:

当单独使用时,"e"这个音有点像英文当中"uh"的发音,类似字母 u 在单词"under"当中的发音。但是,在下面这些音素组合当中,其发音如下所示:

❖ "-ie" sounds like the "ye" in "yet".
"-ie"听起来像字母组合"ye"在单词"yet"当中的发音。
❖ "-ue" sounds like the "we-" in "wet".
"-ue"听起来像字母组合"we-"在单词"wet"中的发音。
❖ "ye" sounds like the "ye" in "yet".
"ye"听起来像字母组合"ye"在单词"yet"中的发音。

- -ian

Despite there is an "a", "-ian" sounds like the word "yen". Similarly, " yan" sounds like the word "yen", too.

尽管这个发音当中有"a",但这个音在发音时很像单词"yen"的发音。同样的情况也发生在拼音"yan"中,也发类似英文的"yen"音。

- -ui

The "-ui" sounds like the word "way". (You might have expected this sound to be spelled as "-uei", but unluckily it isn't. At least it isn't spelled as "weigh".)

这个音发单词"way"的音。(你可能更希望这个音被拼写成"-uei",可惜事实无法如人所愿。起码地,这个音没有拼成为"weight")

The Figure 3.5 is an illustration of the position of the lips and tongue of the mouth and the tip of the tongue in the oral cavity when pronunciation is made. This sketch may help you to correctly grasp the pronunciation essentials of single finals in Chinese Pinyin.

图 3.5 是汉语拼音发音时,嘴唇和舌头以及舌尖在口腔里面的位置示意图。这个草图可能对大家掌握汉语拼音单韵母的发音有所助益。

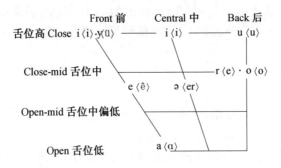

Figure 3.5　Chinese vowel illustration adapted from Google images
图3.5　改编自谷歌的汉语元音舌位图

### 3.2.5　The tone
声调

**1. The concept of tone**
**声调的概念**

Tone refers to the change of the rise and fall of the sound of a Chinese character. It is often said that the intonation of a Chinese character is an integral part of its pronunciation. So it is thought that Chinese is a tonal language, which means that the tone of your voice changes the meaning of the character. Tones are by far one of the biggest obstacles confronted by foreigners when learning Chinese. Getting your tones down early in your studies will pave the way for future success. And, not placing enough importance on your tones will lead to frustration. Chinese are very sensitive to tones. So if your tones are not accurate, more often than not, they will not understand you. As time goes on, the tones you speak will become more and more natural.

声调就是指汉字声调的升降变化。众所周知,汉字声调是整个汉字发音不可分割的一部分。所以,汉语被认为是一种声调语言,意指你的声调变化往往会改变字的意思。迄今为止,声调是外国人学习汉语的最大障碍之一。因此,尽早把声调掌握好,就会为今后成功地掌握汉语铺平道路。反之,如果不给予声调足够的重视,汉语学习就会受挫。中国人对于声调是十分敏感的。所以,声调如果发得不够准确,那么人们多半会不理解你的意思是什么。随着时间的推移,你的声调会越来越自然。

So what is tone? The so-called TONE refers to the change of the volume of a Chinese syllable which can distinguish the meaning of a Chinese character. It is generally believed that different volumes of a Chinese syllable would lead to four changes for pronunciation and therefore there are four tones in Mandarin Chinese. Actually, there are five tones including a so-called "neutral tone". When a syllable is pronounced in different tones, it has different meanings and different Chinese characters. Namely, the same syllable pronounced in such different tones as the first tone, the second tone, the third tone and the fourth tone represent different characters. The classic example used to notice beginning learners of Chinese is the syllable "ma" (see Figure 3.6), which means "mother" if pronounced in the first tone and "horse" if pronounced in the third tone. For another example, "mai" (Figure 3.6) pronounced in the fourth tone means to sell, but in the third tone means to buy.

那么,什么叫声调呢? 所谓声调,就是指可以决定汉字字义的汉字音节的音高之变化。一般人都认为通过改变汉字音节的音高会带来四种变化,因此也就派生出了四种声调。但事实上,汉语中有五种声调,包括一种所谓的"轻声调"。同一个音节发不同的声调,就代表了不同的汉字字意,也对应了不同的汉字。即相同的音节,读第一声和读第二声、第三声或第四声,其所代表的汉字是完全不同的。典型的、用来提醒汉语初学者注意的例字就是音节"ma"(见图 3.6),这个字在读第一声时表示汉字"妈",在读第三声时表示汉字"马"。再举个例字,如果大家用第四声读音节"mai",那就是"卖"的意思;如果大家读成了第三声,那就是"买"的意思了。

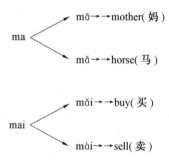

Figure 3.6  Examples of a Chinese character with a different meaning because of a different tone
图 3.6  相同音节不同声调表示不同汉字的例字

People from the nations of alphabetic writing sometimes feel that they cannot hold tones, but this is not exactly what the problem is. After all, speakers of alphabetic writing listen to and use intonation some of the time. For example, consider the difference between a rising tone "Yes?" (as an answer to the door) or a falling tone "Yes!" (as an enthusiastic response to an offer of fair money). The difference between Chinese and English is that in English intonation functions at the sentence level instead of the word level, with the rises and falls of the sentence conveying the emotional impact of the message. The problem for the people from the nations of alphabetic writing in learning Chinese is not hearing intonation per se, but hearing intonation as part of the pronunciation of a character. This is the very phenomenon that Chinese learners from the nations of alphabetic writing need to get used to.

来自表音文字国家的汉语学习者有时会觉着他们掌控不了汉字声调,但这其实并非问题的实质。毕竟这些来自表音文字国家的人有时也会听见声调。例如,英语中用升调读"yes"和用降调读"yes"的区别:前者如回答有人敲门时的"yes"声调,后者如感到别人提供的报价很公平之后给予热情回应的"yes"声调。中文与英文之间的这种声调区别就在于,英文声调存在于句子层面,而不是存在于词汇层面,句子声调的升降变化,表达了信息对情绪的影响。来自表音文字国家的人在学习汉语时所面临的问题不是听到声调本身这个问题,而是对声调是汉字而不是句子的一部分有所迷糊。这正是来自表音文字国家的人学习汉语时需要予以适应的一个现象。

2. The tones of common spoken Chinese
**普通话的声调**

In common spoken Chinese (Mandarin Chinese), most characters are pronounced with one of four tones (Some unaccented syllables are also pronounced with a "light tone"—more about this later). Tone 1, 2, and 4 are relatively straightforward, so there is no need to talk about them. Tone 3 changes according to what follows it, so will require greater elaboration. Let's look at them one by one.

在普通话中,绝大多数汉字都读四种声调之一(有些汉字读"轻声"——后面我们会对此详细介绍)。第一声、第二声和第四声都相对简单,所以无须赘言。第三声则视其后面跟着什么声调的汉字而有所变化。下面我们对这四个声调逐一做介绍。

Here, the Chinese number "一(one, read as /yī/)" "二(two, read as /èr/)" "三(three, read as /sān/)" and "四(four, read as /sì/)" represent Tone 1, Tone 2, Tone 3 and Tone 4 respectively, and a line with an arrow indicates a tone. In addition, we shall use the volume of sound to indicate the weight of the pronunciation, i. e., in the following illustrations, the larger the number from zero to five, the higher the voice volume. Furthermore, people use different Tone Mark placed on a syllable to mark different tones of the syllable in Chinese Pinyin.

在此,我们用汉语数字"一(读 /yī/)""二(读 /èr/)""三(读/sān/)"和"四(读 /sì/)"分别表示第一声、第二声、第三声和第四声,而用带箭头的线条表示声调。除此之外,我们用"音高"来表示发音的轻重,即在下面图例当中,从 0 到 5,数字越大,表示声音音高也就越大。此外,人们在每个音节上画上不同的声调符号,以表示汉语拼音当中这个音节的不同声调。

- Tone 1

一声

Tone 1 is a high-volume level tone (Figure 3.7), like singing a long treble sound. E. g., "mā" is pronounced with Tone#1.

"一声"是音高值最高的平声(图3.7),就像在唱一个长长的高音。如音节"mā"就发一声。

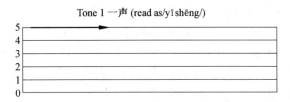

Figure 3.7　Graph of the sound value of Tone 1 and its feature of pronunciation flatness
图 3.7　第一声的音高值及其发音平滑度示例

- Tone 2

二声

Tone 2 is a rising tone (Figure 3.8), like the word "yes" used as a question in answering the door: "Yes?" E. g., "má" is pronounced with Tone 2.

"二声"是一个上升声调(图 3.8),就像有人敲门时回答的"yes?"声调。例如,音节"má"就读第二声。

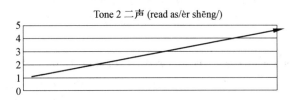

Figure 3.8　Graph of the sound value of Tone 2 and its feature of pronunciation flatness
图 3.8　第二声音高值及其发音平滑度示例

- Tone 3

三声

Tone 3 is usually described as a "falling-rising" tone (Figure 3.9), and this is what it sounds like when a word of English is pronounced in isolation or at the end of a sentence. E. g., "mǎ" is pronounced with Tone 3. However, you will find that if another character follows a Tone 3 character, it becomes a little cumbersome to pronounce a complete "falling-rising" tone. Thus, there are two scenarios in this case.

"三声"通常认为是"降升"调(图 3.9),听起来就像一个英文单词单独发音或这个单词在句子尾部时的发音那样。例如,"mǎ"就发"三声"。不过,如果这个"三声"汉字后面紧跟着一个汉字,那么就不一定非要发一个完整的"先降后升"的"三声"不可了。此时,会有以下两种情况出现。

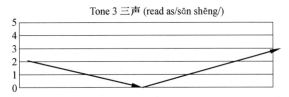

Figure 3.9　Graph of the sound value of Tone 3 and its feature of pronunciation flatness
图 3.9　第三声音高值及其发音平滑度示例

Usually, if a Tone 3 character is followed by another character the rising part drops off (Figure 3.10) and it becomes just a low-falling tone (something like the intonation of a reflective "Hmmm"). A good example is "很(hěn)" in "很快(hěn kuài)" (very fast).

一般来说,如果一个"三声"汉字后面紧跟着另外一个汉字,那么这个"三声"汉字声调的后面上升部分就要略掉不发音了(图3.10)。这样一来,其发音就变成了一个仅有"短促降调"的音节了(有点像英文表示沉思时"Hmmm"的发音)。例如,"hěn kuài(很快)"一词当中"很(hěn)"字的发音就有这个现象。

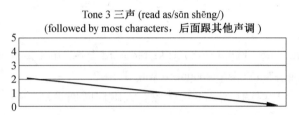

Figure 3.10　The tone of a character with Tone 3 changes with the subsequent character with other tones

图3.10　后面跟其他声调的第三声汉字的音调变化示例

But when one Tone 3 character is followed by another Tone 3 character, the tone of the first character changes to a rising tone (just like Tone 2, Figure 3.11). That's where it gets tricky. Essentially, it is the initial falling part of the tone which is now omitted. A good example phrase for this is "很好(hěn hǎo)" (very good).

但是,当一个"三声"汉字后面也跟着另外一个"三声"汉字时,第一个"三声"汉字的声调就变成了升调(有点像在发"二声",参见图3.11)。实际上就是省略了第一个"三声"汉字后半部分的那个降调。一个很好的例子就是"hěn hǎo"(很好)这个双音节词。

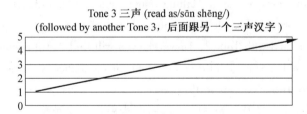

Figure 3.11　The tone of a character with Tone 3 changes because of the subsequent Tone 3 character

图3.11　后面跟第三声汉字的第一个第三声汉字的声调变化示例

Of course, it doesn't matter if you are confused about what variations should be made when the character with Tone 3 is followed by other characters, only needing to know one point will be all right, that is, the pronunciation duration of the character with Tone 3 should not be pronounced as completely as when it is pronounced alone. I. e., at this time, the pronunciation duration of the character with Tone 3 should be pronounced a little shorter and you should

Chapter 3　Basic knowledge
基础知识

quickly transit to read the Chinese character immediately after it.

当然,如果"三声"汉字后面跟着另外一个"三声"汉字,你不知道应该如何变化第一个"三声"汉字的声调时,那也没有关系,你只需知道这一点就可以了,即当第一个"三声"汉字后面跟着另外一个"三声"汉字时,这个"三声"汉字的发音不能完全都发出来。亦即,此时,第一个"三声"汉字的发音时长应该稍微短一点,你应该尽快从第一个"三声"汉字过渡到读第二个"三声"汉字。

- Tone 4

四声

Tone 4 is a falling tone (Figure 3.12), like an enthusiastic affirmation "Yes!". E. g., "mà" is pronounced with Tone 4.

"四声"是一个降调(图3.12),就像热情地肯定性答复"Yes!"一样。例如,"mà"就读"四声"。

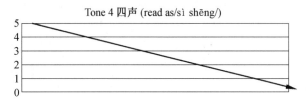

Figure 3.12　Graph of the sound value of Tone 4 and its feature of pronunciation flatness
图3.12　第四声音高值及其发音平滑度示例

- Light tone(also called "silent tone" or "neutral tone")

轻声(亦称"默声"或"中性"声调)

Some unaccented syllables are pronounced with a "light tone" (sometimes called "silent tone" or "neutral tone"). The simplest way to deal with these is to pronounce them in the middle of your voice range—somewhere around 3 on the chart (Figure 3.13)—lightly and with little emphasis. (When written in Pinyin like this one, these syllables of Chinese characters have no tone mark over them.)

所谓"轻声",即指一些无重音音节(有时也被称为"默声"或"中性"声调)。处理这些音节的最简单方法就是在你声音音域的中间部位来发这些汉字的音——几乎就是在图3.13中的音高值3附近来发这些汉字的读音。要发得轻一些、几乎没有重音(书写这些汉字的拼音字母时,在其拼音字母上方就不用标出声调标号了)。

The neutral tone is not independent. It always follows another tone. For example, the syllables without tone marks are pronounced with a light tone. The Chinese usually finish the neutral tone quickly, lightly and shortly. See Table 3.5.

"轻声"是依附性声调。它往往跟在另外一个声调的后面。例如,没有标注音调的音节就发"轻声"。中国人发带这种声调的音时会很快、很轻,也很短。如表3.5所示。

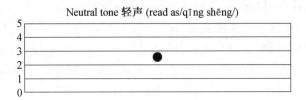

Figure 3.13　Graphic explanation of the sound value of light tone or neutral tone

图 3.13　中性声调音高值图示

Table 3.5　Examples of "light tone"

表 3.5　"轻声"汉字音节举例

| māma | bàba | gēge | jiějie | dìdi |
|---|---|---|---|---|
| 妈妈 | 爸爸 | 哥哥 | 姐姐 | 弟弟 |
| Mother | Father | Brother | (old) Sister | Brother |
| mèimei | wǒmen | nǐmen | tāmen | zěnme |
| 妹妹 | 我们 | 你们 | 他们 | 怎么 |
| (young) Sister | We | You | They | How |

### 3.2.6　Summary
总结

The following figure is the comparison of the sound interval and volume of the four tones and the light tone (Figure 3.14). It is easy to observe that the sound interval of Tone 3 is slightly longer than any other four tones (including the light tone) and that of the light tone is shortest.

图 3.14 是四个声调以及"轻声"的音高值及其抑扬顿挫的变化对比图。从中可以很容易看到"三声"的音程比其他声调的音程要略微长点,而轻声则最短。

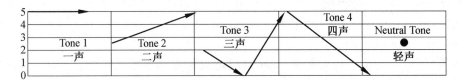

Figure 3.14　Comparison of the sound interval
and volume of the four tones and the light tone

图 3.14　四个声调以及轻声的音程及其音高值变化比较图示

In fact, the pronunciation (Pinyin) of a Chinese character is determined by the two parts of "syllable + tone" (Figure 3.15) which are indispensable. However, the same "syllable + tone" doesn't necessarily refer to a Chinese character because there may be several homonyms. For example, the corresponding character of the sound "yǐ" in Chinese may be "以" or "已".

Similarly, the corresponding word of the sound "ai" in English may be "eye" or "I". The only way to distinguish them is by the context.

事实上,一个汉字的发音(拼音)取决于"音节+声调"这两个部分(图3.15),而这两个部分无法单独存在。不过,同样的"音节+声调"不一定指同一个汉字,因为一个发音可以对应多个汉字。例如,同样是发"yǐ"音,但是其对应的汉字可能是"以",也有可能是"已"。这就像英文中发音"ai",有可能是指单词"eye(眼睛)",也可能是指单词"I(我)"。区别字意的唯一方法就是根据上下文来做出判断。

Figure 3.15　Illustration of the complete composition of Pinyin
图3.15　汉字拼音的完整构成

### 3.2.7　Suggestions for learning tones
声调学习的建议

The natural assumption when first confronted with all these tones is that you need to memorize which tone category each new Chinese character belongs to, i.e., which character is pronounced with Tone 1, which is pronounced with Tone 2 and so forth. However, as you will quickly discover, trying to recall tones in this way when you are trying to say a sentence isn't very efficient; when talking you don't have time to be constantly asking yourself "Is this character pronounced with the first or the fourth tone?" It needs to come out naturally and quickly. So, what should you do?

当你第一次遇到声调时,一般人认为你肯定是想要记住每个汉语生字都发哪个声调,例如,哪个生字是第一声、哪个是第二声等。但是,你会很快发现,当你尝试着想要说一句话时,用这种方式记忆每个汉字的声调信息,其效率是很低的;其实说话时,你是没有时间去不断地问自己"这个字是发第一声呢,还是第四声?"声调发音需要很快、很自然。所以,你该怎么做呢?

One bit of advice is to start with your ears. When Chinese children learn to speak, nobody teaches them which characters are pronounced with Tone 3 and so forth. Rather they listen and learn to say what sounds right. Likewise, to get your tones right without stopping to think before every character, you just need to go with what pronunciation sounds right.

首先,建议你从自己的耳朵开始。当中国孩子学说话时,没有人教他们哪个汉字读第三声或读其他什么声调。他们只是学着听、说那些他们认为正确的发音。同样地道理,要想在说每个字之前不用停下来考虑这个字的正确声调究竟是什么的话,你只需模仿你认为正确的发音就可以了。

The second suggestion is practice, lots of it. The first few times you say anything new, it requires conscious thought, and you may well need to pause to remember which characters are pronounced with which tones. However, after having said a certain character, character combination or phrase a few times, you will speak it naturally and don't need to think about it so much (thus freeing your attention for other problems). Don't practice things just to the point where you can scrape your way through them once; practice them until you can speak them right without thinking.

其次就是建议多做练习。起初在谈论什么新东西的时候,你需要有意识地想一想,或许还需要停下来记住哪些汉字发哪些声调。不过,当把某个汉字、词组、短语重复说了很多遍之后,你可能就自然而然地会说出这些东西而无须想那么多了(这样一来,大家就可以把精力用来应付其他问题了)。建议你做练习时不要浅尝即止,而是要一直练到能够出口成章的程度。

The last suggestion is that don't excessively concern about tones. Yes, you should try to get them right, but you shouldn't become so worried that you are reluctant to speak. Not all of the Chinese could speak Mandarin well.

最后,就是建议你不要过分在意声调。是的,你是得尽量发音正确,但也没必要就此紧张到不敢开口的程度。事实上,在中国,不是所有人都能说好普通话。

Please remember, Chinese people will often understand you quite well even if your tones are wrong, especially if you speak in phrases rather than single characters. (If you speak in single character utterances and get the tone wrong, it may be more difficult for Chinese to understand, especially if the situation or context doesn't make it easy for the listener to guess what you might be trying to say.) It is much better to get a sentence out with the tones wrong than not to open your mouth at all. As long as you keep speaking—and keeping paying attention to how things sound when Chinese people say them—the accuracy of your tones and the naturalness of your pronunciation will continue to improve.

有一点请记住,就是即便你的声调错了,中国人往往也能很好地理解你的意思,尤其是在你用词语而非单个汉字表达意思的时候(如果你使用单个汉字表达意思,并且还把声调发错了,那么中国人也就真的很难理解你的意思了。尤其是在上下文或环境不利于听众揣摩你意思的时候,更是如此)。所以,要说就最好说一个整句,即使声调错了也比始终不开口要强。只要大家坚持不懈地开口说汉语,并始终关注中国人说话时是怎么发音的,那么大家的声调准确性和发音的自然程度就会持续地得到改善。

## 3.3 Strokes and their position relation
## 笔画及笔画间的位置关系

Please have a look at Figure 3.16, the disassembly map of the Chinese character "赢".

# Chapter 3  Basic knowledge
## 基础知识

What can you find out from Figure 3.16?

请看图 3.16 对汉字"赢"的拆解,你能从中看出什么吗?

Obviously, the character "赢" is split finally into many lines and dots. Usually, Chinese characters are made of two kinds of geometric elements which are lines and dots respectively. Although the shapes of lines or dots may be various, every line or dot is made in one breath. That is to say, during the writing of these various lines and dots, their track from the start to the end of the handwriting cannot be interrupted, i.e., these lines or dots are the smallest geometric unit of a Chinese character. Of course, it's easily found that sometimes there are some "middleware" in a Chinese character called COMPONENTs also made of dots or/and various lines, e.g., the five components in the Chinese character "赢" such as 亡, 口, 月, 贝, and 凡.

显然,汉字"赢"最终被拆解成了许多个点和线条。一般来说,汉字都是由两种几何元素组成的,这两种几何元素分别是点和线条。尽管点或线条的形状可能多种多样,但每个点或线条都是一气呵成写完的。即在书写这些点或线条的过程当中,它们的轨迹从落笔起始点到抬笔结束点,中间都不能打断、续写。也就是说,点或线条是构成汉字的最小几何单元。当然,有时汉字中也会有一些由点和线组成的、被称为"部件"的"中间件"。例如,在汉字"赢"中,就有亡、口、月、贝和凡等五个部件。

On those accounts, the line or the dot composing a Chinese character is collectively called a STROKE, the STROKE and the COMPONENT (middleware) are referred to as SCs composing a Chinese character. In other word, it's thought that SC could be any geometrical part of a Chinese character. And certainly, among the SCs of a Chinese character, a STROKE is the smallest unit, namely other SC having more STROKEs than the smallest one (See the illustration in the Figure 3.16 above).

有鉴于此,人们就把构成汉字的点或线条统称为"笔画",而笔画和部件(中间件)则统称为构成汉字的"字形组分"。换句话说,"字形组分"可以是一个汉字的任何一个几何部分。当然,在这些"字形组分"当中,笔画肯定是其中最小的几何单元了,即其他"字形组分"拥有的笔画数量更多(参见图3.16示例)。

Because there may be many strokes in a Chinese character, this gives birth to a concept called POSITION RELATION (PR for short) for any two strokes. And the position relation between strokes in a Chinese character can be essential to its meaning. Actually, there are three ways to combine strokes in a character.

由于一个汉字可能会有很多个笔画,这就诞生了一个叫作"笔画位置关系(PR)"的概念,而汉字笔画之间的这种位置关系对于汉字字意的变化至关重要。事实上,汉字笔画的位置关系一共有三种。

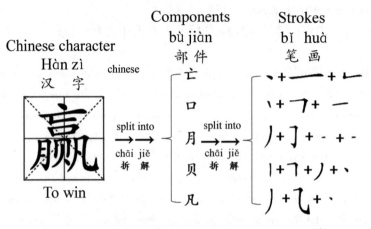

Figure 3.16  The disassembly map of the Chinese character "赢"

图 3.16  汉字"赢"的拆解示例

(1) Adjacent/Noncontact relation (not attached), like "八""儿""二""小" (Table 3.6).

分离关系(即互不接触),如"八""儿""二""小"中的两个笔画之间的关系(表 3.6)。

Table 3.6  Illustration of adjacent/noncontact relation between two strokes

表 3.6  笔画位置之分离关系举例

| bā | ér | èr | xiǎo |
|---|---|---|---|
| 八 | 儿 | 二 | 小 |
| eight | son/child | two | little/small/young |

(2) Intersection relation, like "十""大""九""夫" (Table 3.7).

交叉关系,如"十""大""九""夫"中的一些笔画就互相把另外一个笔画分为了两个部分(表 3.7)。

Table 3.7  Illustration of intersection relation between two strokes

表 3.7  笔画位置之交叉关系举例

| shí | dà | jiǔ | fū |
|---|---|---|---|
| 十 | 大 | 九 | 夫 |
| ten | big | nine | husband |

## Chapter 3　Basic knowledge
### 基础知识

(3) Connecting Relation, like "厂""丁""人""山""天"(Table 3.8).

相连关系,即相互接触但没有把另外一个笔画分为两个部分,如汉字"厂""丁""人" "山""天"中的一些笔画之间就是相连关系(表3.8)。

**Table 3.8　Illustration of connecting relation between two strokes**
**表 3.8　笔画位置之相连关系举例**

| chǎng | dīng | rén | shān | tiān |
|---|---|---|---|---|
| 厂 | 丁 | 人 | 山 | 天 |
| factory | man | human | mountain | sky/heaven |

There are not less than 78 Chinese character strokes written by writing brush, which are listed in the Table 3.9 below.

就毛笔书写的汉字笔画数量而言,其总数不少于78个。表3.9列出了这78个毛笔笔画。

Although there are so many strokes in Chinese characters, it doesn't seem necessary to spend so much time learning how to beautifully handwrite these strokes at the very start of your learning Chinese if you just want to "KEYWRITE" characters with a keyboard in the future (e.g., working in the situation of paperless office). Of course, if you want to write beautiful calligraphy, knowing how to correctly handwrite the strokes in Table 3.9 is essential.

尽管汉字有这么多的笔画,但在大家开始学习汉字的初期,如果将来仅仅是想用键盘 "键写"汉字的话(例如无纸化办公之情形),那么大家则未必需要花费那么多的时间用在 如何把笔画写得漂亮的方面。当然,如果想要写一手漂亮的汉字,那么知道如何正确地书 写表3.9当中的那些笔画就十分必要了。

In fact, as far as we can see, any foreigner who is serious about learning Chinese language should master how to handwrite and keywrite Chinese characters rightly in the Internet Era. This is because both of the two "writing" ways will teach you a lot about how characters work. At least, they will help you recognize characters, which is truly essential besides daily conversations.

其实,在我们看来,在互联网时代,任何一位真想学习汉语的外国人都应该掌握如何 正确地手写和键写汉字。这是因为这两种"书写"汉字的方法都将教会读者许多汉字是 如何应用的知识。至少,这两种汉字"书写"方式将会帮助读者辨认汉字。而辨认汉字这 一点在日常会话之外则非常重要。

**Table 3.9  Various shapes of brush strokes in Chinese characters**
**表3.9  汉字各种形状毛笔笔画表**

| No.编号 | Stroke笔画 | No.编号 | Stroke笔画 | No.编号 | Stroke笔画 | No.编号 | Stroke笔画 |
|---|---|---|---|---|---|---|---|
| 1 | | 21 | | 41 | | 61 | |
| 2 | | 22 | | 42 | | 62 | |
| 3 | | 23 | | 43 | | 63 | |
| 4 | | 24 | | 44 | | 64 | |
| 5 | | 25 | | 45 | | 65 | |
| 6 | | 26 | | 46 | | 66 | |
| 7 | | 27 | | 47 | | 67 | |
| 8 | | 28 | | 48 | | 68 | |
| 9 | | 29 | | 49 | | 69 | |
| 10 | | 30 | | 50 | | 70 | |
| 11 | | 31 | | 51 | | 71 | |
| 12 | | 32 | | 52 | | 72 | |
| 13 | | 33 | | 53 | | 73 | |
| 14 | | 34 | | 54 | | 74 | |
| 15 | | 35 | | 55 | | 75 | |
| 16 | | 36 | | 56 | | 76 | |
| 17 | | 37 | | 57 | | 77 | |
| 18 | | 38 | | 58 | | 78 | |
| 19 | | 39 | | 59 | | | |
| 20 | | 40 | | 60 | | | |

Chapter 3  Basic knowledge
基础知识

The ECCode™ has a companion online dictionary that provides animated demonstrations of how to handwrite Chinese characters (Figure 3.17). Through the animated demonstrations, you can learn how to handwrite these strokes rightly.

实际上,"汉易码™"有一个配套的在线字典可以提供如何正确书写汉字的动画演示(图 3.17)。通过这些动画演示,大家可以学会如何正确地手写这些笔画。

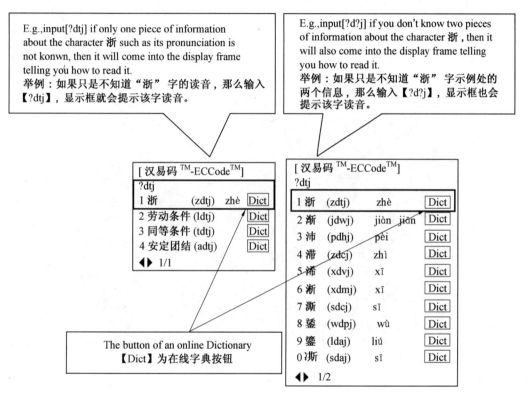

Figure 3.17  Illustrating dictionary lookup method by the ECCode™
图 3.17  图解"汉易码™"查字典方法

Unlike most Chinese-teaching online resources, the ECCode™ integrated with its companion online dictionary would mainly solve the problem which is faced by the most Chinese-learners who are in the conditions of dynamic learning of Chinese Language, e.g., such as those on the shopping street who do not know Chinese characters written on a billboard 40 meters away (Figure 3.18) but want to learn them. That is to say, they almost have no other highly efficient ways to input various Chinese characters on many billboards tens meters away into an information device by a soft or hard keyboard. In other word, the ECCode™ emphasizes the concept of "dynamical independent Chinese learning"—a way to learn Chinese anywhere and anytime as well as not depending on others. In this way, people can be liberated from the study and classroom for learning Chinese. They can acquire their accumulation of

67

Chinese knowledge in an all-round way, and lay the solid foundation of keywriting ability for paperless office in the future.

与其他很多汉语教学在线资源不同,"汉易码™"与配套的在线字典相结合,主要是想要解决许多处于动态汉语学习之中的人所面临的这样一个问题,例如汉语学习者在逛商业街时,想要认识40米之外中文广告牌上的陌生汉字(如图3.18所示),但在这种情况下,他们几乎没有其他高效的方法使其能够在信息设备上用软硬键盘输入各种汉字,以便查字典和学习这些汉字。换句话说,"汉易码™"强调的是"汉语动态自主学习"理念——就是随时随地不依赖于他人的一种汉语学习方式。这样,人们就能够从学习汉语的书房和教室中解放出来,并从生活的方方面面全方位地积累汉语知识了。借此,就为日后无纸化办公奠定了扎实的"键写能力"之基础。

Figure 3.18  One situation of learning Chinese characters anywhere and anytime
图 3.18  随时随地学习汉语的一种场景示例

## 3.4  Five basic strokes and stroke combination
## 5 个基本笔画及笔画组合

### 3.4.1  Five Basic Strokes
### 5 个基本笔画

We've claimed that it's not necessary for you to worry about learning how to write beautiful characters containing so many strokes. The ECCode™ used for keywriting Chinese characters only uses five basic strokes out of so many strokes, which are introduced as follows.

前文曾经说过,不必为如何写出含有那么多笔画的漂亮汉字而纠结。在那么多笔画当中,用于汉字键写的"汉易码™"只选用了5个基本笔画。这5个基本笔画分别介绍如下。

Chapter 3　Basic knowledge
基础知识

(1) Stroke "一"

笔画"横",读作/héng/

The corresponding English title of stroke "一" is horizontal line or horizon; in fact, here it includes the long horizon line, short one, thick one, thin one as well as various oblique ones (Table 3.10).

笔画"一"(横,读/héng/),对应的英文名称叫 horizontal line,或叫 horizon;其实,这里的笔画"横"包括了长横、短横、细横以及各种斜横(参见表 3.10)。

(2) Stroke "丨"

竖,读作/shù/

Stroke "丨", also called vertical stroke, means a vertical line; it includes the long vertical line, short one, thick one, thin one as well as various obliquely vertical lines (Table 3.10).

笔画"丨"(竖,读/shù/),也叫垂直笔画,指垂直的一条线;笔画"竖"实际上包括长竖、短竖、粗竖、细竖以及各种斜竖(参见表 3.10)。

(3) Stroke "丿"

撇,读作/piě/

Stroke "丿" is a left-falling stroke; of course, it also includes various shapes (Table 3.10).

笔画"丿"(撇,读/piě/),即指向左下方落下的笔画;当然,笔画"撇"也包括各种形状(参见表 3.10)。

(4) Stroke "、"

点,读作/diǎn/

Stroke "、" is a dot stroke; of course, it also includes various shapes (Table 3.10).

笔画"、"(点,读/diǎn/),即指英文的 dot;当然,笔画"点"也包括各种形状(参见表 3.10)。

(5) Stroke "一"

折,读作/zhé/

Stroke "一" means a turn line or a line with a hook; it also includes various shapes of curve, including various vertical lines with a right hook (Table 3.10).

笔画"一"(折,读/zhé/),即指弯曲或带钩的线条;笔画"折"同样有各种形状,包括各种带右弯钩的笔画(参见表 3.10)。

## Table 3.10 Table of 5 basic strokes which cover respectively its same type stroke of itself
### 表 3.10　5个基本笔画所代表的同类笔画示例

| No.<br>编号 | Stroke type<br>笔画归类 | Same type stroke<br>同类笔画 | Examples<br>例字 | Calligraphy direction<br>运笔示范 |
|---|---|---|---|---|
| 1 | Horizon<br>héng<br>横<br>(6) | 一 | 二、三、丰 | |
| 2 | | 一 | 士、王、壬 | |
| 3 | | 一 | 土、下、正 | |
| 4 | | 一 | 七、毛、皂 | |
| 5 | | 一 | 虫、好、船 | |
| 6 | | 丶 | 习、冷、圾 | |
| 7 | Vertical<br>shù<br>竖<br>(8) | 丨 | 尘、圭、止 | |
| 8 | | 丨 | 世、甘 | |
| 9 | | 丨 | 古、共 | |

Chapter 3 Basic knowledge
基础知识

Table 3.10(Continued)　表3.10(续)

| No.<br>编号 | Stroke type<br>笔画归类 | Same type stroke<br>同类笔画 | Examples<br>例字 | Calligraphy direction<br>运笔示范 |
|---|---|---|---|---|
| 10 | Vertical<br>shù<br>竖<br>(8) | ∣ | 十、干、中 | |
| 11 | | ∣ | 卜、川、木 | |
| 12 | | 丿 | 子、手、狂 | |
| 13 | | 丁 | 于、乎、予 | |
| 14 | | 丁 | 丁、寸、才 | |
| 15 | Left-falling<br>piě<br>撇<br>(6) | ㇀ | 千、斤、舌 | |
| 16 | | 丿 | 牛、生、年 | |
| 17 | | 丿 | 人、左、少 | |
| 18 | | 丿 | 义、文、父 | |

71

Table 3.10 (Continued)　表3.10(续)

| No. 编号 | Stroke type 笔画归类 | Same type stroke 同类笔画 | Examples 例字 | Calligraphy direction 运笔示范 |
|---|---|---|---|---|
| 19 | Left-falling piě 撇 (6) | ノ | 厂、月 | |
| 20 | | ノ | 大、火、史 | |
| 21 | | ヽ | 八、入、太 | |
| 22 | Dot diǎn 点 (5) | ⌒ | 之、这、廷 | |
| 23 | | ′ | 刃、小、写 | |
| 24 | | ヽ | 斗、头、雨 | |
| 25 | | ヽ | 不、斥、贝 | |
| 26 | Turn zhé 折 (53) | フ | 了、子、矛 | |
| 27 | | フ | 之、乏、芝 | |

Chapter 3  Basic knowledge
基础知识

Table  3.10(Continued)　表3.10(续)

| No. 编号 | Stroke type 笔画归类 | Same type stroke 同类笔画 | Examples 例字 | Calligraphy direction 运笔示范 |
|---|---|---|---|---|
| 28 | Turn zhé 折 (53) | ㄋ | 又、久、夕 | |
| 29 | | フ ㄣ | 专、传、砖 | |
| 30 | | ㄋ | 及、极、建 | |
| 31 | | ㄋ乀 | 过、边、进 | |
| 32 | | ㄟ | 以、衣、农 | |
| 33 | | ㄴ | 瓜、瓦 | |
| 34 | | ㄴ | 长、良 | |
| 35 | | ㄥ | 乡、红、级 | |
| 36 | | ㄥ | 么、台、允 | |

Table 3.10(Continued)　表3.10(续)

| No.编号 | Stroke type 笔画归类 | Same type stroke 同类笔画 | Examples 例字 | Calligraphy direction 运笔示范 |
|---|---|---|---|---|
| 37 | Turn zhé 折 (53) | ㇇ | 计、认、识 | |
| 38 | | ㇕ | 口、五、今 | |
| 39 | | ㇆ | 互、丑 | |
| 40 | | ㇈ | 片、且、直 | |
| 41 | | ㇄ | 山、凶、画 | |
| 42 | | ㇄ | 牙、屯、出 | |
| 43 | | ㇄ | 亡、世 | |
| 44 | | ㇄ | 区、巨、匠 | |
| 45 | | ㇄ | 车、东 | |

# Chapter 3　Basic knowledge
## 基础知识

Table　3.10(Continued)　表3.10(续)

| No.<br>编号 | Stroke type<br>笔画归类 | Same type stroke<br>同类笔画 | Examples<br>例字 | Calligraphy direction<br>运笔示范 |
|---|---|---|---|---|
| 46 | Turn<br>zhé<br>折<br>(53) | ㄴ | 母、每 | |
| 47 | | ㄑ | 女、汝 | |
| 48 | | ㄑ | 如、妈、姐 | |
| 49 | | ㄑ | 妥、安、要 | |
| 50 | | ㄴ | 四、泗 | |
| 51 | | ㄴ | 酉、酒、醋 | |
| 52 | | 乙 | 朵、没、铅 | |
| 53 | | 乙 | 凹 | |
| 54 | | ㄣ | 鼎 | |

Table 3.10(Continued)　表3.10(续)

| No. 编号 | Stroke type 笔画归类 | Same type stroke 同类笔画 | Examples 例字 | Calligraphy direction 运笔示范 |
|---|---|---|---|---|
| 55 | Turn zhé 折 (53) | ㄴ | 兄、巴、巳 | |
| 56 | | ㄴ | 儿、电、兆 | |
| 57 | | ㄟ | 九、丸、乞 | |
| 58 | | ㄟ | 几、凡、机 | |
| 59 | | ㄟ | 飞、气、风 | |
| 60 | | ㄴ | 戈、我、成 | |
| 61 | | ㄴ | 心、必、志 | |
| 62 | | ㄱ | 欠、吹 | |
| 63 | | ㄱ | 买、军、宝 | |

Chapter 3　Basic knowledge
基础知识

Table　3.10(Continued)　表3.10(续)

| No.<br>编号 | Stroke type<br>笔画归类 | Same type stroke<br>同类笔画 | Examples<br>例字 | Calligraphy direction<br>运笔示范 |
|---|---|---|---|---|
| 64 | Turn<br>zhé<br>折<br>(53) | ㄋ | 也、他、池 | 也 |
| 65 | | ㄱ | 四、而、书 | 书 |
| 66 | | ㄱ | 田、回、勿 | 勿 |
| 67 | | ㄱ | 万、方、芳 | 万 |
| 68 | | ㄱ | 习、句、旬 | 习 |
| 69 | | ㄱ | 司、同、因 | 司 |
| 70 | | ㄅ | 永、月、丹 | 永 |
| 71 | | ㄅ | 引、驶 | 引 |
| 72 | | ㄅ | 与、马、鸟 | 马 |

77

Table 3.10(Continued)　表3.10(续)

| No. 编号 | Stroke type 笔画归类 | Same type stroke 同类笔画 | Examples 例字 | Calligraphy direction 运笔示范 |
|---|---|---|---|---|
| 73 | Turn zhé 折 (53) | 勹 | 弗、夷、驾 | 夷 |
| 74 | | 了 | 乃、仍 | 乃 |
| 75 | | 弓 | 汤、杨 | 汤 |
| 76 | | 弓 | 凸 | 凸 |
| 77 | | 了 | 队、阳、阵 | 队 |
| 78 | | 了 | 邓、邮、那 | 邓 |

　　Through Table 3.10, you can find which or how many strokes are merged respectively by every stroke defined by the ECCode™. Here are some simple explanations as follows.

　　通过表3.10，大家可以发现"汉易码™"所定义的笔画合并了哪些笔画，以及"汉易码™"所定义的每种笔画合并了多少个笔画。下面就对此做一些简单的说明。

- There are 6 shapes of horizonal stroke "横(一)"; e.g., the rising stroke "㇀"(提, read as /tí/) is taken as the horizon stroke "一" too, namely, (㇀)=(一) defined by the ECCode™.

　　笔画"横(一)"包含6种类型的"横"；例如，笔画"提(㇀，读作/tí/)"也被视作笔画"横"，亦即"汉易码™"规定(㇀)=(一)。

- There are 8 shapes of vertical stroke "竖(丨)"; e.g., the vertical stroke with a left hook "亅"(左竖钩, read as /zuǒ shù gōu/) is taken as the vertical stroke "丨", namely,

（亅）=（丨）defined by the ECCode™.

笔画"竖"有8种形状；例如，"左竖钩（亅，读作/zuǒ shù gōu/）"被当成了"竖（丨）"，亦即"汉易码™"规定（亅）=（丨）。

- There are 6 shapes of left-falling stroke "撇（丿）".

  笔画"撇（丿）"有6种形状。

- There are 5 shapes of dot stroke "点（丶）"; e. g. , the right-falling stroke "㇏" or "㇏"（捺，read as /nà/）" is taken as the dot stroke "丶", namely, （㇏）=（㇏）=（丶）defined by the ECCode™.

  笔画"丶"有5种形状，例如，笔画"捺（㇏或者㇏，读/nà/）"被当成了笔画"丶"，亦即"汉易码™"规定（㇏）=（㇏）=（丶）。

- There are 53 shapes of turn stroke "折（㇀）", i. e. , as long as a line with turn or a right hook, it is taken as the turn stroke by the ECCode™.

  笔画"折（㇀）"一共有53种形状，即，线条带弯或带右边钩的笔画，"汉易码™"都视其为笔画"折"。

In other word, you can see how many strokes in Table 3. 10 are simplified by the ECCode™! It greatly reduces the difficulty of learner's mastering the keylearning and keywriting of Chinese characters.

换句话说，大家可以看到"汉易码™"简化了表3.10当中的多少个汉字笔画！这也就大大降低了汉语学习者掌握汉字键学和汉字键写的难度。

### 3.4.2 Stroke Combination
笔画组合

Apart from the five basic strokes and related stroke conventions, the ECCode™ introduces a concept of TWO STROKE COMBINATION (TSC for short) to reduce the Rate of Coincidental Code (RCC for short).

除了5个基本笔画及其相关的笔画约定之外，为了减少汉字输入的重码率（RCC），"汉易码™"引进了一个"两笔画组合（TSC）"的概念。

At first, what's the concept of the RCC? The RCC refers to the percentage of the number of Chinese characters with code duplication in the total number of Chinese characters.

首先，什么是重码率？重码率是指有代码重复现象的汉字数量占汉字总数的百分比。

Second, what's the TSC? The TSC means that two strokes are selected out of the five basic strokes mentioned above and made to be combined together to compose a pair of two strokes (see Table 3.11). The concept is more or less like the concept of combination in mathematics. So, it brings another advantage that you don't worry about the problem of micro stroke order you may encounter in the traditional theory of Chinese characters. We will introduce the micro stroke order later.

其次,什么叫两笔画组合？两笔画组合就是指从5个基本笔画当中挑出两个笔画进行配对组合(参见表3.11)。这个笔画组合概念多多少少有点像数学里面的组合概念。所以,这个笔画组合概念带来了另外一个好处,就是大家不必在意传统汉字理论当中遇到的微观笔顺问题(稍后介绍)。

Table 3.11 The combinations of two strokes out of the five basic strokes

表3.11 5个基本笔画中挑出2个笔画的组合

| Basic stroke 基本笔画 | Basic stroke 基本笔画 | | | | |
|---|---|---|---|---|---|
| | 一 | 丨 | 丿 | 丶 | ㇀ |
| 一 | (一一) | (一丨) | (一丿) | (一丶) | (一㇀) |
| 丨 | (丨一) | (丨丨) | (丨丿) | (丨丶) | (丨㇀) |
| 丿 | (丿一) | (丿丨) | (丿丿) | (丿丶) | (丿㇀) |
| 丶 | (丶一) | (丶丨) | (丶丿) | (丶丶) | (丶㇀) |
| ㇀ | (㇀一) | (㇀丨) | (㇀丿) | (㇀丶) | (㇀㇀) |

According to the concept property of combination in mathematics, the combination has nothing to do with the order of its two composed elements. So, two combinations of two strokes, such as the two combinations of stroke (一) and stroke (丿), namely (一丿) and (丿一), have no difference from each other. That is to say, (一丿) = (丿一). Of course, (一一) = (一). And others are analogous. Therefore, Table 3.11 is simplified as Table 3.12.

根据数学当中组合的概念属性,一个组合与两个组合构成元素的顺序无关。所以,两个笔画的两个组合之间没有区别,如笔画"一"与笔画"丿"的两个组合,亦即(一丿)和(丿一)之间没有区别,也就是说,(一丿) = (丿一)。当然,(一一) = (一)。其他以此类推。因此,表3.11就可以简化成下面的表3.12了。

Table 3.12 Simplication of Table 3.11 for two-stroke combinations

表3.12 两笔画组合简化表

| Basic stroke 基本笔画 | Basic stroke 基本笔画 | | | | |
|---|---|---|---|---|---|
| | 一 | 丨 | 丿 | 丶 | ㇀ |
| 一 | (一一)=(一) | (一丨) | (一丿) | (一丶) | (一㇀) |
| 丨 | | (丨丨)=(丨) | (丿丨) | (丨丶) | (丨㇀) |
| 丿 | | | (丿丿)=(丿) | (丶丿) | (丿㇀) |
| 丶 | | | | (丶丶)=(丶) | (丶㇀) |
| ㇀ | | | | | (㇀㇀)=(㇀) |

It's obvious that there are 10 different stroke combinations and 5 basic strokes in Table 3.12, i.e., their codes needing to be remembered. And you will soon see how the basic strokes and the stroke combinations introduced here will be used. Be patient, please!

显然,表 3.12 当中只有 10 个不同笔画的组合以及 5 个基本笔画,即它们的代码需要记住。大家很快就会看到基本笔画和笔画组合概念有什么用处,敬请耐心即可!

Now, let us study some examples based on the concept of TSC and 5 basic strokes as well as related stroke conventions.

现在,基于上述两笔画组合和 5 个基本笔画的概念以及相关的笔画约定,我们来举几个汉字字例进行分析研究。

**Example 3.1**   As to the last two strokes of the character "予" (shown in Figure 3.19 below), their TSC is (一丨) because the stroke "亅" (vertical with left hook) is taken as "丨" in the ECCode™, namely (亅) = (丨).

**例 3.1**   就汉字"予"的最后两个笔画而言(如图 3.19 所示),按照"汉易码™"的笔画约定,笔画"亅"被视作笔画"丨"了,亦即(亅)=(丨),其最后两笔画组合就是(一丨)。

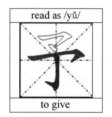

Figure 3.19   Character with the combination of its last two strokes
图 3.19   汉字最后两笔画组合的例字

**Example 3.2**   As to the characters "入" and "八" (shown in Figure 3.20), they can be split into the stroke combination of (丿丶) while encoding the two characters respectively, because the stroke "㇏" (right-falling) is taken as "丶" in the ECCode™, namely (㇏) = (丶).

**例 3.2**   就汉字"入"和汉字"八"来说(如图 3.20 所示),由于"汉易码™"把笔画"㇏"视作笔画"丶",即(㇏)=(丶),所以在对这两个汉字进行计算机编码时都可拆解为笔画组合(丿丶)。

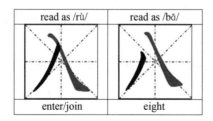

Figure 3 20 Two characters with the stroke combination (丿丶)
图 3.20   笔画组合为(丿丶)的两个汉字字例

**Example 3.3**　As to the character "刁" ( shown in Figure 3.21 ), it can be decomposed into the stroke combination of ( 乛一 ) = ( 一乛 ) because the stroke "⸌" ( rising stroke ) is taken as "一" in the ECCode™, namely (⸌) = ( 一 ).

**例 3.3**　就汉字"刁"而言(如图 3.21 所示),由于"汉易码™"把笔画"⸌"视作笔画"一",即(⸌)=(一),所以这个汉字可以拆解成笔画组合(乛一),也就是(一乛)的笔画组合。

Figure 3.21　A character with the stroke combination ( 一 乛 )
图 3.21　笔画组合为(一乛)的字例

**Example 3.4**　As to the character "儿" ( shown in Figure 3.22 ), it can be split into the stroke combination of ( 丿 乛 ) because the stroke "乚" ( vertical with a curve and a right hook ) being taken as "乛" in the ECCode™, namely ( 乚 ) = ( 乛 ).

**例 3.4**　就汉字"儿"而言(如图 3.22 所示),由于"汉易码™"把笔画"乚"视作笔画"乛",即( 乚 )=( 乛 ),所以汉字"儿"可以拆解成笔画组合(丿乛)。

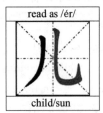

Figure 3.22　A character with the stroke combination ( 丿 乛 )
图 3.22　笔画组合为(丿乛)的字例

**Example 3.5**　As to the character "市" ( shown in Figure 3.23 ), the combination of its first two strokes is ( 丶一 ).

**例 3.5**　就汉字"市"而言(如图 3.23 所示),其前两个笔画组合就是(丶一)。

Figure 3.23　A character with the combination (、一) as its first two strokes

图 3.23　前两笔画组合为(、一)的字例

**Example 3.6**　As to the character "象"(shown in Figure 3.24), the combination of its first two strokes is (丿 ㄋ) and the combination of its last two strokes is (、丿).

例 3.6　就汉字"象"而言(如图 3.24 所示),其前两个笔画组合为(丿ㄋ),最后两个笔画组合为(、丿)。

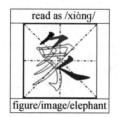

Figure 3.24　The combination of the first or last two strokes of the character "象"

图 3.24　"象"字前两个笔画组合与最后两个笔画组合

**Example 3.7**　As to the character "赢"(shown in Figure 3.25 below), the combination of its first two strokes is (、一) and the combination of its last two strokes is (、ㄋ); because the stroke "乁"(horizon turn with a curve and a right hook) is taken as "ㄋ" regulated by the ECCode™.

例 3.7　就汉字"赢"而言(参见图 3.25),其前两个笔画的组合是(、一);由于"汉易码™"把笔画"乁"视作笔画"ㄋ",所以这个字最后两个笔画的组合就是(、ㄋ)。

Figure 3.25　The combination of the first or last two strokes of the character "赢"

图 3.25　"赢"字的前两个笔画和最后两个笔画的组合图示

## 3.5 Differences between shape constituents and radicals of Chinese characters
## 汉字的字形组分与字根(偏旁部首)的区别

In the ECCode™, the SC is a big concept, which refers to a kind of geometric shape composing a Chinese character, including five basic STROKEs, 10 TSCs and 89 RADICALs, but the radical, including Pianpang Bushou and meaningless middleware, namely semantic, phonetic or meaningless component, is a small one. That is to say, what the extension of the concept SC includes covers what the counterpart of the concept radical includes (Figure 3.26). The concrete difference between them is already shown in previous Figure 3.2. In the context of the ECCode™, components and radicals are almost the same things.

在"汉易码™"中,字形组分是个大概念,即指构成汉字的一种几何形状,它包含5个基本笔画、10个不同笔画的组合以及89个字根;而字根却是个小概念,它包含偏旁部首和没有任何特指含意的中间件(构字部件)。也就是说,字形组分的概念外延包含字根的概念外延(如图3.26所示)。前文图3.2已经展示了它们之间的关系。在"汉易码™"语境之下,部件基本上就是指字根。

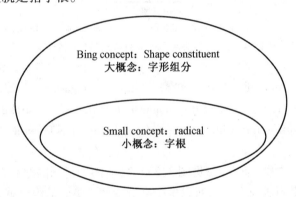

Figure 3.26　Inclusion relationship between constituents and radicals of Chinese characters
图3.26　汉字组分与字根之间的包含关系

Generally, a RADICAL or a COMPONENT is a shared SC by many Chinese characters (Table 3.13 below), and there are more than 200 common radicals in characters. However, the ECCode™ just uses 89 radicals as one or more "letters" of a CCCC. Furthermore, most of the 89 radicals are selected from the most commonly used ones, and only a few ones are defined by the ECCode™.

总的来说,字根或者部件是指许多汉字共享的一个字形成分(如表3.13所示),这样的常用字根汉字当中大致有200多个。不过,"汉易码™"只用了其中的89个字根作为计算机汉字代码的一个或多个"字母"。而且,这89个字根的大多数都选自最常用的字根,只有个别几个字根是"汉易码™"定义的。

Table 3.13   Examples of characters including the radical "亻"
表 3.13   含有"亻"的汉字举例

| Radical, a shared constituent by many characters<br>字根,一种多个汉字共享的汉字组分 | Example<br>例字 |
|---|---|
| 亻 | 你、他、住、们、借、保、做、使、伙、休、仗…… |

### 3.5.1   The key mapping of shape constituents
字形组分键位表

According to the Figure 3.2 above, it's easily concluded that the SCs in the ECCode™ contain the following shape "letters" (Figure 3.27).

根据前面图 3.2,大家可以发现,"汉易码™"的字形组分包括以下几种字形"字母"(参见下面图 3.27)。

- 5 basic strokes, equivalent to 5 "letters" which are constituents of a CCC or a CCCC.
  
  5 个基本笔画,相当于 5 个"字母",是计算机汉字或其代码的组成成分。

- 15 "TSCs" made of two strokes selected out of the five basic strokes, equivalent to 15 "letters" which are constituents of CCCs or CCCCs too; among them, the code-element of a combination made of a basic stroke and itself is the same as the basic stroke's code-element, e.g., [一一] = [一] = H, and only 10 combinations of two different strokes need to be remembered on purpose; here the so-called "code-element" is the code letter of a constituent, which is one of the parts composing a CCCC.
  
  从 5 个基本笔画当中挑出的两笔画"组合"一共有 15 个,相当于 15 个"字母",也是计算机汉字或其代码的组成成分;在这 15 个"字母"当中,有 5 个"字母"是 5 个基本笔画跟其自身"组合"的码元,它们分别与 5 个基本笔画的码元相同。例如,[一一] = [一] = H。这样一来,就只有 10 个不同笔画的两笔画组合之码元需要特别记忆了。在此,所谓"码元",就是指汉字一个组分的字母代码,它是汉字计算机汉字代码的一个组成部分。

- 89 radicals, equivalent to 89 "letters" which are constituents of CCCs or CCCCs too.
  
  89 个字根,相当于 89 个"字母",也是计算机汉字或其代码的组成成分。

```
                    ┌─ A radical → using a letter for the shape constituent
                    │  (also called a shape code-element)
                    │     zì gēn   yòng yī gè zì mǔ biǎo shì zì xíng zǔ fēn   xíng mǎ mǎ yuán
                    │  字根→用一个字母表示字形组分(形码码元)
                    │
Shape constituents  │  A combination of two basic strokes → using a letter for the SC
of Chinese         ─┤  (also called a shape code-element)
characters          │     jī běn bǐ huà zǔ hé    yòng yī gè zì mǔ biǎo shì zì xíng zǔ fēn   xíng mǎ mǎ yuán
 hàn zì zì xíng zǔ fēn │  基本笔画组合→用一个字母表示字形组分(形码码元)
汉字字形组分        │
                    │  A basic stroke → using a letter for the shape constituent
                    │  (also called a shape code-element)
                    │     jī běn bǐ huà    yòng yī gè zì mǔ biǎo shì zì xíng zǔ fēn   xíng mǎ mǎ yuán
                    └─ 基本笔画→用一个字母表示字形组分(形码码元)
```

Figure 3.27 Classification of shape constituents (letters) of the Chinese character

图3.27 汉字字形组分(字母)构成分类示例

Note: The sign of "→" express derivative relationships.

shuō míng  fú hào   biǎo shì pài shēng guān xì
说 明：符 号"→"表 示 派 生 关 系。

In other word, in the ECCode™, there are altogether 104 SCs of Chinese characters which are equivalent to 104 "letters" of CCCs. You need to get familiar with them as soon as possible.

换句话说,在"汉易码™"当中,总共有104个汉字的字形组分,亦即相当于有104个汉字"字母"。对这些汉字"字母",需要大家尽快熟悉起来。

In fact, the 104 SCs of Chinese characters are assigned to 26 English letter keys. The following Table 3.14 is the KEY MAPPING TABLE(KMT for short) of these SCs, almost equivalent to the table of shape "letter" of Chinese characters in the ECCode™(Table 3.14). Just like you need to remember the alphabet for English learning, all you need to do now is to remember which letter key each shape constituent, namely a SC, is on. Of course, there are two tips for memorizing most of the SCs.

实际上,汉字104个字形组分都被分配给26个英文字母键了。表3.14就是字形组分键位表(KMT),相当于"汉易码™"的汉字字形"字母表"。就像学习英文大家需要记忆字母表一样,现在所需要做的就是记住这些字形组分都在哪一个字母键上。当然,这里有两个方法可以帮助大家辅助记忆大多数的字根。

Chapter 3 Basic knowledge
基础知识

Table 3.14 The key mapping table of shape constituents (letters) of Chinese characters in ECCode™
表 3.14 "汉易码™"汉字字形键位(字母)表

| Q 犭 且(目) | W (一乛) 王 | E 耳 阝(卩) 巳(㔾) | R 亻(彳) 人(大) 日(白) | T 扌 土(士) | Y 礻(衤) 月 也 雨 羽 | U 又(夂夊) 九 幺 酉(襾) | I (丨) (冂) | O (丿丨) (丿一) | P (丿) |
|---|---|---|---|---|---|---|---|---|---|

| A (丶一) (丶乛) | S 山(凵) 水(氺氵) 尸(户) 手 | D (丶) 冫(氵) 刂 | F (丿乛) 方 卩 | G 工 广(疒) | H (一) 禾 火 | J 巾 金(钅) 斤 | K 口 可 | L (丨乛) 力(刀) 门 |
|---|---|---|---|---|---|---|---|---|

| Z (乛) 走 辶(廴) 子 竹 | X 心 忄(忄) 小(⺌) | C 艹 厂 寸 虫 | V (丶丿) 灬 丷 | B 宀(宀穴) 贝 巴 | N 女 牛 鸟 | M 马 门 木(木木) 皿(罒) |
|---|---|---|---|---|---|---|

## 3.5.2 Two tips for memorizing the key mapping table
键位表两个辅助记忆方法

In the KMT of the ECCode™ (the Table 3.14 above), there are two phenomena. First, there are some letter keys on which several radicals outside parentheses have the same first letter in their pronunciations; second, some few radicals inside parentheses look like their counterparts in shape outside parentheses. So, two aided memory methods of the KMT (the Table 3.21 above) are born out of the two phenomena.

在"汉易码™"的键位表中(参见上面表 3.14),存在着两个现象。首先,在一些字母键上,有几个括号外面的字根读音之第一个字母都相同;其次,少部分括号里面的字根与其对应的括号外面的字根看上去形状相似。所以,上面键位表 3.14 的两个辅助记忆方法就据此现象而生了。

1. Tip one: phonetic similarity
助记方法 1:音相似

Most radicals (the ones without parenthesis) in Table 3.14 above are matched with English letters according to the first phonemes of the pinyin of the radicals. For example, the radical "土" is read as "tǔ", so its code is the very letter "T", which is also called a SHAPE CODE-ELEMENT (SCE or SC for short) when it is a SC of a character's code, namely, a

87

"letter" of the Chinese character.

在键位表 3.14 当中,许多没有括号的字根都放置在其读音的第一个字母键上了。例如,字根"土"的读音是"tǔ",所以这个字根的代码就是字母"T"了。当这个字根"土"是一个汉字代码的字形组分时,这个字母"T"也被称为这个汉字代码的一个字形码元(汉语简称"形码"),亦即是这个汉字的一个字形"字母"。

Similarly, the codes of the four basic strokes (Table 3.14 above) are also matched by their pronunciation as follows。

同样的,下面 4 个基本笔画的代码(参见表 3.14)也是放置在其读音的第一个字母键上的。

- Letter H for the code of the horizon stroke "一"(横,read as /héng/).
  字母 H 就是笔画"一"(横,读/héng/)的代码。
- Letter P for the code of the left-falling stroke "丿"(撇,read as /piě/).
  字母 P 就是笔画"丿"(撇,读/ piě/)的代码。
- Letter D for the code of the dot stroke "、"(点,read as /diǎn/).
  字母 D 就是笔画"、"(点,读/ diǎn/)的代码。
- Letter Z for the code of the turn stroke "⇁"(折,read as /zhé/).
  字母 Z 就是笔画"⇁"(折,读/zhé/)的代码。

However, among the five basic strokes, there is only an exception of "丨"(竖,read as /shù/) which is represented by the letter "I(i)" because of their shape similarity (Table 3.14 above). And the reason for this arrangement is to reduce the RCC (equivalent to the work of reducing homophone phenomena).

但是,在 5 个基本笔画当中,只有笔画"丨"(竖,读/shù/)是一个例外。因为这个笔画"丨"的形状看上去很像字母"I(i)",所以其代码就是字母"I(i)"了(参见表 3.14)。这样安排的原因就是为了降低汉字代码的重码率(相当于减少"同音字"的现象)。

If you just start to learn Chinese and almost have no idea of Chinese radicals, don't worry about how to read a radical which is placed on its corresponding letter key according to the first letter of its pronunciation. The Table 3.15 below is provided to help you to fast recognize and remember most of them, which is arranged according to the property of phonetic similarity or shape similarity among these radicals.

如果大家刚刚开始学习汉语而对汉字字根几乎没有任何概念意识的话,那么大家也不必为字母键上的字根怎么读而纠结。表 3.15 可以帮助大家快速认记那些音相似的字根。

## Chapter 3  Basic knowledge
基础知识

**Table 3.15  The radicals with the property of phonetic similarity**
**表 3.15  具有音相似属性的字根表**

| No.编号 | Radical 字根 | Pronunciation 读音 | Meaning of the radical 字根含义 | Letter of SCE 形码字母 |
|---|---|---|---|---|
| 1 | 宀 | bǎo gài tóu 宝盖头 | Roof or house, occurring in 它, 家, 安, etc. 房顶,含此字根的汉字有它、家、安等 | B(key) |
| 2 | 贝 | bèi zì páng 贝字旁 | Seashell; money, currency, occurring in 则, 财, 购, etc. 贝壳,含此字根的汉字有钱、财、购等 | |
| 3 | 巴 | bā zì páng 巴字旁 | Greatly desire, anxiously hope, occurring in 爸, 色, 把, etc. 担心无法实现的愿望,含此字根的汉字有爸、色、把等 | |
| 4 | 艹 | cǎo zì tóu 草字头 | Grass, occurring in 花, 共, 世, etc. 草之意,含此字根的汉字有花、共、世等 | C(key) |
| 5 | 厂 | chǎng zì páng 厂字旁 | Residence, cliff, occurring in 原, 历, 压, etc. 居住地、悬崖边等意,含此字根的汉字有原、历、压等 | |
| 6 | 寸 | cùn zì páng 寸字旁 | A unit of length, inch, thumb, occurring in 过, 对, 时, etc. 长度单位、英寸、拇指等意,含此字根的汉字有过、对、时等 | |
| 7 | 虫 | chóng zì páng 虫字旁 | Reptiles, insects, worms, occurring in 虾, 蚁, 虹, etc. 爬行虫类、昆虫、蠕虫等意,含此字根的汉字有虾、蚁、虹等 | |
| 8 | 氵 | sān diǎn shuǐ páng (三)点水旁 | Water, occurring in 江, 活, 范, etc. 水之意,含此字根的汉字有江、活、范等 | D(key) |
| 9 | 刂 | lì dāo páng (利)刀旁 | Knife, occurring in 利, 型, 剑, etc. 刀之意,含此字根的汉字有利、型、剑等 | |

Table 3.15(Continued) 表3.15(续)

| No. 编号 | Radical 字根 | Pronunciation 读音 | Meaning of the radical 字根含义 | Letter of SCE 形码字母 |
|---|---|---|---|---|
| 10 | 耳 | ěr duo páng 耳朵旁 | Ear, handle, occurring in 取、联、最, etc. 耳朵、手柄等意,含此字根的汉字有取、联、最等 | E(key) |
| 11 | 阝 | | Mound, city, occurring in 防、阻、院、邦、那、郊, etc. 土丘、城池等意,含此字根的汉字有防、阻、院、邦、那、郊等 | |
| 12 | 方 | fāng zì páng 方字旁 | Direction, power, side, square, occurring in 放、族、施, etc. 方向、权势、侧面、正方形等意,含此字根的汉字有放、族、施等 | F(key) |
| 13 | 足 | zú zì páng 足字旁 In the ECCode™, using the first letter of word Foot as a mnemonic, "汉易码™"中,使用英文单词Foot的第一个字母作为助记方法 | Foot, occurring in 路、跑、露, etc. 足之意,含此字根的汉字有路、跑、露等 | F(key) |
| 14 | 工 | gōng zì páng 工字旁 | Worker, work, profession, trade, craft, skill, labor, occurring in 功、式、江、空, etc. 干活的人、干活、职业、贸易、手艺、技能、劳力等意,含此字根的汉字有功、式、江、空等 | G(key) |
| 15 | 广 | guǎng zì páng 广字旁 | Wide, surname Guang, numerous, to spread, occurring in 应、府、度, etc. 宽、广姓、许多、拓展等意,含此字根的汉字有应、府、度等 | |
| 16 | 禾 | hé mù páng 禾木旁 | Grain, cereal, occurring in 利、和、种, etc. 粮食、谷物等意,含此字根的汉字有利、和、种等 | H(key) |
| 17 | 火 | huǒ zì páng 火字旁 | Fire, occurring in 灯、灿、烛, etc. 火之意,含此字根的汉字有灯、灿、烛等 | |

Chapter 3 Basic knowledge
基础知识

Table 3.15(Continued) 表3.15(续)

| No. 编号 | Radical 字根 | Pronunciation 读音 | Meaning of the radical 字根含义 | Letter of SCE 形码字母 |
|---|---|---|---|---|
| 18 | 巾 | jīn zì páng 巾字旁 | A piece of cloth, occurring in 布、市、帽, etc. 织物之意,含此字根的汉字有布、市、帽等 | J(key) |
| 19 | 金 | jīn zì páng 金字旁 | Metals in general, money, gold, occurring in 鑫、鉴, etc. 金属、金钱、金子等意,含此字根的汉字有鑫、鉴等 | |
| 20 | 斤 | jīn zì páng 斤字旁 | The shape of an Oracle Bone Inscription, like an axe, meaning "chop", occurring in 近、斥、欣, etc. 一个甲骨文,其字形像一把斧头,表示"砍"之意,含此字根的汉字有近、斥、欣等 | |
| 21 | 钅 | jīn zì páng 金字旁 | Metal, gold, occurring in 钢、钦、铃, etc. 金属、金子等意,含此字根的汉字有钢、钦、铃等 | |
| 22 | 口 | kǒu zì páng 口字旁 | Mouth, occurring in 吃、喝、中, etc. 嘴巴之意,含此字根的汉字有吃、喝、中等 | K(key) |
| 23 | 可 | kě zì páng 可字旁 | Approve, but, can, may, need, yet, occurring in 哥、寄、倚, etc. 赞同、转折、允许、能够、需要、但是等意,含此字根的汉字有哥、寄、倚等 | |
| 24 | 力 | lì zì páng 力字旁 | Power, capability, influence, occurring in 办、加、动, etc. 能力、才能、影响力等意,含此字根的汉字有办、加、动等 | L(key) |
| 25 | 马 | mǎ zì páng 马字旁 | Horse, occurring in 骑、驰、驾, etc. 马之意,如骑、驰、驾等 | M(key) |
| 26 | 门 | mén zì kuàng 门字框 | Door, occurring in 问、闭、闯, etc. 门之意,含此字根的汉字有问、闭、闯等 | |
| 27 | 木 | mù zì páng 木字旁 | Wood, tree, occurring in 朴、杜、栋, etc. 木质、树木等意,含此字根的汉字有朴、杜、栋等 | |
| 28 | 皿 | mǐn zì dǐ 皿字底 | Dish, occurring in 孟、猛、益, etc. 餐具之意,含此字根的汉字有孟、猛、益等 | |

Table 3.15(Continued)　表3.15(续)

| No.<br>编号 | Radical<br>字根 | Pronunciation<br>读音 | Meaning of the radical<br>字根含义 | Letter of SCE<br>形码字母 |
|---|---|---|---|---|
| 29 | 女 | nǚ zì páng<br>女字旁 | Woman, daughter, female, occurring in 妈、按、她, etc.<br>妇女、女儿、雌性等意,含此字根的汉字有妈、按、她等 | N(key) |
| 30 | 牛 | niú zì páng<br>牛字旁 | Cattle, occurring in 牡、物、牲, etc.<br>牲畜之意,含此字根的汉字有牡、物、牲等 | |
| 31 | 鸟 | niǎo zì páng<br>鸟字旁 | Bird, occurring in 鹅、鸡、鸭, etc.<br>鸟禽之意,含此字根的汉字有鹅、鸡、鸭等 | |
| 32 | 犭 | fǎn quǎn páng<br>(反)犬旁 | Dog, animal, occurring in 狂、独、狠, etc.<br>狗、动物等意,含此字根的汉字有狂、独、狠等 | Q<br>(key) |
| 33 | 且 | qiě zì páng<br>且字旁 | Even, just, occurring in 县、助、粗, etc.<br>还、姑且之意,含此字根的汉字有县、助、粗等 | |
| 34 | 亻 | dān rén zì páng<br>(单)人字旁 | Person, occurring in 仁、位、你, etc.<br>人之意,含此字根的汉字有仁、位、你等 | R<br>(key) |
| 35 | 人 | rén zì páng<br>人字旁 | Person, human being, occurring in 两、众、提, etc.<br>人、人类等意,含此字根的汉字有两、众、提等 | |
| 36 | 日 | rì zì páng<br>日字旁 | Sun, occurring in 晚、旺、晴, etc.<br>太阳之意,含此字根的汉字有晚、旺、晴等 | |
| 37 | 山 | shān zì páng<br>山字旁 | Hill, mountain, occurring in 凯、岁、密, etc.<br>山坡、山峰等意,含此字根的汉字有凯、岁、密等 | |
| 38 | 水 | shuǐ zì dǐ<br>水字底 | Liquid, water, occurring in 浆、泵、腺, etc.<br>河川、水流等意,含此字根的汉字有浆、泵、腺等 | S(key) |
| 39 | 尸 | shī zì páng<br>尸字旁 | Corpse, body, occurring in 屋、尽、尿, etc.<br>尸体、体格之意,含此字根的汉字有屋、尽、尿等 | |

Table 3.15(Continued) 表3.15(续)

| No. 编号 | Radical 字根 | Pronunciation 读音 | | Meaning of the radical 字根含义 | Letter of SCE 形码字母 |
|---|---|---|---|---|---|
| 40 | 手 | shǒu zì páng 手字旁 | | A bunch of fives, fist, hand, manus, mauley, pud, occurring in 拳,拿,掌, etc. 张开的手掌、拳头、手、前肢、前脚等意,含此字根的汉字有拳、拿、掌等 | S(key) |
| 41 | 扌 | tí shǒu páng 提手旁 | | Hand, occurring in 扛,担,摘, etc. 手之意,含此字根的汉字有扛、担、摘等 | T(key) |
| 42 | 土 | tǔ zì páng 土字旁 | | Soil, earth, occurring in 地,场,城, etc. 土壤、灰尘等意,含此字根的汉字有地、场、城等 | |
| 43 | 又 | yòu zì páng 又字旁 | similar to the pronunciation of the letter U 类似英文字母U的发音 | Also, again, occurring in 对,双,难, etc. 也、再次之意,含此字根的汉字有对、双、难 | U(key) |
| 44 | 尢 | yóu zì páng 尢字旁 | | Lame, weak, occurring in 尤,尨,尬, etc. 坡脚、羸弱之意,含此字根的汉字有尤、尨、尬等 | |
| 45 | 幺 | yāo zì páng 幺字旁 | | One, youngest, occurring in 幼,幻,幽, etc.; Silk, occurring in 红,约,纯, etc. 数量"一"、最小的等意,含此字根的汉字有幼、幻、幽等; 丝之意,含此字根的汉字有红、约、纯等 | |
| 46 | 酉 | yǒu zì páng 酉字旁 | | 10th terrestrial branch, a wine vessel, occurring in 酸,酿,酬, etc. 排序为10的地支、盛酒器皿等意,含此字根的汉字有酸、酿、酬等 | |
| 47 | 王 | wáng zì páng 王字旁 | | King, great, occurring in 玩,珍,班, etc. 国王、伟大等意,含此字根的汉字有玩、珍、班等 | W(key) |

Table 3.15 (Continued)  表3.15(续)

| No.<br>编号 | Radical<br>字根 | Pronunciation<br>读音 | Meaning of the radical<br>字根含义 | Letter of SCE<br>形码字母 |
|---|---|---|---|---|
| 48 | 心 | xīn zì dǐ<br>心字底 | Mind, occurring in 忘, 想, 恋, etc.<br>心理之意,含此字根的汉字有忘、想、恋等 | X(key) |
| 49 | 忄 | shù xīn páng<br>(竖)心旁 | Heart, occurring in 怀, 快, 性, etc.<br>心之意,含此字根的汉字有怀、快、性等 | |
| 50 | 小 | xiǎo zì páng<br>小字旁 | Small, little, tiny, occurring in 尖, 京, 你, etc.<br>小、细小、微少等意,含此字根的汉字有尖、京、你等 | |
| 51 | 衤 | yī zì páng<br>衣字旁 | Clothes, occurring in 初, 袖, 被, etc.<br>衣服之意,含此字根的汉字有初、袖、被等 | Y(key) |
| 52 | 月 | yuè zì páng<br>月字旁 | Moon, flesh, occurring in 肚, 明, 胖, etc.<br>月亮、肉等意,含此字根的汉字有肚、明、胖等 | |
| 53 | 也 | yě zì páng<br>也字旁 | Also, likewise, too, either, occurring in 他, 她, 地, etc.<br>也、同样地等意,含此字根的汉字有他、她、地等 | |
| 54 | 雨 | yǔ zì tóu<br>雨字头 | Rain, occurring in 雪, 霜, 雷, etc.<br>雨水之意,含此字根的汉字有雪、霜、雷等 | |
| 55 | 羽 | yǔ zì páng<br>羽字旁 | Feather, plume, wing, occurring in 翩, 翠, 翼, etc.<br>皮革、羽毛、翅膀等意,含此字根的汉字有翩、翠、翼等 | |
| 56 | 走 | zǒu zì páng<br>走字旁 | Walk, go, pad, track, wend, occurring in 起, 越, 赴, etc.<br>走、走着去、衬垫、足迹、行进等意,含此字根的汉字有起、越、赴等 | Z(key) |
| 57 | 子 | zǐ zì páng<br>子字旁 | Child, occurring in 孔, 孙, 孩, etc.<br>孩子之意,含此字根的汉字有孔、孙、孩等 | |
| 58 | 竹 | zhú zì tóu<br>竹字头 | Bamboo, occurring in 笑, 笔, 笛, etc.<br>竹子之意,含此字根的汉字有笑、笔、笛等 | |
| 59 | 辶 | zǒu zì dǐ<br>走字底 | Walk, occurring in 过, 还, 送, etc.<br>走之意,含此字根的汉字有过、还、送等 | |

2. Tip two: shape similarity
助记方法 2：形相似

Some radicals (see Table 3.14 above) with parentheses look similar to the radicals they are next to. For example, the radical "白" in brackets looks like the radical "日" (read as /rì/) outside brackets, so letter "R" is the corresponding SCE for both radicals.

在键位表 3.14 里,英文字母键上在括号里面的"汉易码™"字根看上去很像其括号外面的字根。例如,括号里面的字根"白",看上去形状很像字根"日"(读/rì/)。所以,字母 R 就成为这两个字根的字形码元。

Here is an explanation that because the inventor of the ECCode™ wants to reduce the RCC, some radicals do not configure English letter keys according to the above two tips. For example, "又" (read as /yòu/) is represented by U since the two Chinese & English symbols have similar pronunciations. Considering that Y is matched with a couple of radicals, matching "又" with U rather than Y would reduce the RCC. Similarly, the radical "𧾷" (read as /zú/) is placed on letter key F because the radical means "foot" and the first letter of its English matching word "Foot" is F —this is a variation of the memory tip of phonetic similarity. In addition, there is a radical "㔾" which looks like the lowercase letter "e", so it is placed on the letter E and the radical "⊐" is also placed on the letter E because of its similarity to the shape of the radical "㔾".

这里解释一下,由于发明人想减少汉字的重码率,所以少部分字根的字形码元没有依照上述两个助记方法来配置英文字母键。例如,由于汉字"又"(读作/yòu/)的发音跟字母 U 的读音很相似,所以其字形码元就是字母 U 了。考虑到字母 Y 键上已经配置了很多字根,所以把字根"又"放在字母 U 键上,而不是放在字母 Y 键上,这样可以减少汉字代码的重码率。同样地,字根"𧾷"(读作/zú/)被放置在字母 F 键上是因为这个字根的英文单词 Foot 的第一个字母是 F——这也是"音相似"助记方法的一个变种。另外还有一个字根"㔾"外观像小写字母"e",所以就放在字母 E 键上了,而字根"⊐"与字根"㔾"形状也相似,所以也把字根"⊐"放在字母 E 键上了。

In order to help to remember the radicals with the property of shape similarity, the ECCode™ also gives another fast recognition memory Table (see Table 3.16) for these radicals.

为了帮助大家记住形相似的字根,"汉易码™"也提供了快速认记这些字根的形相似字根表(表3.16)。

Table 3.16 The radicals with the property of shape similarity
表3.16 形相似字根表

| No. 编码 | Radicals 字根 | The radicals with the property of shape similarity 形相似字根 | Meaning of the radical 字根含义 | Letter of SCE 形码字母 |
|---|---|---|---|---|
| 60 | 冖 | 宀 | Cover, occurring in 写, 军, 冠, etc.<br>盖子之意,含此字根的汉字有写、军、冠等 | B(key) |
| 61 | 穴 | | cavity, acupuncture point, hole, cave, occurring in 空, 穿, 穷, etc.<br>洞穴、巢穴、穴位、洞穴等意,含此字根的汉字有空、穿、穷等 | |
| 62 | 冫 | 氵 | Ice, occurring in 冰, 冷, 次, etc.<br>冰冷之意,含此字根的汉字有冰、冷、次等 | D(key) |
| 63 | 卩 | 阝 | Seal, occuring in 卫, 印, 却, etc.<br>密封、印章之意,含此字根的汉字有卫、印、却等 | |
| 64 | 㔾 | Looks like "e" 外观像英文小写字母"e" 巳 | Genuflected, kneel down, occurring in 犯, 创, etc; storehouse, occurring in 仓, 危, etc.<br>跪姿、跪着等意,含此字根的汉字有犯、创等;储藏之意,含此字根的汉字有仓、危等 | E(key) |
| 65 | ⺕ | | A constituent of many characters, occurring in 导, 强, 管, etc.<br>许多汉字的构成部件,含此字根的汉字有导、强、管等 | |
| 66 | 疒 | 广 | Sickness, occurring in 病, 疾, 痛, etc.<br>疾病之意,含此字根的汉字有病、疾、痛等 | G(key) |
| 67 | 刀 | 力 | Knife, old coin, measure, occurring in 初, 剪, 劫, etc.<br>刀、旧时硬币、度量等意,含此字根的汉字有初、剪、劫等 | L(key) |
| 68 | 朩 | 木 | Peel the stem of, occurring in 条, 亲, 茶, etc.<br>去皮的茎,含此字根的汉字有条、亲、茶等 | M(key) |
| 69 | 朿 | | Occurring in 策, 棘, 涑, etc.<br>许多汉字的构成部件,含此字根的汉字有策、荆、涑等 | |
| 70 | 罒 | 皿 | Net, occurring in 罗, 罝, 罪, etc.<br>网之意,含此字根的汉字有罗、罝、罪等 | Q(key) |
| 71 | 目 | 且 | Eyes, occurring in 盯, 眼, 睛, etc.<br>眼睛之意,含此字根的汉字有盯、眼、睛等 | |

# Chapter 3  Basic knowledge
基础知识

Table 3.16(Continued)　表3.16(续)

| No. 编码 | Radicals 字根 | The radicals with the property of shape similarity 形相似字根 | Meaning of the radical 字根含义 | Letter of SCE 形码字母 |
|---|---|---|---|---|
| 72 | 彳 | 亻 | Step, occurring in 徒、行、征, etc.<br>步伐之意,含此字根的汉字有徒、行、征等 | R(key) |
| 73 | 大 | 人 | Big, large, occurring in 太、达、关, etc.<br>体积大、数量大等意,含此字根的汉字有太、达、关等 | |
| 74 | 白 | 日 | White, occurring in 皂、晃、皇, etc.<br>白之意,含此字根的汉字有皂、晃、皇等 | |
| 75 | 凵 | 山 | Receptacle, occurring in 出、凶、恼, etc.<br>容器、插座之意,含此字根的汉字有出、凶、恼等 | |
| 76 | ⺀ | 水 | Occurring in 脊, etc.<br>构成汉字的部件,含此字根的汉字有"脊"字等 | S(key) |
| 77 | 氺 | | Occurring in 求、康, etc.<br>构成汉字的部件,含此字根的汉字有求、康等 | |
| 78 | 户 | 尸 | Door, household, occurring in 房、扁、扇, etc.<br>房门、房间等意,含此字根的汉字有房、扁、扇等 | |
| 79 | 士 | 土 | Bachelor, person, scholar, soldier, occurring in 志、壮、任, etc.<br>单身汉、人、学者、士兵等意,含此字根的汉字有志、壮、任等 | T(key) |
| 80 | 夂 | 又 | Follow, slow, occurring in 冬、处、夏, etc.<br>跟随、流淌等意,含此字根的汉字有冬、处、夏等 | U(key) |
| 81 | 攵 | | Rap, tap, occurring in 收、改、教, etc.<br>交谈、轻敲等意,含此字根的汉字有收、改、教等 | |
| 82 | 覀 | 酉 | Cover, occurring in 覆、漂、腰, etc.<br>盖子之意,含此字根的汉字有覆、漂、腰等 | |
| 83 | ⺌ | V | Light, occurring in 光、哨、党, etc.<br>光线之意,含此字根的汉字有光、哨、党等 | V(key) |
| 84 | 丷 | | Grass, straw, herbs, weeds, occurring in 关、养、业, etc.<br>草、吸管、草本植物等意,含此字根的汉字有关、养、业等 | |
| 85 | ⺍ | | Occurring in 受、爱、应, etc.<br>构成汉字的部件,含此字根的汉字有受、爱、应等 | |

Table 3.16(Continued) 表3.16(续)

| No.<br>编码 | Radicals<br>字根 | The radicals with the property of shape similarity<br>形相似字根 | Meaning of the radical<br>字根含义 | Letter of SCE<br>形码字母 |
|---|---|---|---|---|
| 86 | 少 | 小 | Few, less, inadequate, occurring in 省、吵、秒, etc.<br>少、不足等意,含此字根的汉字有省、吵、秒等 | X(key) |
| 87 | 礻 | 衤 | Show, occurring in 礼、社、祖, etc.<br>展示之意,含此字根的汉字有礼、社、祖等 | Y(key) |
| 88 | 廴 | 辶 | Occurring in 建、廷、延, etc.<br>构成汉字的部件,含此字根的汉字有建、廷、延等 | Z(key) |

### 3.5.3 Shape constituents requiring special memory and their code-elements
需要专门记忆的字形组分及其代码

There are 11 SCs and their shape code-elements, namely "letters" of Chinese characters, which need to be remembered on purpose in the ECCode™. They are 1 radical code-element (see Table 3.17) and 10 combination code-elements (see Table 3.18). And the large bold letters in the cell of the Table 3.18 are the shape code-elements of stroke category in the same cell respectively.

在"汉易码™"中,一共有11个字形组分——亦即汉字"字母"——及其字形码元需要专门记忆一下。这11个字形码元分别是1个字根码元(参见表3.17)和10个不同笔画组合的字形码元(参见表3.18)。表3.18中每一个格子里面的粗体字母就是这个格子里面笔画类字形组分的码元。

Table 3.17 The radical and its code-element which need to be remembered on purpose
表3.17 一个需要费心记忆的字根及其码元

| No.<br>编号 | Radical<br>字根 | Explanation<br>解释说明 | Meaning<br>含义 | 形码字母<br>Letter of SC |
|---|---|---|---|---|
| 89 | 冂 | This radical is "丨 + 乛", and as to the capital letter L, if being read in Chinese while writing, it is pronounced "竖折" (shù zhé, means vertical fold), so the radical is placed on the L key—associative memory method<br>这个字根的写法是"丨+乛",大写字母"L"若边写边读则读为"竖折",故放在L键——联想记忆法 | Borders, occurring in 冈、网, etc.<br>边界之意,含此字根的汉字有冈、网等 | L(key) |

Table 3.18  Ten combinations of two different strokes, five combinations of one stroke and itself and their code-elements

表 3.18  10 个不同笔画组合以及 5 个基本笔画与自身的组合及其码元

| Basic stroke 基本笔画 | Basic stroke 基本笔画 | | | | |
|---|---|---|---|---|---|
| | 一 | 丨 | 丿 | 丶 | ㇕ |
| 一 | (一 一)=(一)=H | (一 丨)= I | (一 丿)= O | (一 丶)= A | (一 ㇕)= W |
| 丨 | | (丨 丨)=(丨)= I | (丿 丨)= O | (丨 丶)= X | (丨 ㇕)= L |
| 丿 | | | (丿 丿)=(丿)= P | (丶 丿)= V | (丿 ㇕)= F |
| 丶 | | | | (丶 丶)=(丶)= D | (丶 ㇕)= A |
| ㇕ | | | | | (㇕ ㇕)=(㇕)= Z |

## 3.6  Structures of Chinese characters in the ECCode™
## "汉易码™"定义的汉字结构

In the traditional Chinese character theory, there are more than 13 kinds of structures of Chinese characters. The ECCode™ simplifies them into two categories and four subcategories as follows.

在传统汉字理论当中,有多达 13 种汉字结构。"汉易码™"把它们简化成了如下所述的两大类四小类。

### 3.6.1  Category 1: Detached Chinese Characters
### 类别 1:分体字

A DETACHED CHINESE CHARACTER(DCC for short) defined by the ECCode™ refers to such three categories of Chinese written symbols shown in Table 3.19 below as that their composed parts obviously separate or do not touch each other. In other word, the so-called DCC is meant that any stroke included in one of the parts composing the DCC does not contact or cross with another stroke included in another part also composing the DCC.

"汉易码™"所定义的"分体字"(DCC)是指表 3.19 所示的三种汉字,其各个组成部分明显地相互分离而没有互相接触。换句话说,所谓分体字,即意味着构成这类汉字的一个部分当中的任何一个笔画与其他部分当中的任何一个笔画都不接触或不相交。

**Table 3.19　Classification of Detached Chinese Characters**
**表 3.19　分体字分类表**

Category 1: Detached Chinese Characters (DCC for short)
*lèi bié　fēn tǐ zì　yīng wén suō xiě*
类别 1:分体字(英文缩写 DCC)

| Subcategory 1:<br>Left-right structure<br>*xiǎo lèi　zuǒ yòu jié gòu*<br>小类 1:左右结构 | Subcategory 2:<br>Two-upper-and-one-lower structure<br>*xiǎo lèi　shàng èr xià yī jié gòu*<br>小类 2:上二下一结构 | Subcategory 3:<br>One-upper-and-two-lower structure<br>*xiǎo lèi　shàng yī xià èr jié gòu*<br>小类 3:上一下二结构 |
|---|---|---|
| A　B | A　B₁<br>　B₂ | A<br>B₁　B₂ |

Examples of Detached Chinese Characters
*fēn tǐ zì jǔ lì*
分体字举例

| 提他她浙摊你鸽乱胡<br>准淮海持川船把吧扒<br>新汉韩朝加欧 | 坚督哭樊繁热些想帮您望<br>楚熊照熟整奖努警贺集售<br>货暂赞毕梦 | 花范筑赢舞箱药品筷符众<br>森赢羡笑前 |

For instance, in character "韭" (read as /jiǔ/, fragrant-flowered garlic), the two strokes "丨" (竖, read as /shù/) above the stroke "一" (横, read as /héng/) all contact with the stroke "一", so this character "韭" is not a DCC of two-upper-and-one-lower structure and it belongs to one kind of the structures called mixed Chinese character which will be introduced later.

例如,在汉字"韭"(读/jiǔ/,指韭菜)里面,笔画"一"上面的两个笔画"丨"都与之接触,所以这个"韭"字就不是"上二下一结构"的分体字了,而是下面将要介绍的杂合体字。

Again for example, in character "品" (read as /jí/, clamor, noise, public opinion), i.e., there are four "口" in this character—two "口" above and two "口" below. Because any stroke in one "口" does not contact with any stroke in other "口", this character is a DCC of two-upper-and-one-lower structure—the two "口" below are seen as a whole. That is to say, when a character can be taken as one of both the two-upper-and-one-lower and the one-upper-and-two-lower structures, users should give priority to encoding it as the two-upper-and-one-lower structure. This often happens in traditional Chinese characters, and in this case, the software provides fault-tolerant code.

又比如,汉字"品"(读作/jí/,意思是喧闹、噪声、民意)有四个"口"——上下各有两个"口"。由于每个"口"中任何一个笔画与其他"口"中的笔画都没有接触,所以这个汉

Chapter 3　Basic knowledge
基础知识

字"品"就是一个"上二下一结构"的分体字。也就是说,当一个汉字既可以视作"上二下一结构"也可以视作"上一下二结构"的分体字时,用户应该优先把它当作"上二下一结构"的分体字进行编码。这种情况常常出现在繁体字当中,针对这种情况,也有容错码可用。

### 3.6.2　Category 2：Mixed Chinese Character
### 类别 2：杂合体字

All Chinese characters not belonging to the DCCs defined by the ECCode™ in Table 3.19 above are called MIXED CHINESE CHARACTERs (MCC for short). This category of Chinese characters is almost impossible to express all of their structures just by only with one graph. So, we use the following square diagram or an apple in Table 3.20 below to abstractly express the concept of MCCs.

所有不属于上面表 3.19 中"汉易码™"定义的分体字都叫"杂合体字"(英文缩写 MCC)。这类汉字几乎很难用一个图形来表达其所有的结构,所以我们用表 3.20 所示的方块图或一个苹果来抽象地表达杂合体字这个概念。

**Table 3.20　Abstract graphic expression of Mixed Chinese Characters**
**表 3.20　杂合体字的抽象表达方式**

Category 2：Mixed Chinese Characters (MCC for short)
lèi  bié　　zá  hé  tǐ  zì　yīng wén suō xiě
类别 2：杂合体字(英文缩写 MCC)

Subcategory 4：Mixed Chinese Characters
xiǎo lèi　　zá  hé  tǐ  zì
小类 4：杂合体字

 Or
=

Examples of Mixed Chinese Characters
zá  hé  tǐ  zì  jǔ  lì
杂合体字举例

电天不儿么生午下车果面气少水我小中爸店多见看医在怎字八本出东飞高个关后几今京九开来老里了六买米年女著尊幽……

## 3.7 Stroke order and macro stroke order
## 笔顺与宏观笔顺

STROKE ORDER (SO for short) refers to the order in which the strokes of a Chinese character are written. Here are some rules about SO and the number in each blank area, namely in a stroke, surrounded by the closed black line in a character stands for the SO shown in Table 3.21 below.

笔顺是指构成汉字诸多笔画的书写顺序。下面表3.21中介绍了几个有关笔顺的规则,其中每个字里面由线条围成的空白处(亦即一个笔画里面)的数字代表了这个笔画的书写顺序。

**Table 3.21 General rules of stroke order**
**表3.21 笔顺的一般规则**

| | Stroke order rule 笔顺规则 | Example 字例 | |
|---|---|---|---|
| 1 | Horizon first, vertical second<br>xiān héng hòu shù<br>先横后竖 | 十 | 下 |
| 2 | Left-falling first, right-falling second<br>xiān piě hòu nà<br>先撇后捺 | 人 | 八 |
| 3 | From top to bottom<br>xiān shàng hòu xià<br>先上后下 | 三 | 多 |

# Chapter 3  Basic knowledge
基础知识

Table 3.21 （Continued）  表3.21(续)

| | Stroke order rule<br>笔顺规则 | Example<br>字例 |
|---|---|---|
| 4 | From left to right<br>xiān zuǒ hòu yòu<br>先左后右 | 他 朝 |
| 5 | Horizon first, left-falling second<br>xiān héng hòu piě<br>先横后撇 | 厂 大 |
| 6 | From outside to inside<br>xiān wài hòu lǐ<br>先外后里 | 月 风 |
| 7 | Outside first, inside next, closure last<br>xiān wài hòu lǐ, zuì hòu fēng kǒu<br>先外后里,最后封口 | 日 四 |
| 8 | Center first, sides second<br>xiān zhōng jiān hòu liǎng biān<br>先中间后两边 | 小 水 |

From Table 3.21 above we can draw two conclusions concerning the DCCs of which structures are shown in Figure 3.28 ~ 3.30 as follows.

从上面表 3.21 中,我们可以归纳出有关下面图 3.28 ~ 3.30 所示分体字的两个如下结论。

(1) The left part of subcategory 1 (Figure 3.28) written before its right part, i.e., the correct order is to write the left part first, then the middle part if there is a middle part, and finally the right part; e.g., as to character "胡", the left part (A) "古" is written first and then the right part (B) "月".

在如图 3.28 所示的第一小类分体字中,先左后右,亦即先写左边的 A 部分,然后写中间部分后——如果这个字有中间部分的话,最后写右边的 B 部分。例如,对于汉字"胡",就是先写左边 A 部分的"古",后写右边 B 部分的"月"。

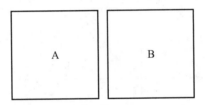

Figure 3.28    Left-right structure
图 3.28    左右结构汉字

(2) Part A of subcategory 2 (Figure 3.29) or subcategory 3 (Figure 3.30) is written first, then part $B_1$, and part $B_2$ finally.

对于图 3.29 中的小类 2 或图 3.30 中的小类 3 分体字而言,A 部分先写,其次写 $B_1$ 部分,最后写 $B_2$ 部分。

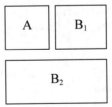

Figure 3.29    Two-upper-and-one-lower structure
图 3.29    "上二下一"结构示例

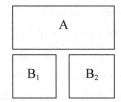

Figure 3.30  One-upper-and-two-lower structure
图3.30 "上一下二"结构示例

**Example 3.8**  As to the character "想", part A "木" is written first, then part $B_1$ "目", and finally part $B_2$ "心".

例3.8  对于汉字"想",先写 A 部分的"木",然后写 $B_1$ 部分的"目",最后写 $B_2$ 部分的"心"。

**Example 3.9**  As to the character "符", part A "⺮" is written first, then the part $B_1$ "亻", and finally the part $B_2$ "寸".

例3.9  对于汉字"符",先写 A 部分的"⺮",其次写 $B_1$ 部分的"亻",最后写 $B_2$ 部分的"寸"。

In general, we can call the rule of which part in the DCCs to be written first as MACRO STROKE ORDER(MaSO for short) because it still essentially a problem of SO, but only for the components made of strokes instead of strokes themselves. Accordingly, we call the SO for strokes themselves as MICRO STROKE ORDER(MiSO for short), e.g., perhaps there are problems faced by you of SO inside every part of DCCs. It is obvious that in the ECCode™ the MiSO is not important because of the introduced concept of TSC. In fact, you can almost ignore this problem of MiSO while using the ECCode™ to keywrite Chinese characters.

总体而言,我们可以把分体字当中哪个部分先写这个规则称为"宏观笔顺",因为它毕竟本质上还是一个笔顺问题,但其针对的却是笔画构成的部件而非针对笔画本身了。相应地,我们把针对笔画本身的笔顺规则称为"微观笔顺"。例如,在书写分体字时,每个部件部分内部或许都存在着笔顺问题。但很显然,在"汉易码™"中,由于引入了两笔画组合这个概念而导致微观笔顺不是那么重要了。即事实上,人们在用"汉易码™"键写汉字时,几乎可以忽略掉微观笔顺问题。

# Review 3
# 复习题3

Q1: What two attributes of Chinese characters are embodied in the concept of Chinese character constituents introduced in this book? (Clue: See Figure 3.2)

思考题1:本书所介绍的汉字组分概念体现了汉字的哪两种属性?(提示:参考图3.2)

Q2: Why don't you have to worry about being able to speak standard Mandarin Chinese?
思考题2：为什么说不必为能不能说一口标准的普通话担心？

Q3: Do you know which three constituents make up a Pinyin of most Chinese characters? To sum up, what is the main meaning of the statement that "Hanyu Pinyin is of very limited help to foreigners learning Chinese to recognize new characters"?

思考题3：你知道大多数汉字的拼音是由哪三个部分组成的吗？请总结一下，"汉语拼音对于初学汉语的外国人认识生字的帮助非常有限"这个说法主要是指什么意思？

Q4: As to the character "韭"（read as /jiǔ/, a pictograph, fragrant-flowered garlic）, please answer the questions as follows:
思考题4：就汉字"韭"（读/jiǔ/,一个象形文字,指韭菜），请回答以下问题：

① Which two strokes have the Adjacent/Noncontact relation? How many pairs of such relations are there in "韭"? 哪两个笔画之间的位置关系属于"分离关系"？有多少对笔画拥有这种分离关系？

② Which two strokes have the Intersection relation? How many pairs of such relations are there in "韭"? 哪两个笔画之间的位置关系属于"交叉关系"？有多少对笔画拥有这种分离关系？

③ Which two strokes have the Connecting relation? How many pairs of such relations are there in "韭"? 哪两个笔画之间的位置关系属于"相连关系"？有多少对笔画拥有这种分离关系？

Q5: How many components (middleware) are there in Figure 3.31?
思考题5：图3.31中汉字"哭"有多少个中间件（部件）？

Figure 3.31　The Chinese character "哭"
图3.31　汉字"哭"

Q6: Please decompose the character "哭" shown in Figure 3.31 above into components and finally decompose it into lines and dots if there are.
思考题6：请把图3.31中的汉字"哭"拆解成中间件,并最后把"哭"字拆解成为点和

Chapter 3　Basic knowledge
基础知识

线条——如果有"点"的话。

Q7：In the character shown in Figure 3.31 above, how many pairs of two strokes are adjacent/noncontact relation, intersection relation or connecting relation?

思考题7：在汉字"哭"里面(参见图3.31)，有多少对笔画是分离关系，多少对是交叉关系，多少对是连接关系？

Q8：Please write out the five basic strokes in the ECCode™. And what kind of basic stroke is "━"？What kind of basic stroke is "╲"？What kind of basic strokes is "亅"？

思考题8：请写出"汉易码™"认定的5个基本笔画。其中，"━"是哪种基本笔画？"╲"是哪种基本笔画？"亅"是哪种基本笔画？

Q9：Except the five basic strokes recognized by the ECCode™, what conventions for other strokes in the Chinese characters are there in the ECCode™? I.e., which basic strokes do other strokes in Chinese characters belong respectively to which of the five basic strokes defined by the ECCode™?

思考题9：除"汉易码™"认定的5个基本笔画之外，"汉易码™"对其他传统认知中的笔画做了哪些归属约定？

Q10：What's the meaning for the TWO-STROKE COMBINATION in the context of the ECCode™?

思考题10："汉易码™"语境当中的"笔画组合"是什么意思？

Q11：In the ECCode™, is the code of the combination of one basic stroke and itself the same with the one of the basic stroke itself?

思考题11：在"汉易码™"当中，一个基本笔画与其自身的笔画组合之代码跟这个基本笔画的代码相同吗？

Q12：How many combinations of two different basic strokes are there in the ECCode™?

思考题12："汉易码™"当中，两个不同笔画的组合有多少个？请写出这些不同笔画的组合。

Q13：In the character "予"，what's the combination of the first two strokes of it?

思考题13：在汉字"予"当中，前两个笔画的组合是什么？

Q14：In the character "私"，what's the combination of the last strokes of it?

思考题 14：在汉字"私"当中，最后两个笔画的组合是什么？

Q15：In the character "九", what's the combination of the two strokes composing it?
思考题 15：在汉字"九"当中，构成这个汉字的两个笔画的组合是什么？

Q16：Both of the characters "刁" and "刀" have two strokes. According to the rule of the ECCode™, is the combination of the two strokes in each character composing each of the two characters same with each other? Please write out respectively the combination of the two strokes in each character.
思考题 16：汉字"刁"与汉字"刀"都有两个笔画，根据"汉易码™"的规则，这两个汉字各自所有的两个笔画的组合是一样的吗？请分别写出这两个汉字的笔画组合。

Q17：Please make a comparison, see what the relation between the combination of the two strokes in character "儿" or "九" and the combination of the first two strokes in the character "象" is.
思考题 17：比较一下，看看"儿""九"这两个汉字的两笔画组合与汉字"象"的前两个笔画的笔画组合之间有什么关系？

Q18：What's the stroke combination of the first and the second strokes in the character "与"? Which keyboard letter is assigned to this stroke combination?
思考题 18：汉字"与"的第一、第二笔画形成的笔画组合是什么？是放在哪个英文字母键上的？

Q19：What's the stroke combination of the first and the second strokes in the character "川"? Which keyboard letter is assigned to this stroke combination?
思考题 19：汉字"川"的第一、第二笔画形成的笔画组合是什么？是放在哪个英文字母键上的？

Q20：What's the stroke combination of the last two strokes in the character "风"? Which keyboard letter is assigned to this stroke combination?
思考题 20：汉字"风"的最后两个笔画形成的笔画组合是什么？是放在哪个英文字母键上的？

Q21：What's the shape constituent in a Chinese character? And in the ECCode™, what's a radical?
思考题 21：什么是汉字的字形组分？在"汉易码™"中，字根是什么？

Q22：Please point out what a shared radical the following Chinese characters include.

# Chapter 3 Basic knowledge
## 基础知识

思考题22：请指出以下汉字中都包含了什么字根。

①藤、苏、莎、萨、节、菌、蒋、蒜、英、药、若、荣、茹、蓉、蒂、董、花、获、荷、苦、茶、菜、草、茨、葱、蔡、藏、芙、芬、芳、范、菲。

②简、竺、算、笼、策、答、筝。

③铁、钱、铭、钦、铜、错、锣、铺、钩、钉、钢、铅、镜、铁。

④列、则、刎、刑、划、创、刘、刚、刻。

Q23：How many shape constituents or "letters" of Chinese characters are there in the Key Mapping Table (Table 3.4) of the ECCode™? Among them, how many basic strokes, stroke combinations, and radicals?

思考题23："汉易码™"的键位表(表3.14)当中,一共包含了多少个字形组分或"汉字字母"？其中,基本笔画有多少个、笔画组合多少个、字根多少个？

Q24：As to some radicals in the KMT (Table 3.14) of the ECCode™, what's the phenomenon of PHONEME SIMILARITY?

思考题24：对于"汉易码™"的键位表(表3.14)中的一些字根来说,"音相似"是一个什么现象？

Q25：As to some radicals in the KMT (Table 3.14) of the ECCode™, what's the phenomenon of SHAPE SIMILARITY?

思考题25：对于"汉易码™"的键位表(表3.14)中的一些字根来说,"形相似"是一个什么现象？

Q26：What the feature of DCC defined by the ECCode™? What are its sub categories?

思考题26："汉易码™"定义的分体字具有什么特点？它有几个小类？

Q27：What are the mixed Chinese characters in the ECCode™?

思考题27：在"汉易码™"中,什么叫杂合体字？

Q28：In the ECCode™, is the character "韭" a character of the "two-upper-and-one-lower structure"?

思考题28：在"汉易码™"当中,汉字"韭"是"上二下一体"结构吗？

Q29：What is the macro writing order of some DCCs defined by the ECCode™? Based on the concept of macro stroke order in the ECCode™, how many pieces of middleware or components in the character "鼐"? Please write out these components sequentially.

思考题29："汉易码™"定义的一些分体字的宏观书写顺序是指什么？基于"汉易码™"宏观笔顺的概念,汉字"鼐"有几个构字中间件？请依次写出这些构字部件。

Q30: Through the four Chinese characters "田""由""甲", and "申", can you realize the important meaning of the positional relationship concept of the strokes in a Chinese character?

思考题30：通过"田""由""甲""申"这四个汉字,你能够体会到汉字笔画的位置关系这个概念的重要意义吗？

Q31: Please point out the difference between the five Chinese characters "戍""戌""戊""戒", and "戎".

思考题31：请指出这5个汉字的区别："戍""戌""戊""戒"和"戎"。

Q32: Generally, in the ECCode™, which of a radical and a two-stroke combination in a Chinese character contains more strokes?

思考题32：一般来说,在"汉易码™"当中,字根与汉字当中的两笔画组合,哪个含有的笔画数量更多？

Q33: In the ECCode™, can you point out what the relation between the concept of position relation between a two-stroke in a Chinese character and the concept of Detached Chinese Characters is? I. e., in the ECCode™, could the concept of Detached Chinese Characters be given birth to if there doesn't exist the concept of position relation between a two-stroke in a Chinese character?

思考题33：在"汉易码™"当中,你能指出汉字当中两笔画位置关系概念与分体字概念的关系吗？也就是说,"汉易码™"当中,如果没有汉字中两笔画位置关系这个概念,会产生分体字这个概念吗？

# Chapter 4  How to input a Chinese character without knowing its pronunciation
# 如何输入不知道读音的汉字

In literacy, the biggest disadvantage of Chinese Pinyin (a system of Romanized spelling used to transliterate Chinese characters into the Roman alphabet) is that even if you are very familiar with it, you can't pronounce this Chinese character right with Chinese Pinyin if you run into a Chinese character you don't know how to read it. What we do here is to solve this problem as well as its derivative keywriting problem by a general keyboard.

在识字方面,拼音(一种把汉字转换成罗马字的拼写系统)的一个最大问题就是,即使你对其十分熟悉,但如果你遇到一个不会读的汉字,那么你也无法知道这个汉字该如何发音。而我们在此所要做的,就是要解决这个问题,并解决由此衍生出来的用普通键盘键写汉字的问题。

So, from now on, we will really start the journey to solve the two basic problems mentioned above of Chinese keylearning & keywriting, and all the previous contents are the foundation of this chapter.

所以,从现在开始,我们才将真正开始解决前面所提汉字键学与汉字键写这两个基本问题的旅程,而之前的所有内容都是为本章做一个基础性的铺垫。

## 4.1 A brief introduction to the encoding theory of the Easy Chinese Code (ECCode™)
## "汉易码™"编码理论概要

In the ECCode™, a Computer Chinese Character Code (CCCC) is a letter code that is made of a Phonetic Code-Element (abbreviated as "Phonetic Code", PC for short) and no more than 3 Shape Code-Elements (abbreviated as "Shape Code", SC for short), i.e., a character code is composed of no more than four constituent "letters" of the Chinese character (Figure 4.1).

在"汉易码™"中,计算机汉字代码就是由一个字音码元(简称"音码")和不超过3个字形码元(简称"形码")所构成的一个字母代码,也可说汉字代码是由不超过4个汉字组分"字母"所构成的一个代码(参见图4.1)。

Specifically, a computer Chinese character code in the ECCode™ is composed of no more than four letters as follows.

具体来说,"汉易码™"中一个计算机汉字代码由以下不超过4个的字母构成。

# A Crash Course on Keylearning and Keywriting for Chinese
## 汉字键学与键写简明教程

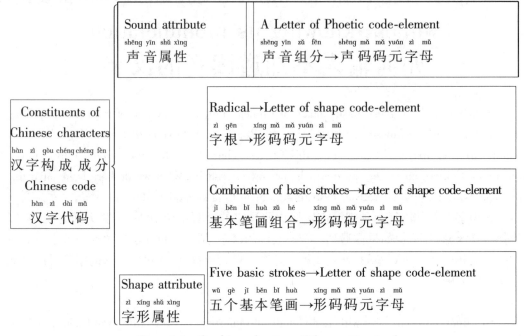

Figure 4.1　Graphic explanations of the constituents of
a computer Chinese character code

图 4.1　计算机汉字代码的构成组分图解

Notes：

说明：

1. A letter composing the code of a Chinese character is called a code-element.

构成汉字代码组成成分的单个字母都叫"码元"。

2. The sign of "→" express derivative relationships.

符号→表示派生关系。

（1）A letter of PHONETIC CODE-ELEMENT(PC for short, referring to Phonetic Code). It is the first letter of the pronunciation of the Chinese character; of course, you can use the question mark [?] to take the place of PC as a constituent of a Chinese character if you do not know how to pronounce it. I. e., a computer Chinese character code in the ECCode™ cannot be without the part equivalent to the pronunciation code-element even if the question mark has to be taken as the part of Phonetic Code which you don't know (and finally you can learn how to read it from the companion online dictionary).

字音码元字母(缩写PC,意指音码PC),就是汉字读音的第一个字母。当然,如果大家不会读这个汉字,也可用问号键"?"代替这个字音码元。也就是说,"汉易码™"的计算机汉字代码不能没有相当于读音的这个部分,哪怕你使用"?"键代替读音也行(最后在线字典可以告诉大家如何读这个汉字）。

（2）No more than three letters of SHAPE CODE-ELEMENTs. Each of them is also called a Shape Code (SC for short), which is the code letter of a shape constituent in Table 3.14 composing a Chinese character or a CCCC.

不超过3个的字形码元字母。每个字形码元也被称为形码（缩写SC），它们都是构成汉字的、表3.14中字形组分的代码字母。

That is to say, people can use no more than 4 letters (code-elements) to type in a Chinese character by the ECCode™ (see latter examples). However, how many shape codes a Chinese character should use depends on the synthetic action of the encoding rules, the encoding formula and the number of its strokes. In other words, as to the 104 character shape constituents (i.e., Chinese "letters") in Table 3.14, how to use them, i.e., under what circumstance should a radical, a combination of two strokes, or a basic stroke be used? It is the big problem which we should solve. Therefore, it is necessary to formulate a set of encoding rules first.

也就是说，人们借助于"汉易码™"可以使用不超过4个字母（码元）来输入一个汉字（参见后面诸多例子）。不过，一个汉字应该使用多少个形码则有赖于编码规则、编码公式以及笔画数量的综合作用。换句话说，如何使用表3.14中那104个构成汉字的字形组分（即汉字"字母"），亦即应该在什么情况下使用字根、笔画组合或者基本笔画呢？这个问题就是我们应该予以解决的一个大问题。所以，这就十分有必要首先建立一套编码规则。

## 4.2 Probability thinking of Easy Chinese Code and four encoding rules
## "汉易码™"中的概率思想及四个编码规则

As everyone knows that a Chinese character is entirely different from an English word, but the application of a computer is mainly based on the usage habit of the Western keyboard. In light of these two facts, when a Chinese character is transformed into an alphabetic code made of no more than 4 letters, the Chinese character information contained in each letter should be maximized as much as possible. This is the probability thinking of the ECCode™ for Chinese character encoding and also the starting point for its inventor to make encoding rules.

众所周知，汉字与英文单词完全不同，但计算机的应用却主要是基于西文键盘的使用习惯。基于这两个基本事实，当我们要把一个汉字转换成不超过4个字母的代码时，每个字母所包含的汉字信息量应该尽可能地最大化。这就是"汉易码™"针对汉字编码的概率思想，也是其发明人制定编码规则的出发点。

In fact, how to decompose a Chinese character into different shape constituents included in

Table 3.14 is decided by the four rules as follows.

实际上,如何把一个汉字拆分成表 3.14 中的不同字形组分,取决于以下四个编码规则。

### RULE 1: THE PRIORITY RULE
guī zé　　　yōu xiān lǜ
规则 1:优先律

The PRIORITY rule states that the PRIORITY should be given to using the shape constituents contained in a Chinese character with more strokes when disassembling it into several shape constituents contained in Table 3.14 and inputting it into a computer. That is, when a Chinese character is inputted into a computer, the following two regulations of the PRIORITY rule should be observed.

优先律是指在把一个汉字拆解为表 3.14 中的若干个字形组分并需要把这个汉字输入进计算机时,用户应该优先使用这个汉字所含有的表 3.14 中那个笔画数量多的字形组分。也就是说,当用户需要把汉字输入计算机时,应该遵守优先律的以下两个要求。

(1) Never divide the radical in Table 3.14 into stroke combinations or basic strokes, namely using a radical prior to using a combination of two strokes or a basic stroke while encoding a Chinese character.

不要把表 3.14 中的字根拆解成笔画组合或基本笔画,即给汉字编码时优先使用字根而不是笔画组合或者基本笔画。

When encoding each of no more than three shape constitutes, if a radical code-element, namely a shape constituent of radical, is available, a shape code-element of a stroke-combination or a basic stroke should not be used; if neither of the other two codes respectively corresponding with the two shape constituents except for a basic stroke is available (see Figure 4.1 above), you have to consider the shape code-element of the basic stroke.

在对不超过三种字形组分的每一个字形组分进行编码时,如果有字根码元——即有一个字根类字形组分——可用,就不要使用笔画组合或基本笔画码元;如果除基本笔画码元之外其他两种字形组分之码元都不存在(参见上文图 4.1),那么就只能使用基本笔画码元了。

For example, the radical "木 (read as /mù/, meaning wood)" is one of shape constituents contained in Table 3.14 whose shape code-element is available, so it could be split into neither any combination of two strokes nor several basic strokes.

例如,字根"木(读作/mù/,意指木头)"就是表 3.14 中的一个字形组分,其字形码元可用,所以这个字根"木"既不能拆分成笔画组合,也不能拆成几个基本笔画。

Chapter 4  How to input a Chinese character without knowing its pronunciation
如何输入不知道读音的汉字

Another example, the character "九 ( read as /jiǔ/, meaning nine or ninth)" doesn't include any radical contained in Table 3.14 but the two strokes "丿" and "一 ( see the previous convention about the ownership of basic strokes of the stroke cluster with various turns except for the left vertical hook)", therefore, only the combination of two strokes "丿" and "一" rather than the two independent basic strokes could be used as a shape constituent, of course, only its shape code-element is available.

再举一例,汉字"九(读作/jiǔ/,意指数字9或第9)"中除了两个笔画"丿"和"一(参见前面有关除左竖钩外各种带弯钩的笔画族之基本笔画归属的约定)",就没有任何表3.14中的字根了。因此,只有两笔画"丿"和"一"的组合而不是独立的两个基本笔画可以用作字形组分。当然,该汉字在编码时也只有这个笔画组合的代码可以使用了。

Third example, the character "三 ( read as /sān/, meaning third)" doesn't have any radical either contained in Table 3.14, but it is made of three "一 ( read as /héng/, meaning the stroke horizontal)" strokes. Taking the PRIORITY rule here into account, using a stroke combination with more strokes should be given priority over using any basic stroke while encoding the character. Thus, after taking a combination of two strokes from the character "三", it has been left only one stroke "一". On those accounts, there are only two shape constituents in the character "三", which are the two stroke combination (一一) and the basic stroke "一" respectively, their corresponding shape code-elements are all "H".

例三,汉字"三(读作/sān/,意指数字3或第3)",也没有表3.14当中的任何字根,而是由三个笔画"一(读作/héng/,意即笔画'横')"构成。此处考虑到优先律规则,在给汉字"三"编码时,笔画数量更多的笔画组合(一一)就比独立的基本笔画(一)具有取码的优先权了。如此一来,在从汉字"三"中拿走两笔画组合之后,只剩下一个笔画"一"了。因此,汉字"三"当中只有两个字形组分,即分别是两笔画组合"一一"和基本笔画"一",其对应的形码都是字母"H"。

(2) Using a radical with more strokes prior to using a radical with less strokes.
优先取码笔画多的字根。

When there are more than one radical or radical code-element available, according to the PRIORITY rule, the radical or radical code-element with more strokes should be chosen. For instance, in the Chinese character "木", there are two radicals in Table 3.14 which are respectively "木" and "人". Although the two radicals' code-elements are same with each other, the letter "M", in view of that the radical "木" has more strokes than the radical "人", according to this PRIORITY rule, using the radical "木" should be given priority over using the radical "人" while encoding the character. Thus, users shouldn't disassemble the radical "木" into the basic stroke "一" and the radical "人".

当有不止一个字根或字根码元可用时,根据优先律规则,应该选用笔画数多的字根或

115

字根码元。例如,汉字"木"有表 3.14 中的两个字根,即字根"木"和字根"朩"。尽管这两个字根码元相同,都是字母 M,但考虑到字根"木"比字根"朩"含有更多的笔画,根据优先律规则,在给这个汉字编码时,就应该优先选择字根"木"作为取码对象。因此,用户不应把字根"木"拆分成基本笔画"一"和字根"朩"。

### RULE 2: THE INTEGRITY RULE

guī zé wán zhěng lǜ
规则 2:完 整 律

The INTEGRITY rule merely repeats some content of the PRIORITY from another angle, i. e., the radical in Table 3.14 cannot be divided into stroke combinations and several basic stroke, nor can it be divided into simple basic strokes. This is another way of saying the first connotation of the PRIORITY rule above. Please refer to the previous example, involving the PRIORITY rule, about the difference between the radical "木" and the radical "朩".

完整律只是从另一个角度重复了优先律的部分内容,即表 3.14 中的字根既不能拆分成笔画组合和几个基本笔画,也不能拆分成单纯的基本笔画。这就是上述优先律第一个内涵的另外一种说法。请参考上文有关字根"木"与"朩"之区别的、涉及优先律的示例。

### RULE 3: THE SINGLE RULE

guī zé dān yī lǜ
规则 3:单 一 律

For each character, the SINGLE rule states that the code-element for a radical, a stroke combination, or a basic stroke in the character can be used only once. For example, in the character "字", there are two radicals "宀" and "子", both contained in Table 3.14. So, as to every code-element of the character "字", including one phonetic code-element or one question mark "?" (if users do not know how to read it) and two shape code-elements of "宀" and "子", each of them can be used only once. That is to say, the code for "字" should be "ZBZ" rather than "ZBBZ" or "ZBZZ" (the first "Z" for the phonetic code-element, "B" for the shape code-element of the radical "宀", and the other "Z(s)" for the shape code-element of the radical "子").

就每个汉字而言,单一律是指汉字中的字根或笔画组合或基本笔画的码元只能被使用一次。例如,汉字"字"有两个表 3.14 中的字根"宀"和字根"子"。所以,就汉字"字"的每一个码元而言,包括一个字音码元或问号(如果不知道该怎么读这个汉字的话)以及两个字根"宀"和"子"的码元,每一个码元只能使用一次。也就是说,汉字"字"的代码是"ZBZ"而不是"ZBBZ"或"ZBZZ"(第一个 Z 代表字音码元,B 代表字根"宀"的字形码元,其他 Z 代表字根"子"的字形码元)。

Chapter 4　How to input a Chinese character without knowing its pronunciation
　　　　　如何输入不知道读音的汉字

## RULE 4: THE STROKE ORDER RULE
　　　guī zé　　　　bǐ shùn lǜ
规则 4:笔顺律

The STROKE ORDER rule refers to the macroscopic consistency between the encoding order of each shape constituent of a Chinese character and the stroke order of the character writing.

笔顺律是指汉字每个字形组分的编码顺序与汉字书写的笔顺在宏观方面要保持一致。

For example, in the character "题", from the view of macro stroke order, the first part "是" in the character should be written first, the second part "页" in it should be written later. Another example is shown in Figure 4.2.

例如,在汉字"题"中,从宏观笔顺的角度来看,其第一个部分"是"应该先写,其第二个部分"页"应该后写。图 4.2 是另外一个例子。

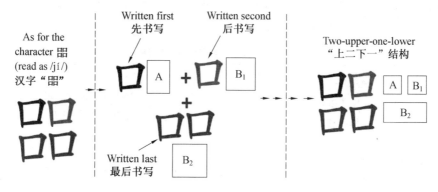

Figure 4.2　Illustration of the macro stroke order of the character "品"

图 4.2　汉字"品"宏观笔顺示例

Here are some examples for choosing the shape code-element for each character under the four rules.

下面是依据上述四个编码规则来为每个字选择字形码元的一些汉字编码举例。

**Example 4.1**　In "百" (read as /bǎi/, meaning hundred, Table 4.1), according to the STROKE ORDER rule, the first shape code-element is not that of the combination ( 一 丿) because the radical "白" (read as /bái/) is one of the radicals listed in Table 3.14 and "白" occupies the stroke " 丿". Although "日" is also a radical in Table 3.14, it has fewer strokes than the radical "白". So, the radical "白" and its corresponding shape code-element should be chosen as the second shape constituent as well as its shape code in accordance with the priority rule. As a result, the first shape constituent and its corresponding shape code of the

117

character are respectively "一" and "H", and the complete code of the character "百" is "BHR" rather than "BHHR" or "BHRR" (according to the SINGLE rule). If you do not know how to read "百", its code could also be "? HR".

**例 4.1** 在汉字"百"(读作/bǎi/,意指 100)中,依据笔顺规则,由于"白(读作/bái/)"是表 3.14 键位表当中的一个字根,所以根据完整律,这个汉字的第一个字形码元就不能是第一个笔画所在的笔画组合(一丿)的代码了——因为"丿"被字根"白"占用了。尽管"日"也是表 3.14 键位表中的一个字根,但"日"的笔画数量比"白"少。所以,根据优先律,编码时应该选用字根"白"及其字形码元作为"百"字的第二个字形组分及其形码。因此,汉字"百"的第一个字形组分及其形码分别是"一"和"H",而汉字"百"的完整编码就是 BHR,而不是 BHHR,也不是 BHRR(参见单一律)。如果你不知道这个汉字"百"该怎么读,那么其代码也可以是"? HR"。

After all, the shape constituents of "百" = "(一)" + "白" and "百" ≠ "(一丿)" + "日".

总之,"百"的字形组分="(一)"+"白","百"≠"(一丿)"+"日"。

Table 4.1 The computer code of **"百"**
表 4.1 汉字"百"的计算机代码

| bǎi / Hundred | Standard code in the ECCode™ 标准代码 | Dictionary inquiry code without knowing its pronunciation 不知道读音时的字典查询码 |
|---|---|---|
| | BHR | ? HR |
| | | Used for looking it up in the e-dictionary at the website: 用于在下面网址上查字典: www.fingerchinese.com |

**Example 4.2** In "米" (read as /mǐ/, meaning a kind of food, rice, Table 4.2), it seems that both radicals "⺍" and "木" in Table 3.14 can be taken as its shape constituents. However, choosing "⺍" as the radical would take one stroke "一" from "木" and disassemble the radical "木". Since the radical "木" has more strokes than the radical "⺍" and the integrity of radical "木" should be ensured first based on the PRIORITY rule and the INTEGRITY rule. Therefore, the first shape code-element employed should be the letter "V" which is the shape code for the shape constituent, namely two stroke combination, (、丿). The second shape code-element should be "M", namely the code of the radical "木"

Chapter 4  How to input a Chinese character without knowing its pronunciation
如何输入不知道读音的汉字

which is one of the shape code-elements of the character "米". As a result, the complete code of the character "米" is "MVM" rather than "MVVM" or "MVMM". If you do not know how to read "米", its code could also be "? VM".

**例 4.2**  在汉字"米"(读作/mǐ/,意指一种粮食,大米)中,似乎有键位表 3.14 中字根"⸺"和字根"木"。但是,如果选用字根"⸺",就要从字根"木"中抽走一个笔画"一",进而拆散了字根"木"。因为字根"木"的笔画数量比字根"⸺"要多,所以,根据优先律和完整律,应该优先确保字根"木"的完整性而不能拆开它。因此,第一个字形码元应该是两笔画组合(、丿)的码元即字母 V。第二个字形码元当然就是汉字"米"的字形组分即字根"木"的代码 M 了。结果,汉字"米"的完整代码就是 MVM,而不是 MVVM,也不是 MVMM。如果大家不会读这个汉字"米",那么其代码也可以是"? VM"。

After all, "米" ≠ "⸺" + "朩", "米" = "(、丿)" + "木".
总之,"米" ≠ "⸺" + "朩","米" = "(、丿)" + "木"。

Table 4.2  The computer code of "米"
表 4.2  汉字"米"的计算机代码

| mǐ | Standard code in the ECCode™ 标准代码 | Dictionary inquiry code without knowing its pronunciation 不知道读音时的字典查询码 |
|---|---|---|
| 米 | MVM | ? VM |
| Rice | | Used for looking it up in the e-dictionary at the website: 用于在下面网址上查字典: www.fingerchinese.com |

**Example 4.3**  In "秦" (read as /qín/, meaning family name or place name, Table 4.3), according to the encoding rules of the ECCode™, its three shape code-elements are respectively "H" for "一一" (not "一"), "R" for "大" (not "人") and "H" for "禾" (not "木"). So, the standard code of "秦" is "QHRH". If you do not know how to read "秦", its code could also be "? HRH".

**例 4.3**  在汉字"秦(读作/qín/,姓及地名)"当中,根据"汉易码™"编码规则,其三个字形码元分别是 H 为"一一"(而非"一")的代码、R 为"大"(而非"人")的代码,以及禾"(而非"木")的代码 H。所以,汉字"秦"的标准代码是 QHRH;如果大家不会读这个字,那么其代码也可以是"? HRH"。

## Table 4.3 The computer code of "秦"
### 表4.3 汉字"秦"的计算机代码

| qín | Standard code in the ECCode™ 标准代码 | Dictionary inquiry code without knowing its pronunciation 不知道读音时的字典查询码 |
|---|---|---|
| 秦 | QHRH | ? HRH |
| family name or place name | | Used for looking it up in the e-dictionary at the website: 用于在下面网址上查字典: www.fingerchinese.com |

Sometimes, when two radicals that share the same stroke have the same number of strokes, you should follow the STROKE ORDER rule to decide which radical should be chosen as a constituent of the character's shape code. For example, in the traditional Chinese character "東" (read as /dōng/, meaning east, Table 4.4), the radical "日" and the radical "木" both have 4 strokes and they share the fourth-from-last stroke "一 (héng)" of the character. According to Rule 4 (the STROKE ORDER rule), Rule 1 (the PRIORITY rule) and Rule 2 (the INTEGRITY rule), the integrity of the radical "日" should be ensured because the radical "日" is written before the radical "木". Therefore, the standard code for the character "東" is "DHRM". Among the four code-elements:

有时候,两个字根既共享了一个笔画又有相同的笔画数量,你就应该根据笔顺来决定先用哪一个字根作为汉字代码的形码组分。例如,在繁体字"東"(读作"/dōng/",意指东方)里面,字根"日"和字根"木"都有4个笔画,而且这两个字根共享了这个汉字的倒数第四个笔画"一(横)"。根据编码规则4(笔顺律)、规则1(优先律)和规则2(完整律),因为先要写"日"而后写"木",并且不能拆散先写的字根"日",因此,这个繁体字"東"的标准码就是DHRM,其中:

D—phonetic code-element, the first letter of this character's pronunciation.
D是字音码元,即"東"的发音的第一个字母。

H—the first shape code-element of "東", also the code of the basic stroke "一", mark as "shape 1".
H是"東"的第一个字形码元,也就是基本笔画"一"的代码,标记为"形码1"。

# Chapter 4  How to input a Chinese character without knowing its pronunciation
## 如何输入不知道读音的汉字

R—the second shape code-element of "東", also the code of the radical "日", mark as "shape 2".

R 是"東"的第二个字形码元,也就是字根"日"的代码,标记为"形码2"。

M—the third shape code-element of "東", also the code of the radical "朩", mark as "shape 3".

M 是"東"的第三个字形码元,也就是字根"朩"的代码,标记为"形码3"。

Of course, if you don't know its pronunciation, its dictionary inquiry code could be "? HRM".

当然,如果你不知道这个字的读音,那么其字典查询代码也可是"? HRM"。

Besides, the ECCode™ also provides fault-tolerant codes for such words.

此外,"汉易码™"对于这类汉字也大都提供了容错码。

Table 4.4  The computer code of traditional Chinese character "東"

表 4.4  繁体字"東"的计算机代码

| dōng | Shape 1<br>形码 1 | Shape 2<br>形码 2 | Shape 3<br>形码 | Standard code | Inquiry code |
|---|---|---|---|---|---|
| 東 | (一) | 日 | 朩 | DHRM | ? HRM |
| East | Horizon | sun | No meaning | | |

## 4.3  A coding formula of Chinese characters in ECCode™
## "汉易码™"编码公式

### 4.3.1  The Encoding Law
### 编码规律

There is a LAW of VISUAL MEMORY(LVM for short) which refers to some content characteristics that people remember by impression after having a look at geometric objects or portraits. Specifically speaking, many people can remember the external features of Chinese characters (their outer parts) but often cannot remember the internal details (their inner parts).

有一种视觉记忆规律,指的是人们看一眼几何物体或画像,就能够凭着印象记住一些内容特征。具体地说,就是指很多人能够记住汉字的外围特征(汉字的外部),而常常记不住这个汉字的内部细节(汉字的内部)。

For example, cast a glance at the following character (Figure 4.3), then close your eyes and think about what you have remembered. Generally, you maybe have only remembered such as "穴" and "辶" along the periphery of the character but nothing else.

例如,大家看一眼下面这个汉字(图4.3),然后闭起眼睛想一下自己都记住了些什么东西。一般来说,除了处于这个汉字外围的"穴"和"辶",估计大家什么都没有记住。

Figure 4.3 biáng biáng miàn, the name of a kind of Chinese noodles
图4.3 biáng biáng 面,一种中国面条的名称

Therefore, based on the LVM, for the convenience of users to encode a character, the EC-Code$^{TM}$ generally takes the shape constituents along the periphery of the character as its sources of shape code-elements (or shape codes).

所以,基于这个视觉记忆规律,为了便于用户对汉字进行编码,"汉易码$^{TM}$"一般都是在汉字的外围选用字形组分作为其字形码元(形码)的出处。

Note that this phenomenon or the LVM is very important for your understanding of the encoding formula of the ECCode$^{TM}$. So, this regular pattern is called "the ENCODING LAW".

注意,这个视觉记忆现象或规律对于帮助大家理解"汉易码$^{TM}$"的编码公式非常重要。所以,这个视觉记忆规律就被称为"编码规律"。

### 4.3.2 The location of encoded object (shape constituent) in Detached Chinese Characters
分体字中编码对象(亦即字形组分)的大致位置

So called ENCODED OBJECT or ENCODED CONSTITUENT refers to a phonetic constituent or a shape constituent in a Chinese character needing to be encoded.

所谓编码对象或编码组分,就是指汉字中需要编码的字音组分或字形组分。

As to the Table 3.19, considering the encoding law above, we can mark out the general site ($S_{x=1,2,or3}$) for each encoded constituent or object of a Detached Chinese Character as follow (Table 4.5 below). That is, $S_1$, $S_2$, and $S_3$ (namely $S_{x=1,2,or3}$) indicate respectively the locations of three encoded shape constituents in a Chinese character.

就表3.19而言,鉴于上述编码规律,我们可以标示出分体字每个编码组分或编码对象的大致位置($S_{x=1,2,or3}$,如表4.5所示)。也就是说,$S_1$,$S_2$,和$S_3$(即$S_{x=1,2,or3}$)分别表示汉字当中三个字形编码对象的大致位置。

Chapter 4　How to input a Chinese character without knowing its pronunciation
如何输入不知道读音的汉字

**Table 4.5**　**The general site（$S_x$）** for each encoding constituent of the Detached Chinese Character
表 4.5　分体字中每个编码组分的大致位置

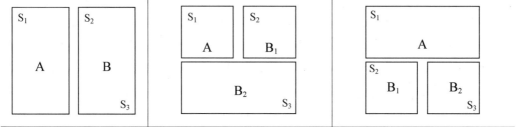

Among Table 4.5:
在表 4.5 当中:

$S_1$ is the site for the first encoded shape object (namely a shape constituent) of a DCC, i. e., $S_1$ is the place where the first stroke of part A locates.

$S_1$是分体字第一个字形编码对象(字形组分)的所在位置,即$S_1$是 A 部分第一个笔画所在位置。

$S_2$ is the site for the second encoded shape object (namely a shape constituent) of a DCC, i. e., $S_2$ is the place where the first stroke of part B or $B_1$ locates.

$S_2$是分体字第二个字形编码对象(字形组分)的所在位置,即$S_2$是 B 或 $B_1$部分的第一个笔画所在位置。

$S_3$ is the site for the third encoded shape object (namely a shape constituent) of a DCC.

123

In other words, $S_3$ is the place where the last stroke of part B or $B_3$ locates. Please note that $S_3$ only represents the place where the shape constituent of the last stroke of the character locates rather than the place where the constituent of the "bottom" stroke of the character locates.

$S_3$是分体字第三个字形编码对象(字形组分)的所在位置,即$S_3$是B或$B_2$部分的最后一个笔画所在位置。注意,$S_3$仅代表该字最后一个笔画所属字形组分所在的位置,而不是指"最底部"笔画所属字形组分所在的位置。

Of course, there may be no $S_3$ and $S_2$ if there are not enough strokes in a DCC. For example, in the characters 九, 儿, 刁, etc., there are no encoded shape constituents whose locations are represented respectively by $S_3$ and $S_2$ because these characters have too less strokes, and the characters 办, 丸, 台, etc. have no encoded shape constituent whose location is represented by $S_3$ because the number of strokes in this character is too small to form the third encoded shape component.

当然,如果一个分体字的笔画数量不多的话,也就不一定有$S_3$或$S_2$了。例如,在"九、儿、刁"等汉字当中,由于这些汉字的笔画数量太少了,所以这些汉字就没有第三和第二个编码对象落脚的位置$S_3$和$S_2$了,而在汉字"办、丸、台"等汉字当中,由于这些汉字的笔画数量少到无法构成第三个字形编码组分,所以这些汉字也就没有第三个字形编码组分落脚的位置$S_3$了。

### 4.3.3 The location of encoded object (shape constituent) in the Mixed Chinese Character
**杂合体字中编码对象(字形组分)的大致位置**

Similarly, as to the Table 3.20, also considering the encoding law above, we can mark out the general site ($S_{x=1, 2, or 3}$) for each encoded shape constituent of a Mixed Chinese Character as follow (shown as Table 4.6 below).

同样的,就表3.20而言,也是鉴于上述编码规律,我们可以大致标出杂合体字里面各个字形编码组分的大致位置如表4.6所示.

**Table 4.6** Nonfigurative sketch for the general site ($S_x$) for each encoding constituent of an MCC
**表4.6 杂合体字中每个编码组分大致位置的抽象示意图**

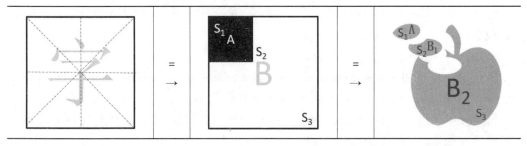

Chapter 4　How to input a Chinese character without knowing its pronunciation
如何输入不知道读音的汉字

Among Table 4.6:
在表4.6中：

$S_1$ is the place for the first encoded shape object or encoded shape constituent of MCC. In other words, the shape constituent whose location is represented by $S_1$ includes the first stroke of part A. That is, if the mixed character is regarded as an "apple", then $S_1$ is equivalent to the position of the bitten part of the "apple", which contains the first stroke of the Chinese character.

$S_1$是杂合体字第一个字形编码对象或字形编码组分的大致位置。换句话说，位置$S_1$所代表的字形组分包含杂合体字 A 部分的第一个笔画。也就是说，如果把这个杂合体字当作是一个"苹果"的话，那么$S_1$就相当于"苹果"被咬掉的那个部分所在的位置，这个"被咬掉"的部分包含这个汉字的第一个笔画。

$S_2$ is the place for the second encoded shape object or encoded shape constituents of MCC and also the site for the first encoded one where the first stroke of part B locates. In other words, the part whose location is represented by $S_2$ includes the first stroke of the part B that is left after the first bitten part of this character having been taken with its location represented by $S_1$. Namely, part B just likes the rest of the "apple" which has been bitten the first time, and $S_2$ equivalent to the site representing the second bitten part of the "apple", which contains the first stroke of the part B.

$S_2$是杂合体字第二个字形编码对象或字形编码组分的位置，也是包含 B 部分第一个笔画的、B 部分第一个字形编码对象所在的位置。即$S_2$是整个汉字位于$S_1$处的第一个字形编码组分被拿走之后所剩下的那个 B 部分的第一个笔画所在的位置。这个 B 部分就像是表4.6中那个"苹果"被咬掉第一口后所剩下的那个部分。

$S_3$ is the site for the third encoded shape object or encoded shape constituents of MCC. In other words, $S_3$ represents the part which includes the last stroke of part B and which is also the remaining part after the first two bitten parts of this character having been taken with their locations represented respectively by $S_1$ and $S_2$. Please note that $S_3$ only represents the place where the shape constituent containing the last stroke of the character locates, rather than the place where the shape constituent containing the "bottom" stroke of the character locates.

$S_3$是杂合体字第三个字形编码对象或字形编码组分的位置。即$S_3$代表那个包含 B 部分最后一个笔画的、已经被吃掉了两口的那个"苹果"的"剩余部分"。注意，$S_3$仅代表该字最后一个笔画所属字形编码组分所在的位置，而不是指"最底部"笔画所在字形编码组分所在的位置。

Of course, there may be no $S_3$ or $S_2$ if there are not enough strokes in an MCC. For instance, as to the Chinese characters "一、二、三、台, etc.", all of these characters definitely have no $S_3$ because of their less strokes, and some of these characters even have no $S_2$

125

either because of their further less strokes in them.

当然了，如果这个杂合体字的笔画数量不多的话，那么也就可能没有 $S_3$ 或 $S_2$ 了。例如，对于"一、二、三、台"等汉字而言，所有这些汉字都肯定没有 $S_3$，因为它们的笔画比较少。而其中有些汉字的笔画更少，所以连 $S_2$ 都没有。

Actually, there may be no $S_3$ or $S_2$ if there are not enough strokes in a Chinese character, no matter the DCC or the MCC.

事实上，无论分体字还是杂合体字，如果笔画不够多的话，$S_3$ 和 $S_2$ 都有可能不存在。

Meantime, $S_{x1,2,or3}$ in both Table 4.5 and Table 4.6 represents one of places where the shape constituents locate respectively, namely the place where a radical, a stroke combination, or a basic stroke locates, and the four encoding rules mentioned above decide which shape constituent would be chosen and encoded.

同时，在表4.5和表4.6当中，$S_{x=1,2,or3}$ 表示字形组分的位置，即表示字根、笔画组合或基本笔画这三种字形组分之一的位置。而四个编码规则则决定了究竟选用哪一个字形组分作为编码对象。

### 4.3.4　The encoding formula
### 编码公式

The encoding formula of the ECCode™ is an encoding way used to guide you to encode a Chinese character according to the encoding rules of the ECCode™ mentioned above. The formula is as follow (Figure 4.4).

"汉易码™"的编码公式是用于指导大家根据上述编码规则编制汉字代码的一种编码方法。这个编码公式如图4.4所示。

The code of a Chinese character = phonetic code + start code of A ($S_1$ belonging to the part A)
　　　　　　　　　　　　　　　　　+ start code of B ($S_2$ belonging to the part $B_1$)
　　　　　　　　　　　　　　　　　+ end code of B ($S_3$ belonging to the part $B_2$)

汉字代码 = 声码 + A部分前码($S_1$) + B部分前码($S_2$)
　　　　　+ B部分末码($S_3$)

Figure 4.4　The encoding formula of ECCode™
图4.4　"汉易码™"编码公式

Each variable (code-element) in the formula above can be substituted by the question mark "?", but the variable order cannot be changed.

上面编码公式当中每个变量(即代码码元)都可以用问号键"?"代替，但不能改变变量的排序。

## 4.4 Supplemental provision on the structure of Detached Chinese Character
## 对分体字的补充规定

Supplemental provisions on the structure of Chinese characters are mainly aimed at Detached Chinese Characters (DCC). They are introduced as follows(see Table 4.7).

有关汉字结构的补充规定主要是针对分体字(DCCs)而制定的。这些补充规则如下所列(参见表4.7)。

(1) While keeping the integrity of a radical in the KMT shown as Table 3.14, as to a DCC, there should be no less than 2 strokes in part A. For examples, in the character "川" of left-right structure, part A is the combination ( 丿丨 ); in the character "坚" of two-upper-and-one-lower structure, part A is the combination ( 丨丨 ).

在确保字根完整的情况下,分体字A部分的笔画不能少于2个。例如,在左右结构的汉字"川"里面,A部分就是笔画组合(丿丨);在上二下一结构的汉字"坚"里面,A部分就是笔画组合(丨丨)。

(2) The strokes in part A should always be written before the strokes in part B (Macro stroke order rule). For example, in the character "起", the part A "走" should be written before the part B "巳" even though the last stroke of the part A is extended towards the right bottom. Another example, in the character "督", the part A "未" should be written before part $B_1$ "又" and part $B_2$ "目". And as for the character "范", the part A "艹" is written before the part $B_1$ "氵" and the part $B_2$ "巳". In practice, there are many such characters.

A部分的笔画总是比B部分的笔画先写(即宏观笔顺原则)。例如,在汉字"起"中,尽管A部分"走"的最后一个笔画要向右下方延伸,但该字就是要先书写A部分的"走"然后书写B部分的"巳"。又比如,"督"字的A部分"未"就比$B_1$部分的"又"和$B_2$部分的"目"要先书写。而对于汉字"范"来说,A部分的"艹"就要比$B_1$部分的"氵"和$B_2$部分的"巳"先书写。事实上,这样的字还有很多。

(3) In characters with the shape like "题" "赵" "毯", etc., such left parts as "是" "走" "毛" are always written first but with the last stroke of these parts extended to the lower right. Therefore, the characters like them are regarded as the left-right structure (see Figure 3.28 above).

在形状像"题""赵""毯"等的汉字当中,"是""走""毛"等左边位置的汉字部分总是先书写,只是这些部分的最后一笔画都向右下方做了延伸,所以,像这样结构的汉字就都被视作左右结构(参见前面图3.28)。

(4) In characters with the shape like "邀" "逛", etc., such bottom parts as "辶" "廴" are always written at the end, so the characters like them are regarded as the structure of two-upper-and-one-lower structure (see the Figure 3.29 above).

在形状像"邀""逛"等的汉字当中,人们总是最后写处于底部位置的"辶""廴"等汉字部分,所以,汉字中所有像这样结构的汉字都被视作"上二下一"结构(参见前面图3.29)。

Table 4.7    The demonstrations of supplemental provision 1~4 on DCC
表4.7    针对分体字的补充规定之字例

| Examples 字例 | Split 拆分 | Part A A部分 | Part B B部分 | Examples 字例 | Split 拆分 | Part A A部分 | Part B B部分 |
|---|---|---|---|---|---|---|---|
| 川 | → | 刂 | 丨 | 题 | → | 是 | 页 |
| 坚 | | 刂 | 圣 | 赵 | | 走 | 乂 |
| 提 | | 扌 | 是 | 毯 | | 毛 | 炎 |
| 陪 | | 阝 | 音 | 邀 | | 臱 | 辶 |
| 浙 | | 氵 | 折 | 逛 | | 犭 | 辶 |

(5) For left-right structure characters, if part B is a radical, a combination of two strokes, or a basic stroke, the second shape code, namely the code of the shape constituent located at the place $S_2$, should be taken in the remaining section of the part A (equivalent to part $A_2$) according to the stroke order in order to expand the encoded information quantity of Chinese characters and reduce the rate of coincidental code.

就左右结构汉字而言,如果B部分是一个字根,或者是一个两笔画组合,再或者是一个基本笔画,那么依照笔顺,其第二个形码——即这个形码对应$A_2$部分的字形编码组分所在位置$S_2$——应该继续在A的剩余部分(相当于$A_2$)中选取,以便扩大汉字的编码信息量信息量、降低重码率。

In other words, if the part B of a Chinese character can supply only one code-element (and no extra shape constituent is available), which means part B is made up of only a radical, a stroke combination, or a basic stroke, you should continue to take the second shape code of the shape constituent whose place is at $S_2$ in the remaining section of part A according to the stroke order; and the second shape code ($S_2$) should come from the part A that is left after the first shape code ($S_1$) of part A having been taken. These supplemental provisions are designed to reduce the rate of coincident code in the ECCode™.

换句话说,如果 B 部分的字形组分只够取一个码元(就没有字形组分可用了),这就意味着 B 部分只由一个字根或一个笔画组合或一个基本笔画构成。此时,你应该根据笔顺规则继续在 A 的剩余部分取第二个形码(即对位置 $S_2$ 上的字形组分进行编码);即 A 部分这个第二个形码应该从 A 部分被取走第一个形码($S_1$)之后所剩下的那个部分中选取。这个补充规则也是为了降低重码率而设计的。

**Example 4.4** In the character "鸽" (read as /gē/, meaning a bird's name), part B only has the radical "鸟" recognized by the ECCode™, which can provide only one code "N". So, after taking the letter "R" as the first shape code of the radical "人" in part A "合", you should continue to take the second shape code in the left section (口) of part A according to the STROKE ORDER rule. The second shape code in part A should be "H" that is the code of the basic stroke "一" because "口" in the left section (口) of part A is the radical which cannot be divided into strokes according to the INTEGRITY rule. As a result, the code of "鸽" is "GRHN" (see Table 4.8 below).

例 4.4 在汉字"鸽"(读作/gē/,一种鸟的名称)中,B 部分只有一个字根"鸟",这个字根"鸟"只能贡献一个字形码元 N。所以,在对 A 部分"合"中的字根"人"取码 R 之后,用户应该在 A 部分剩余的部分"口"当中依照笔顺继续以第二个字形作为编码对象进行取码。由于 A 部分取走字根"人"之后就只剩下"口"了,而"口"里有一个字根"口",根据完整律,不能把字根"口"拆散成笔画,所以第二个字形组分码元只能是 A 部分剩余的部分"口"里的笔画"一"的代码 H。所以,汉字"鸽"的代码就是 GRHN(参见表 4.8)。

**Example 4.5** In the character "印", you should take shape codes from (丿 一) and (一) in part A, and (卩) in part B (see the Table 4.8 below).

例 4.5 在汉字"印"当中,用户应该在 A 部分取笔画组合(丿 一)、单个笔画(一)和 B 部分的字根"卩"作为这个汉字的三个字形编码组分或字形编码对象(参见表 4.8)。

Table 4.8 The demonstrations of supplemental provision 5 on DCC
表4.8 分体字补充规则5字例

| Examples 例字 | Phonetic code-element 音码码元 | | Shape code-elements 形码码元 | | | ECCode 汉易码 |
|---|---|---|---|---|---|---|
| | Read as: 读作: | code-element 码元 | $S_1$ | $S_2$ | $S_3$ | |
| 鸽 | gē | G | R | H | N | GRHN |
| 印 | yìn | Y | F (丿一) | H (一) | E | YFHE |

(6) when a character can be taken as one of both the two-upper-and-one-lower and the one-upper-and-two-lower structure, you should give priority to taking it as the two-upper-and-one-lower structure because of encoding a Chinese character according to macro stroke order.

当一个汉字既可以被视作"上二下一结构"汉字，又可以被视作"上一下二"结构时，因为编码是依照宏观笔顺对字形组分进行取码的，所以你得优先把这个汉字视作"上二下一"结构来对其进行编码。

### 4.4.1 Examples of encoding Detached Chinese Characters (DCC)
分体字编码范例

Let's take a look at some examples of how to use the encoding rules and the encoding formula to encode Chinese characters. Before explaining the examples, Let's give a brief description of some of the signs in the example.

下面我们来看一些如何运用编码规则和编码公式来对汉字进行编码的示例。在讲解示例之前，我们先对示例中的一些标示做一个简单的说明。

Chapter 4  How to input a Chinese character without knowing its pronunciation
如何输入不知道读音的汉字

- Hollow strokes, such as "⬭", indicate that such strokes are not used in Chinese character encoding, i. e., they belong to the part that the character encoding formula does not collect its character information.

  像"⬭"这样的空心笔画,表示这些笔画在汉字编码当中没有被使用,即这些笔画属于该字编码不予采集其信息的那一部分。

- At the same time, the shape constituent strokes (namely macro stroke order) of a Chinese character are written in the same order of the character encoding.

  同时,汉字字形组分的笔画书写顺序(即宏观笔顺)与汉字编码的顺序一致。

- If the number of strokes is large enough in a Chinese character, there will be a second shape encoded object (at position $S_2$) and even a third shape encoded object (at position $S_3$). It's hoped that the situation should be paid attention to.

  如果汉字笔画数量足够多,相应地就会有第二个字形编码对象(位于 $S_2$ 位置处)甚至有第三个字形编码对象(位于 $S_3$ 位置处),关于这种情况,希望给予关注。

- The symbol "→" means the order of the encoded shape constituents or encoded shape objects.

  符号"→"表示字形编码组分或字形编码对象的取码顺序。

- Besides, the parenthese in the illustrating tables of example Chinese characters indicate that the stroke or the stroke combination in it is not a radical.

  此外,汉字示例表当中的括号表示,放置其中的笔画或笔画组合不是一个字根。

**Example 4.6**  The encoded shape constituents of the character "川" = ( 丿丨) + ( 丨) and is read as /chuān/. Its phonetic code-element is "C" or "?" (substitute code when it cannot be read). Its standard Chinese code is "COI" and its dictionary query code is "? OI" according to the supplemental provision 1 on DCC (Table 4.9).

**例4.6**  汉字"川"的字形编码组分=( 丿丨)+( 丨),读作"chuān",其字音码元是"C"或者"?"(不会读音时的替代码);根据分体字补充规则1,其标准代码是COI,字典查询码则是"? OI"(参见表4.9)。

Table 4.9  The disassembly of "川" and its coding demon.
表4.9  汉字"川"的拆解及其编码示例

| Character example 例字 | Structure 汉字结构 | Phonetic code-element 字音码元 | | code-element of shape constituents 字形码元 | | ECCode 汉易码 |
|---|---|---|---|---|---|---|
| | | Read as: 读作： | code-element 音码 | $S_1$ 形码1 | $S_2$ 形码2 | |
| 川 | $S_1$ A, $S_2$ B, $S_3$ | chuān | C | 丿 | 丨 | COI |
| | | Unknown 不知读音 | ? | 川 (丿丨) | 丨 (丨) | ? OI |

**Example 4.7**  The encoded shape constituents of the character "坚" = (丨丨) + (又) + (土) and is read as /jiān/. Its phonetic code-element is "J" or "?". Its standard Chinese code is "JIUT" and its dictionary query code is "? IUT" according to the supplemental provision 1 on DCC. It is a left-right structure character (Table 4.10).

例4.7  汉字"坚"的字形编码组分=(丨丨)+(又)+(土),读作/jiān/,其字音码元是"J"或者是"?";根据分体字补充规则1,这个左右结构汉字的标准代码是"JIUT",字典查询码是"? IUT"(参见表4.10)。

Table 4.10  The disassembly of "坚" and its coding demon.
表4.10  汉字"坚"的拆解及其编码示例

| Character example 例字 | Structure 汉字结构 | Phonetic code-element 字音码元 | | code-element of shape constituents 字形码元 | | | ECCode 汉易码 |
|---|---|---|---|---|---|---|---|
| | | Read as: 读作： | code-element 音码 | $S_1$ 形码1 | $S_2$ 形码2 | $S_3$ 形码3 | |
| 坚 | $S_1$ A, $S_2$ B, $S_3$ | jiān | J | I | U | T | JIUT |
| | | Unknown 不知读音 | ? | 刂 (丨丨)= (丨) | 又 | 土 | ? IUT |

**Example 4.8**  The encoded shape constituents of the character "你" = (亻) + (丿一) + (小) and is read as /nǐ/. Its phonetic code-element is "N" or "?". Its standard Chinese code is "NRFX" and its dictionary query code is "? RFX" according to the supplemental provision

Chapter 4  How to input a Chinese character without knowing its pronunciation
如何输入不知道读音的汉字

1 on DCC. It is a two-upper-one-lower structure character (Table 4.11).

**例4.8**  汉字"你"的字形编码组分=（亻）+（丿㇇）+（小），读作/nǐ/，其字音码元是"N"或者是"？"，根据分体字补充规则1，这个"左右结构"汉字的标准代码是"NRFX"，字典查询码是"？RFX"（参见表4.11）。

Table 4.11  The disassembly of "你" and its coding demon.
表4.11  汉字"你"的拆解及其编码示例

| Character example 例字 | Structure 汉字结构 | Phonetic code-element 字音码元 | | code-element of shape constituents 字形码元 | | | ECCode 汉易码 |
|---|---|---|---|---|---|---|---|
| | | Read as: 读作： | code-element 音码 | $S_1$ 形码1 | $S_2$ 形码2 | $S_3$ 形码3 | |
| | | nǐ | N | R | F | X | NRFX |
| | | Unknown 不知读音 | ? | 亻 | ㇇ (丿㇇) | 小 | ? RFX |

**Example 4.9**  The encoded shape constituents of the character "他" = （亻）+（也）and is read as /tā/. Its phonetic code-element is "T" or "?". Its standard Chinese code is "TRY" and its dictionary query code is "? RY". It is a left-right structure character (Table 4.12).

**例4.9**  汉字"他"的字形编码组分=（亻）+（也），读作/tā/，其字音码元是"T"或者是"？"，其标准代码是"TRY"，字典查询码是"？RY"，这是个左右结构的汉字（参见表4.12）。

Table 4.12  The disassembly of "他" and its coding demon.
表4.12  汉字"他"的拆解及其编码示例

| Character example 例字 | Structure 汉字结构 | Phonetic code-element 字音码元 | | code-element of shape constituents 字形码元 | | ECCode 汉易码 |
|---|---|---|---|---|---|---|
| | | Read as: 读作： | code-element 音码 | $S_1$ 形码1 | $S_2$ 形码2 | |
| | | tā | T | R | Y | TRY |
| | | Unknown 不知读音 | ? | 亻 | 也 | ? RY |

133

**Example 4.10** The encoded shape constituents of the character "她" =（女）+（也）and is read as /tā/. Its phonetic code-element is "T" or "?". Its standard Chinese code is "TNY" and its dictionary query code is "? NY". It is a left-right structure character (Table 4.13).

**例4.10** 汉字"她"的字形编码组分=（女）+（也），读作/tā/，其字音码元是"T"或者是"?"，其标准代码是"TNY"，字典查询码是"? NY"，这是个左右结构的汉字(参见表4.13)。

Table 4.13　The disassembly of "她" and its coding demon.

表4.13　汉字"她"的拆解及其编码示例

| Character example 例字 | Structure 汉字结构 | Phonetic code-element 字音码元 | | code-element of shape constituents 字形码元 | | ECCode 汉易码 |
|---|---|---|---|---|---|---|
| | | Read as: 读作： | code-element 音码 | $S_1$ 形码1 | $S_2$ 形码2 | |
| 她 | $S_1$ A / $S_2$ B / $S_3$ | tā | T | N | Y | TNY |
| | | Unknown 不知读音 | ? | 女 | 也 | ? NY |

**Example 4.11** The encoded shape constituents of the character "妈" =（女）+（马）and is read as /mā/. Its phonetic code-element is "M" or "?". Its standard Chinese code is "MNM" and its dictionary query code is "? NM". It is a left-right structure character (Table 4.14).

**例6** 汉字"妈"的字形编码组分=（女）+（马），左右结构汉字，读作/mā/，其字音码元是"M"或者是"?"，其标准代码是"MNM"，字典查询码是"? NM"（参见表4.14）。

Table 4.14　The disassembly of "妈" and its coding demon.

表4.14　汉字"妈"的拆解及其编码示例

| Character example 例字 | Structure 汉字结构 | Phonetic code-element 字音码元 | | code-element of shape constituents 字形码元 | | ECCode 汉易码 |
|---|---|---|---|---|---|---|
| | | Read as: 读作： | code-element 音码 | $S_1$ 形码1 | $S_2$ 形码2 | |
| 妈 | $S_1$ A / $S_2$ B / $S_3$ | mā | M | N | M | MNM |
| | | Unknown 不知读音 | ? | 女 | 马 | ? NM |

Chapter 4　How to input a Chinese character without knowing its pronunciation
如何输入不知道读音的汉字

**Example 4.12**　The encoded shape constituents of the character "吗" =（口）+（马） and is read as /mā/. Its phonetic code-element is "M" or "?". Its standard Chinese code is "MKM" and its dictionary query code is "? KM". It is a left-right structure character (Table 4.15).

例 4.12　汉字"吗"的字形编码组分=（口）+（马），左右体字，读作/mā/，字音码元是"M"或者是"?"；其标准代码是"MKM"，字典查询码是"? KM"（参见表4.15）。

Table 4.15　The disassembly of "吗" and its coding demon.
表 4.15　汉字"吗"的拆解及其编码示例

| Character example 例字 | Structure 汉字结构 | Phonetic code-element 字音码元 | | code-element of shape constituents 字形码元 | | ECCode 汉易码 |
|---|---|---|---|---|---|---|
| | | Read as: 读作: | code-element 音码 | $S_1$ 形码1 | $S_2$ 形码2 | |
| 吗 | $S_1$ A / $S_2$ B / $S_3$ | mā | M | K | M | MKM |
| | | Unknown 不知读音 | ? | 口 | 马 | ? KM |

**Example 4.13**　The encoded shape constituents of the character "码" =（丿一）+（口）+（马） and is read as /mǎ/. Its phonetic code-element is "M" or "?". Its standard Chinese code is "MOKM" and its dictionary query code is "? OKM" according to the supplemental provision 1 on DCC. It is a left-right structure character (Table 4.16).

例 4.13　汉字"码"的字形编码组分=（丿一）+（口）+（马），左右体字，读作/mǎ/，字音码元是"M"或者是"?"；根据分体字补充规则1，其标准代码是"MOKM"，字典查询码是"? OKM"（参见表4.16）。

135

Table 4.16 The disassembly of "码" and its coding demon.
表 4.16 汉字"码"的拆解及其编码示例

| Character example 例字 | Structure 汉字结构 | Phonetic code-element 字音码元 | | code-element of shape constituents 字形码元 | | | ECCode 汉易码 |
|---|---|---|---|---|---|---|---|
| | | Read as: 读作: | code-element 音码 | $S_1$ 形码1 | $S_2$ 形码2 | $S_3$ 形码3 | |
| 码 | $S_1$ A / $S_2$ B | mǎ | M | O | K | M | MOKM |
| | | Unknown 不知读音 | ? | 丿 (一丿) | 口 | 马 | ? OKM |

**Example 4.14** The encoded shape constituents of the character "印" = (丿 ㇇) + (一) + (卩) and is read as /yìn/. Its phonetic code-element is "Y" or "?". Its standard Chinese code is "YFHE" and its dictionary query code is "? FHE" according to the PRIORITY rule and the INTEGRITY rule. It is a left-right structure character (Table 4.17).

例 4.14 汉字"印"的字形编码组分 =(丿 ㇇)+(一)+(卩),左右结构汉字,读作 /yìn/,其字音码元是"Y"或者是"?";根据优先律和完整律,其标准代码是"YFHE",字典查询代码是"? FHE"(参见表4.17)。

Table 4.17 The disassembly of "印" and its coding demon.
表 4.17 汉字"印"的拆解及其编码示例

| Character example 例字 | Structure 汉字结构 | Phonetic code-element 字音码元 | | code-element of shape constituents 字形码元 | | | ECCode 汉易码 |
|---|---|---|---|---|---|---|---|
| | | Read as: 读作: | code-element 音码 | $S_1$ 形码1 | $S_2$ 形码2 | $S_3$ 形码3 | |
| 印 | $S_1$ A / $S_2$ B | yìn | Y | F | H | E | YFHE |
| | | Unknown 不知读音 | ? | ⺈ | 一 | 卩 | ? FHE |

Chapter 4  How to input a Chinese character without knowing its pronunciation
如何输入不知道读音的汉字

**Example 4.15**  The encoded shape constituents of the character "朝" = (丨一) + (日) + (月). It is a polyphonic character and is read as /cháo/ or /zhāo/. Its phonetic code-element is "C", "Z" or "?". Its standard Chinese code is "CIRY" or "ZIRY" and its dictionary query code is "? IRY" according to the supplemental provision 1 on DCC. It is a left-right structure character (Table 4.18).

**例 4.15**  汉字"朝"的字形编码组分=(丨一)+(日)+(月),左右结构汉字,读作/cháo/或/zhāo/(多音字),所以其字音码元是"C"或"Z"或者是"?";根据分体字补充规则1,其标准代码是"CIRY"或"ZIRY",字典查询码是"? IRY"(参见表4.18)。

Table 4.18 The disassembly of "朝" and its coding demon.
表 4.18  汉字"朝"的拆解及其编码示例

| Character example 例字 | Structure 汉字结构 | Phonetic code-element 字音码元 | | code-element of shape constituents 字形码元 | | | ECCode 汉易码 |
|---|---|---|---|---|---|---|---|
| | | Read as: 读作: | code-element 音码 | $S_1$ 形码1 | $S_2$ 形码2 | $S_3$ 形码3 | |
| 朝 | $S_1$ $S_2$ A B $S_3$ | cháo or zhāo | C or Z | I | R | Y | CIRY or ZIRY |
| | | Unknown 不知读音 | ? | 十 (一丨) | 日 | 月 | ? IRY |

**Example 4.16**  The encoded shape constituents of the character "乱" = (丿一) + (丨) + (乚) and is read as /luàn/. Its phonetic code-element is "L" or "?". Its standard Chinese code is "LOIZ" and its dictionary query code is "? OIZ" according to the supplemental provision 1 on DCC. It is a left-right structure character (Table 4.19).

**例 4.16**  汉字"乱"的字形编码组分=(丿一)+(丨)+(乚),左右结构汉字,读作/luàn/,其字音码元是"L"或者是"?";根据分体字补充规则1,其标准代码是"LOIZ",字典查询码是"? OIZ"(参见表4.19)。

Table 4.19 The disassembly of "乱" and its coding demon.

表 4.19 汉字"乱"的拆解及其编码示例

| Character example 例字 | Structure 汉字结构 | Phonetic code-element 字音码元 | | code-element of shape constituents 字形码元 | | | ECCode 汉易码 |
|---|---|---|---|---|---|---|---|
| | | Read as: 读作: | code-element 音码 | $S_1$ 形码1 | $S_2$ 形码2 | $S_3$ 形码3 | |
| 乱 | $S_1$ A / $S_2$ B $S_3$ | luàn | L | O | I | Z | LOIZ |
| | | Unknown 不知读音 | ? | 二 (一丿) | 丨 (丨) | 乚 (⼄) | ? OIZ |

**Example 4.17** The encoded shape constituents of the character "故" = (丨一) + (口) + (攵) and is read as /gù/. Its phonetic code-element is "G" or "?". Its standard Chinese code is "GIKU" and its dictionary query code is "? IKU" according to the supplemental provision 5 on DCC. It is a left-right structure character (Table 4.20).

例 4.17 汉字"故"的字形编码组分 = (丨一) + (口) + (攵),左右结构汉字,读作 /gù/,其字音码元是"G"或者是"?";根据分体字补充规则5,其标准代码是"GIKU",字典查询码是"? IKU"(参见表4.20)。

Table 4.20 The disassembly of "故" and its coding demon.

表 4.20 汉字"故"的拆解及其编码示例

| Character example 例字 | Structure 汉字结构 | Phonetic code-element 字音码元 | | code-element of shape constituents 字形码元 | | | ECCode 汉易码 |
|---|---|---|---|---|---|---|---|
| | | Read as: 读作: | code-element 音码 | $S_1$ 形码1 | $S_2$ 形码2 | $S_3$ 形码3 | |
| 故 | $S_1$ A / $S_2$ B $S_3$ | gù | G | I | K | U | GIKU |
| | | Unknown 不知读音 | ? | 十 (一丨) | 口 | 攵 | ? IKU |

Chapter 4　How to input a Chinese character without knowing its pronunciation
如何输入不知道读音的汉字

**Example 4.18**　The encoded shape constituents of the character "题" = (日) + (一丿) + (贝) and is read as /tí/. Its phonetic code-element is "T" or "?". Its standard Chinese code is "TROB" and its dictionary query code is "? ROB" according to the supplemental provision 3 on DCC. It is a left-right structure character (Table 4.21).

例 4.18　汉字"题"的字形编码组分=(日)+(一丿)+(贝),左右结构汉字,读作/tí/,其字音码元是"T"或者是"?";根据分体字补充规则 3,其标准代码是"TROB",字典查询码是"? ROB"(参见表 4.21)。

Table 4.21　The disassembly of "题" and its coding demon.
表 4.21　汉字"题"的拆解及其编码示例

| Character example 例字 | Structure 汉字结构 | Phonetic code-element 字音码元 | | code-element of shape constituents 字形码元 | | | ECCode 汉易码 |
|---|---|---|---|---|---|---|---|
| | | Read as： 读作： | code-element 音码 | S₁ 形码1 | S₂ 形码2 | S₃ 形码3 | |
| 题 | S₁ S₂ A B S₃ | tí | T | R | O | B | TROB |
| | | Unknown 不知读音 | ? | 日 | 丆 (一丨) | 贝 | ? ROB |

**Example 4.19**　The encoded shape constituents of the character "赵" = (走) + (丶丿) and is read as /zhào/. Its phonetic code-element is "Z" or "?". Its standard Chinese code is "ZZV" and its dictionary query code is "? ZV" according to the supplemental provision 3 on DCC. It is a left-right structure character (Table 4.22).

例 4.19　汉字"赵"的字形编码组分=(走)+(丶丿),左右结构汉字,读作/zhào/,其字音码元是"Z"或者是"?";根据分体字补充规则 3,其标准代码是"ZZV",字典查询码是"? ZV"(参见表 4.22)。

Table 4.22  The disassembly of "赵" and its coding demon.
表4.22  汉字"赵"的拆解及其编码示例

| Character example 例字 | Structure 汉字结构 | Phonetic code-element 字音码元 | | code-element of shape constituents 字形码元 | | ECCode 汉易码 |
|---|---|---|---|---|---|---|
| | | Read as: 读作： | code-element 音码 | $S_1$ 形码1 | $S_2$ 形码2 | |
| 赵 | $S_1$ $S_2$ A B $S_3$ | zhào | Z | Z | V | ZZV |
| | | Unknown 不知读音 | ? | 走 | 乂 (丶丿) | ? ZV |

**Example 4.20** The encoded character "毯" = (丿一) + (火) + (火) and is read as /tǎn/. Its phonetic code-element is "T" or "?". Its standard Chinese code is "TOHH" and its dictionary query code is "? OHH" according to the supplemental provision 3 on DCC. It is a left-right structure character (Table 4.23).

例4.20  汉字"毯" = (丿一) + (火) + (火),左右结构汉字,读作/tǎn/,其字音码元是"T"或者是"?";根据分体字补充规则3,其标准代码是"TOHH",字典查询码是"? OHH"(参见表4.23)。

Table 4.23  The disassembly of "毯" and its coding demon.
表4.23  汉字"毯"的拆解及其编码示例

| Character example 例字 | Structure 汉字结构 | Phonetic code-element 字音码元 | | code-element of shape constituents 字形码元 | | | ECCode 汉易码 |
|---|---|---|---|---|---|---|---|
| | | Read as: 读作： | code-element 音码 | $S_1$ 形码1 | $S_2$ 形码2 | $S_3$ 形码3 | |
| 毯 | $S_1$ $S_2$ A B $S_3$ | tǎn | T | O | H | H | TOHH |
| | | Unknown 不知读音 | ? | 二 (丿一) | 火 | 火 | ? OHH |

Chapter 4  How to input a Chinese character without knowing its pronunciation
如何输入不知道读音的汉字

**Example 4.21**　The encoded shape constituents of the character "邀" =（白）+（攵）+（辶）and is read as /yāo/. Its phonetic code-element is "Y" or "?". Its standard Chinese code is "YRUZ" and its dictionary query code is "? RUZ" according to the supplemental provision 4 on DCC. It is a two-upper-and-one-lower structure character（Table 4.24）.

例 4.21　汉字"邀"的字形编码组分 =（白）+（攵）+（辶），上二下一结构汉字，读作 /yāo/，其字音码元是"Y"或者是"?"；根据分体字补充规则4，其标准代码是"YRUZ"，字典查询码是"? RUZ"（参见表4.24）。

Table 4.24　The disassembly of "邀" and its coding demon.
表4.24　汉字"邀"字的拆解及其编码示例

| Character example 例字 | Structure 汉字结构 | Phonetic code-element 字音码元 | | code-element of shape constituents 字形码元 | | | ECCode 汉易码 |
|---|---|---|---|---|---|---|---|
| | | Read as: 读作: | code-element 音码 | $S_1$ 形码1 | $S_2$ 形码2 | $S_3$ 形码3 | |
| | $S_1$ A　$S_2$ B$_1$　B$_2$　$S_3$ | yāo | Y | R | U | Z | YRUZ |
| | | Unknown 不知读音 | ? | 白 | 攵 | 辶 | ? RUZ |

**Example 4.22**　The encoded shape constituents of the character "逛" =（犭）+（王）+（辶）and is read as /guàng/. Its phonetic code-element is "G" or "?". Its standard Chinese code is "GQWZ" and its dictionary query code is "? QWZ" according to the supplemental provision 4 on DCC. It is a two-upper-and-one-lower structure character（Table 4.25）.

例 4.22　汉字"逛"的字形编码组分 =（犭）+（王）+（辶），上二下一结构汉字，读作 /guàng/，其字音码元是"G"或者是"?"；根据分体字补充规则4，其标准代码是"GQWZ"，字典查询码是"? QWZ"（参见表4.25）。

Table 4.25　The disassembly of "逛" and its coding demon.
表4.25　汉字"逛"的拆解及其编码示例

| Character example 例字 | Structure 汉字结构 | Phonetic code-element 字音码元 | | code-element of shape constituents 字形码元 | | | ECCode 汉易码 |
|---|---|---|---|---|---|---|---|
| | | Read as: 读作： | code-element 音码 | $S_1$ 形码1 | $S_2$ 形码2 | $S_3$ 形码3 | |
| 逛 | $S_1$ A / $S_2$ $B_1$ / $B_2$ $S_3$ | guàng | G | Q | W | Z | GQWZ |
| | | Unknown 不知读音 | ? | 犭 | 王 | 辶 | ? QWZ |

**Example 4.23**　The encoded shape constituents of the character "哭" = (口) + (口) + (、) and is read as /kū/. Its phonetic code-element is "K" or "?". Its standard Chinese code is "KKKD" and its dictionary query code is "? KKD" according to the PRIORITY rule and the INTEGRITY rule. It is a two-upper-and-one-lower structure character (Table 4.26).

例 4.23　汉字"哭"的字形编码组分=(口)+(口)+(、),上二下一结构汉字,读作/kū/,其字音码元是"K"或者是"?";根据优先律和完整律,其标准代码是"KKKD",字典查询码是"? KKD"(参见表 4.26)。

Table 4.26　The disassembly of "哭" and its coding demon.
表4.26　汉字"哭"的拆解及其编码示例

| Character example 例字 | Structure 汉字结构 | Phonetic code-element 字音码元 | | code-element of shape constituents 字形码元 | | | ECCode 汉易码 |
|---|---|---|---|---|---|---|---|
| | | Read as: 读作： | code-element 音码 | $S_1$ 形码1 | $S_2$ 形码2 | $S_3$ 形码3 | |
| 哭 | $S_1$ A / $S_2$ $B_1$ / $B_2$ $S_3$ | kū | K | K | K | D | KKKD |
| | | Unknown 不知读音 | ? | 口 | 口 | (、) | ? KKD |

**Example 4.24**　The encoded shape constituents of the character "器" = (口) + (口) + (口) and is read as /xiāo/. Its phonetic code-element is "X" or "?". Its standard Chinese code is "XKKK" and its dictionary query code is "? KKK" according to the PRIORITY rule

# Chapter 4 How to input a Chinese character without knowing its pronunciation
## 如何输入不知道读音的汉字

and the INTEGRITY rule. It is a two-upper-and-one-lower structure character (Table 4.27).

**例 4.24** 汉字"嚣"的字形编码组分=(口)+(口)+(口),是上二下一结构汉字,读作/xiāo/,其字音码元是"X"或者是"?";根据优先律和完整律,其标准代码是"XKKK",字典查询码是"?KKK"(参见表4.27)。

**Table 4.27 The disassembly of "嚣" and its coding demon.**
**表 4.27 汉字"嚣"的拆解及其编码示例**

| Character example 例字 | Structure 汉字结构 | Phonetic code-element 字音码元 | | code-element of shape constituents 字形码元 | | | ECCode 汉易码 |
|---|---|---|---|---|---|---|---|
| | | Read as: 读作: | code-element 音码 | $S_1$ 形码1 | $S_2$ 形码2 | $S_3$ 形码3 | |
| 嚣 | $S_1$ A $S_2$ $B_1$ / $B_2$ $S_3$ | xiāo | X | K | K | K | XKKK |
| | | Unknown 不知读音 | ? | 口 | 口 | 口 | ? KKK |

In such kind of characters as "嚣", its part A and part B are shown as follows (see Table 4.28) according the writing order of the character and the macro stroke order rule.

在像"嚣"这类汉字当中,其A部分和B部分的划分方法如表4.28所示。

**Table 4.28 Part A and part B of "嚣"**
**表 4.28 汉字"嚣"的 A 和 B 两个部分的划分示例**

| Character example 例字 | Part A A部分 | Part B B部分 |
|---|---|---|
| 嚣 | Structure 汉字结构 $S_1$ A / $S_2$ $B_1$ / $B_2$ $S_3$ / B = $B_1$ + $B_2$ | |
| | 口 | 嚣 |

**Example 4.25** The encoded shape constituents of the character "架" = (力) + (口) + (木) and is read as /jià/. Its phonetic code-element is "J" or "?". Its standard Chinese code is "JLKM" and its dictionary query code is "? LKM" according to the PRIORITY rule and the INTEGRITY rule. It is a two-upper-and-one-lower structure character (Table 4.29).

例4.25　汉字"架"的字形编码组分=(力)+(口)+(木)，是上二下一结构汉字，读作/jià/，其字音码元是"J"或者是"?"；根据优先律和完整律，其标准代码是"JLKM"，字典查询码是"? LKM"（参见表4.29）。

Table 4.29　The disassembly of "架" and its coding demon.
表4.29　汉字"架"的拆解及其编码示例

| Character example 例字 | Structure 汉字结构 | Phonetic code-element 字音码元 | | code-element of shape constituents 字形码元 | | | ECCode 汉易码 |
|---|---|---|---|---|---|---|---|
| | | Read as: 读作： | code-element 音码 | $S_1$ 形码1 | $S_2$ 形码2 | $S_3$ 形码3 | |
| 架 | $S_1$ $S_2$ A $B_1$ $B_2$ $S_3$ | jià | J | L | K | M | JLKM |
| | | Unknown 不知读音 | ? | 力 | 口 | 木 | ? LKM |

**Example 4.26** The encoded shape constituents of the character "赢" = (丶一) + (月) + (丶㇕) and is read as /yíng/. Its phonetic code-element is "Y" or "?". Its standard Chinese code is "YAYA" and its dictionary query code is "? AYA" according to the PRIORITY rule and the INTEGRITY rule. It is a one-upper-and-two-lower structure character (Table 4.30).

例4.26　汉字"赢"的字形编码组分=(丶一)+(月)+(丶㇕)，上一下二结构分体字，读作/yíng/，其字音码元是"Y"或者是"?"；根据优先律和完整律，其标准代码是"YAYA"，字典查询码是"? AYA"（参见表4.30）。

Chapter 4 How to input a Chinese character without knowing its pronunciation
如何输入不知道读音的汉字

Table 4.30 The disassembly of "赢" and its coding demon.
表 4.30 汉字"赢"的拆解及其编码示例

| Character example 例字 | Structure 汉字结构 | Phonetic code-element 字音码元 | | code-element of shape constituents 字形码元 | | | ECCode 汉易码 |
|---|---|---|---|---|---|---|---|
| | | Read as: 读作: | code-element 音码 | $S_1$ 形码1 | $S_2$ 形码2 | $S_3$ 形码3 | |
| | | | | A | Y | A | |
| 赢 | $S_1$ A $S_2$ $B_1$ $B_2$ $S_3$ | yíng | Y | 亠 (丶一) | 月 | 乙 (丶一) | YAYA |
| | | Unknown 不知读音 | ? | | | | ? AYA |

In such a kind of characters as "赢", its part A and part B are shown as follows (Table 4.31).

在像"赢"这类汉字当中,其 A 部分和 B 部分的划分方法如表 4.31 所示。

Table 4.31 Part A and part B of "赢"
表 4.31 汉字"赢"的 A 部分和 B 部分划分方法示例

| Character example 例字 | Part A A 部分 | Part B B 部分 |
|---|---|---|
| | Structure 汉字结构 | |
| 赢 | $S_1$ A $S_2$ $B_1$ $B_2$ $S_3$ $B = B_1 + B_2$ | |
| | 言 | 朋凡 |

145

**Example 4.27** The encoded shape constituents of the character "霞" = (雨) + (⊐) + (又) and is read as /xiá/. Its phonetic code-element is "X" or "?". Its standard Chinese code is "XYEU" and its dictionary query code is "? YEU" according to the PRIORITY rule and the INTEGRITY rule. It is a one-upper-and-two-lower structure character (Table 4.32).

例4.27 汉字"霞"的字形编码组分=(雨)+(⊐)+(又),上一下二结构分体字,读作/xiá/,其字音码元是"X"或者是"?";根据优先律和完整律,其标准代码是"XYEU",字典查询码是"? YEU"(参见表4.32)。

Table 4.32 The disassembly of "霞" and its coding demon.
表4.32 汉字"霞"的拆解及其编码示例

| Character example 例字 | Structure 汉字结构 | Phonetic code-element 字音码元 | | code-element of shape constituents 字形码元 | | | ECCode 汉易码 |
|---|---|---|---|---|---|---|---|
| | | Read as: 读作: | code-element 音码 | $S_1$ 形码1 | $S_2$ 形码2 | $S_3$ 形码3 | |
| 霞 | $S_1$ A / $S_2$ $B_1$ $B_2$ $S_3$ | xiá | X | Y | E | U | XYEU |
| | | Unknown 不知读音 | ? | 雨 | ⊐ | 又 | ? YEU |

**Example 4.28** The encoded shape constituents of the character "范" = (艹) + (氵) + (㔾) and is read as /fàn/. Its phonetic code-element is "F" or "?". Its standard Chinese code is "FCDE" and its dictionary query code is "? CDE" according to the PRIORITY rule and the INTEGRITY rule. It is a one-upper-and-two-lower structure character (Table 4.33).

例4.28 汉字"范"的字形编码组分=(艹)+(氵)+(㔾),上一下二结构分体字,读作/fàn/,其字音码元是"F"或者是"?";根据优先律和完整律,其标准代码是"FCDE",字典查询码是"? CDE"(参见表4.33)。

Chapter 4  How to input a Chinese character without knowing its pronunciation
如何输入不知道读音的汉字

**Table 4.33  The disassembly of "范" and its coding demon.**
**表 4.33  汉字"范"的拆解及其编码示例**

| Character example 例字 | Structure 汉字结构 | Phonetic code-element 字音码元 | | code-element of shape constituents 字形码元 | | | ECCode 汉易码 |
|---|---|---|---|---|---|---|---|
| | | Read as: 读作: | code-element 音码 | $S_1$ 形码1 | $S_2$ 形码2 | $S_3$ 形码3 | |
| | | fàn | F | C | D | E | FCDE |
| | | Unknown 不知读音 | ? | 艹 | 氵 | 巳 | ? CDE |

**Example 4.29**  The encoded shape constituents of the character "茄" = (艹) + (力) + (口) and is read as /qié/. Its phonetic code-element is "Q" or "?". Its standard Chinese code is "QCLK" and its dictionary query code is "? CLK" according to the PRIORITY rule and the INTEGRITY rule. It is a one-upper-and-two-lower structure character (Table 4.34).

例 4.29  汉字"茄"的字形编码组分 = (艹) + (力) + (口),上一下二结构分体字,读作/qié/,其字音码元是"Q"或者是"?";根据优先律和完整律,其标准代码是"QCLK",字典查询码是"? CLK"(参见表 4.34)。

**Table 4.34  The disassembly of "茄" and its coding demon.**
**表 4.34  汉字"茄"的拆解及其编码示例**

| Character example 例字 | Structure 汉字结构 | Phonetic code-element 字音码元 | | code-element of shape constituents 字形码元 | | | ECCode 汉易码 |
|---|---|---|---|---|---|---|---|
| | | Read as: 读作: | code-element 音码 | $S_1$ 形码1 | $S_2$ 形码2 | $S_3$ 形码3 | |
| | | qié | Q | C | L | K | QCLK |
| | | Unknown 不知读音 | ? | 艹 | 力 | 口 | ? CLK |

**Example 4.30**  The encoded shape constituents of the character "茫" = (艹) + (氵) + (一丿) and is read as /máng/. Its phonetic code-element is "M" or "?". Its standard Chinese code is "MCDW" and its dictionary query code is "? CDW" according to the PRIORITY rule and the INTEGRITY rule. It is a one-upper-two-lower structure character (Table 4.35).

**例 4.30**  汉字"茫"的字形编码组分=(艹)+(氵)+(一丿),上一下二结构分体字,读作/máng/,其字音码元是"M"或者是"?";根据优先律和完整律,其标准代码是"MCDW",字典查询码是"? CDW"(参见表 4.35)。

Table 4.35  The disassembly of "茫" and its coding demon.
表 4.35  汉字"茫"的拆解及其编码示例

| Character example 例字 | Structure 汉字结构 | Phonetic code-element 字音码元 | | code-element of shape constituents 字形码元 | | | ECCode 汉易码 |
|---|---|---|---|---|---|---|---|
| | | Read as: 读作: | code-element 音码 | $S_1$ 形码1 | $S_2$ 形码2 | $S_3$ 形码3 | |
| 茫 | $S_1$ A / $S_2$ $B_1$ $B_2$ $S_3$ | máng | M | C | D | W | MCDW |
| | | Unknown 不知读音 | ? | 艹 | 氵 | 匚 (一丿) | ? CDW |

**Example 4.31**  The encoded shape constituents of the character "准" = (氵) + (亻) + (土) and is read as /zhǔn/. Its phonetic code-element is "Z" or "?". Its standard Chinese code is "ZDRT" and its dictionary query code is "? DRT" according to the PRIORITY rule and the INTEGRITY rule. It is a left-right structure character (Table 4.36).

**例 4.31**  汉字"准"的字形编码组分=(氵)+(亻)+(土),左右结构汉字,读作/zhǔn/,其字音码元是"Z"或者是"?";根据优先律和完整律,其标准代码是"ZDRT",字典查询码是"? DRT"(参见表 4.36)。

Chapter 4  How to input a Chinese character without knowing its pronunciation
如何输入不知道读音的汉字

Table 4.36  The disassembly of "准" and its coding demon.
表 4.36  汉字"准"的拆解及其编码示例

| Character example 例字 | Structure 汉字结构 | Phonetic code-element 字音码元 | | code-element of shape constituents 字形码元 | | | ECCode 汉易码 |
|---|---|---|---|---|---|---|---|
| | | Read as: 读作: | code-element 音码 | S₁ 形码1 | S₂ 形码2 | S₃ 形码3 | |
| 准 | A B (S₁ S₂ S₃) | zhǔn | Z | D | R | T | ZDRT |
| | | Unknown 不知读音 | ? | 冫 | 亻 | 土 | ?DRT |

In such kind of characters as "准", its part A and part B are shown as follows (Table 4.37).

在像"准"这类左右结构汉字中,其 A 部分和 B 部分的划分方法如表 4.37 所示。

Table 4.37  Part A and Part B of "准"
表 4.37  像"准"一类左右结构汉字的 A 部分和 B 部分的划分方法

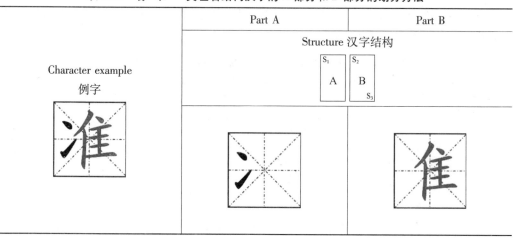

**Example 4.32**  The encoded shape constituents of the character "续" = (幺) + (一丨) + (大) and is read as /xù/. Its phonetic code-element is "X" or "?". Its standard Chinese code is "XUIR" and its dictionary query code is "? UIR" according to the PRIORITY rule and the INTEGRITY rule. It is a left-right structure character (Table 4.38).

例 4.32  汉字"续"的字形编码组分 =(幺)+(一丨)+(大),左右结构汉字,读作 /xù/,其字音码元是"X"或者"?";根据优先律和完整律,其标准代码是"XUIR",字典查询码是"? UIR"(参见表 4.38)。

149

**Table 4.38** The disassembly of "续" and its coding demon.

表 4.38 汉字"续"的拆解及其编码示例

| Character example 例字 | Structure 汉字结构 | Phonetic code-element 字音码元 | | code-element of shape constituents 字形码元 | | | ECCode 汉易码 |
|---|---|---|---|---|---|---|---|
| | | Read as: 读作: | code-element 音码 | $S_1$ 形码1 | $S_2$ 形码2 | $S_3$ 形码3 | |
| 续 | A B (S₁ S₂ S₃) | xù | X | U | I | R | XUIR |
| | | Unknown 不知读音 | ? | 幺 | 十 (一丨) | 大 | ? UIR |

**Example 4.33** The encoded shape constituents of the character "掉" = (扌) + (一丨) + (一丨) and is read as /diào/. Its phonetic code-element is "D" or "?". Its standard Chinese code is "DTII" and its dictionary query code is "? TII" according to the PRIORITY rule and the INTEGRITY rule. It is a left-right structure character (Table 4.39).

例 4.33 汉字"掉"的字形编码组分=(扌)+(一丨)+(一丨),左右结构汉字,读作/diào/,其字音码元是"D"或者"?";根据优先律和完整律,其标准代码是"DTII",字典查询码是"? TII"(参见表 4.39)。

**Table 4.39** The disassembly of "掉" and its coding demon.

表 4.39 汉字"掉"的拆解及其编码示例

| Character example 例字 | Structure 汉字结构 | Phonetic code-element 字音码元 | | code-element of shape constituents 字形码元 | | | ECCode 汉易码 |
|---|---|---|---|---|---|---|---|
| | | Read as: 读作: | code-element 音码 | $S_1$ 形码1 | $S_2$ 形码2 | $S_3$ 形码3 | |
| 掉 | A B (S₁ S₂ S₃) | diào | D | T | I | I | DTII |
| | | Unknown 不知读音 | ? | 扌 | 卜 (一丨) | 十 (一丨) | ? TII |

Chapter 4  How to input a Chinese character without knowing its pronunciation
如何输入不知道读音的汉字

**Example 4.34**  The encoded shape constituents of the character "被" = ( 衤 ) + ( 丿 一 ) + ( 又 ) and is read as /bèi/. Its phonetic code-element is "B" or "?". Its standard Chinese code is "BYFU" and its dictionary query code is "? YFU" according to the PRIORITY rule and the INTEGRITY rule. It is a left-right structure character (Table 4.40).

例 4.34  汉字"被"的字形编码组分 = ( 衤 ) + ( 丿 一 ) + ( 又 ),左右结构汉字,读作/bèi/,其字音码元是"B"或者"?";根据优先律和完整律,其标准代码是"BYFU",字典查询码是"? YFU"(参见表 4.40)。

Table 4.40  The disassembly of "被" and its coding demon.
表 4.40  汉字"被"的拆解及其编码示例

| Character example 例字 | Structure 汉字结构 | Phonetic code-element 字音码元 | | code-element of shape constituents 字形码元 | | | ECCode 汉易码 |
|---|---|---|---|---|---|---|---|
| | | Read as: 读作: | code-element 音码 | $S_1$ 形码1 | $S_2$ 形码2 | $S_3$ 形码3 | |
| 被 ($S_1$ A / $S_2$ B / $S_3$) | | bèi | B | Y | F | U | |
| | | Unknown 不知读音 | ? | 衤 | 厂 (丿一) | 又 | ? YFU |

Through the examples above, it's seen that the reason for choosing a code-element of a shape constituent respectively in Part A and Part B of left-right structure, or Part A, Part $B_1$, and Part $B_2$ of the other two structures of Detached Chinese Characters instead of choosing all code-elements of shape constituents in the same part is to spread and expand the scope of Chinese character information grabbing in order to reduce the rate of coincidental code of Chinese characters.

通过以上举例可以看出,之所以在左右结构汉字中从 A 部分和 B 部分,在其他两种分体字当中从 A 部分与 $B_1$、$B_2$ 各部分分别选择字形组分码元,而不是集中在同一个部分选择所有字形组分码元,就是要分散和扩大汉字信息攫取的范围,以便降低重码率。

### 4.4.2 Examples of encoding Mixed Chinese Characters (MCC)
杂合体字编码范例

Similarly, the method of probabilistic grasping of Chinese character information used in Detached Chinese Character encoding is also used in Mixed Chinese Character encoding. But it is more complex for the MCC because of its heterozygous feature. Furthermore, almost a quarter of the Chinese characters are the MCC defined by the ECCode$^{TM}$. However, there is a basic clue telling you how to disassemble an MCC, which is to see whether the first or the second stroke of an MCC is a constituent of a radical in the ECCode$^{TM}$ or not.

同样地,在杂合体字当中,也采用了分体字编码时所用的那种概率攫取汉字信息的方法。但是,由于杂合体字本身的特点,其情形稍微复杂一些。更有甚者,大约四分之一的汉字都是"汉易码$^{TM}$"所定义的杂合体字。不过,依然有一条线索可资使用,就是要弄清楚这个杂合体字当中包含第一个或第二个笔画的那个部分是不是"汉易码$^{TM}$"的一个字根的组成部分。

Generally speaking, while encoding a MCC, you should gradually become familiar with the Figure 4.5 below which is the encoding flow chart of a MCC. Or conversely, it doesn't matter if you can't remember the flowchart shown as the Figure 4.5 below at a glance. In practice, you will become familiar with the flowchart when you encode Chinese characters against it during encoding exercises.

总地来说,在给杂合体字编码时,你要对图4.5逐渐熟悉起来,这是杂合体字的编码流程图。反过来说,看一眼却记不住这个流程图也没有关系,实际上,你在编码练习时时常对照这个流程图进行汉字编码,就会逐渐熟悉这个流程图了。

Specifically, the following points are worth paying attention to.
具体来说,下面几点值得关注。

(1) If the first and the second strokes compose a radical contained by the ECCode$^{TM}$, according to the PRIORITY rule and the INTEGRITY rule, you should pose the radical's code as the MCC's first shape code-element. Correspondingly, the radical's place is the $S_1$ in Part A—just like the place of the "first bitten part" of the apple (Figure 4.6).

如果这个杂合体字的第一和第二个笔画都是"汉易码$^{TM}$"字根的一个组分部分,根据优先律和完整律,那么你应该选用这个字根作为这个杂合体字的第一个字形码元,相应地,这个字根的位置就是A部分当中的$S_1$处——就像图4.6那个苹果中被咬"第一口"所处的位置。

(2) If not, you should see further that if the second stroke composes a radical in the ECCode$^{TM}$ according to the PRIORITY rule and the INTEGRITY rule. If not either, you should

Chapter 4  How to input a Chinese character without knowing its pronunciation
如何输入不知道读音的汉字

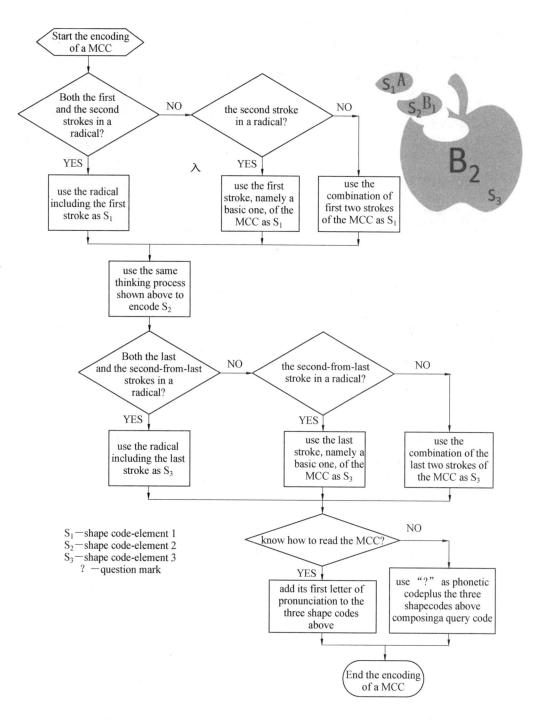

Figure 4.5  The encoding flow chart of the Mixed Chinese Character

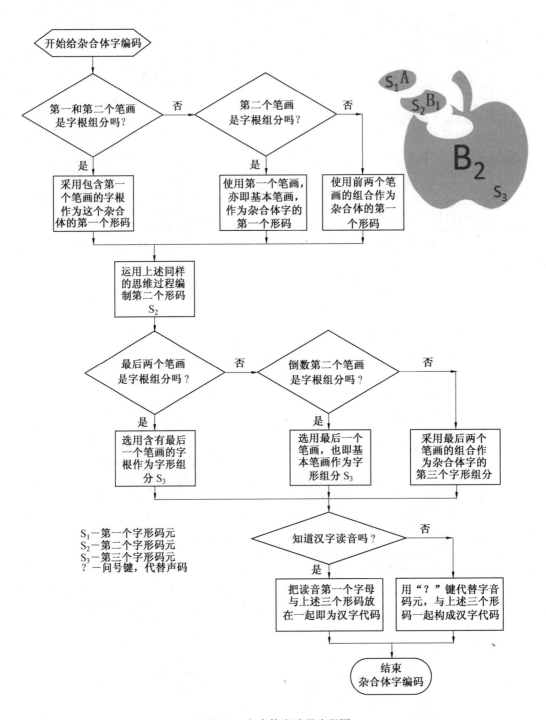

图4.5 杂合体字编码流程图

use the code of the combination of the first two strokes as its first shape code-element. Correspondingly, the place both the first and the second strokes locate is the $S_1$ in the Part A—also like the place of the "first bitten part" of the apple (Figure 4.6).

如果第一个笔画不是"汉易码™"字根的组成部分,那么根据优先律和完整律,大家要进一步弄清楚第二个笔画是否是"汉易码™"字根的一个组成部分。如果第二个笔画也不是字根的组成部分,那么你要选用前两个笔画的组合作为这个杂合体字的第一个字形码元。相应地,这两个笔画所在的位置就是 A 部分中的 $S_1$ 所在位置——也相当于那个苹果被咬第一口所在的位置(参见图4.6)。

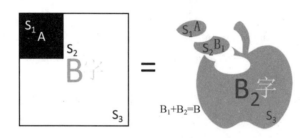

Figure 4.6　A nonfigurative expression of an MCC
图4.6　杂合体字的抽象图示法

(3) If the second stroke composes a radical included in the ECCode™, according to the PRIORITY rule and the INTEGRITY rule, you can only use the first stroke of this MCC, namely a basic stroke, as its first shape constituent, correspondingly, the code of the first stroke is the first shape code-element of the character. And the place where the first stroke stands is $S_1$ in Part A of the character (equivalent to the "first bitten part" of the apple). According to the PRIORITY rule and the INTEGRITY rule, you should use the radical including the second stroke as its second encoded shape constituent. And its second shape code-element is very the code of the radical containing the second stroke. Thus, the place where the radical locates is the $S_2$ in Part B of the character.

如果第二个笔画是"汉易码™"字根的一部分,根据优先律和完整律,你就只能把第一个笔画——亦即基本笔画——作为这个杂合体字的第一个字形码元组分了。相应地,第一个笔画的代码就是这个汉字的第一个形码了。而第一个笔画所处位置就是 A 部分的 $S_1$ 所在位置(相当于那个苹果被咬的第一口所在位置)。根据优先律和完整律,你得选用包含第二个笔画的字根为这个杂合体字的第二个字形编码组分,其第二个形码也就是这个含有第二个笔画的字根的代码。为此,这个含有第二个笔画的字根所在位置就是这个汉字 B 部分的 $S_2$ 所在位置。

(4) After the encoding of the first shape code-element is finished, as to the first two strokes of the Rest Part of the MCC (the Rest Part equivalent to the Part B of the character,

also like the remaining part of the apple after taking only one bite), namely for its second shape constituent (equivalent to the shape constituent located at $S_2$ in the Part B of the character) as well as its shape code-element, you have to repeat the first encoding steps above.

在第一个形码取码完成之后,这个杂合体字相当于苹果被咬掉一口后所剩下的汉字部分的前两个笔画,亦即对这个杂合体的第二个字形编码组分及其代码而言,大家得重复上面第一个编码的步骤。其中,第二个字形组分相当于位于 B 部分的 $S_2$ 所在位置,也是这个杂合体字被取走第一个字形编码对象之后所剩下部分的第一个笔画所在的位置。

(5) For the last encoded shape constituent as well as its shape code-element of the MCC (corresponding the $S_3$ in Part B of the character, see the Figure 4.6), you have to use the encoded shape constituent including the last stroke of the MCC as the source of its last shape code-element, which may be one of a radical, a combination or a basic stroke according to the priority rule and the INTEGRITY rule.

对于这个杂合体字的最后一个字形组分及其代码,其相当于 B 部分字形组分所在的 $S_3$ 位置(参见图 4.6),你得以这个杂合体字包含最后一个笔画的字形组分作为其最后一个字形码元的出处。根据优先律和完整律,这个字形组分可能是一个字根,可能是一个笔画组合,甚至也可能只是一个基本笔画。

Now, let's look at some examples of encoding MCCs.

下面,我们就介绍一些杂合体字的编码例子。

**Example 4.35** For the MCC "春" (read as /chūn/), according to the PRIORITY rule and the INTEGRITY rule as well as the SINGLE rule, its encoding process is shown as follows (Table 4.41).

例 4.35 针对杂合体字"春"(读作/chūn/),根据优先律和完整律以及单一律,其编码过程如下(参见表 4.41)。

**Step 1** Both of the first stroke "一" and the second stroke "一" in "春" do not compose a radical contained by the KMT in the ECCode™, so the first encoded shape constituent of "春" is the stroke combination of "一(read as/héng/)" and "一", namely the two stroke combination of (一一) equivalent to the Part A in the "apple" (see Table 4.41), its corresponding shape code-element $S_1$ is "héng's code" H. Note, the codes of both the stroke (一) and the two stroke combination (一一) are all H.

步骤1 "春"的前两个笔画在这里不是"汉易码™"键位表里面任何一个字根的组分,所以,"春"的第一个字形编码组分是两个"一"笔画的组合(一一),相当于"苹果"的 A 部分(参见表 4.41),其相应的形码 $S_1$ 就是笔画组合(一一)的代码 H。注意,笔画(一)与笔画组合(一一)的代码都是 H。

# Chapter 4  How to input a Chinese character without knowing its pronunciation
如何输入不知道读音的汉字

**Step 2**  After the first shape constituent (一一) having been encoded (taken away from "春"), according to the SINGLE rule, the second encoded shape constituent or encoded shape object should come from the rest part of "春", namely 夯, and the second encoded shape constituent containing the first stroke of 夯 is the radical "大" in the KMT of the ECCode™, which equivalently occupies the part $B_1$ in the "apple" (see Table 4.41). So the second shape code-element of "春" ($S_2$) is the code of radical "大" in the KMT (see Table 3.14 above), i.e., its code is letter "R" because of its shape similarity to the radical "人".

**步骤 2**  在"春"被取走第一个字形组分(一一)之后,根据"单一律"规则,第二个字形编码组分或字形编码对象应该源自"春"所剩下的"夯"部分。而含有"夯"中第一个笔画的字形编码组分是"汉易码™"键位表里面的字根"大"——相当于表4.41当中"苹果"的 $B_1$ 部分。所以"春"的第二个形码($S_2$)就是键位表里面字根"大"的代码(参见前文表3.14,由于字根"大"与字根"人"形相似,所以其代码就是字根"人"的代码R。

**Step 3**  The last stroke (一), the second-from-last stroke (一) and the other two strokes compose the radical "日" in the KMT (the Table 3.14 above), so the third encoded shape constituent ($S_3$) is the radical "日" which equivalently occupies the Part $B_2$ in the "apple" (see Table 4.41), and correspondingly the third shape code-element of "春" ($S_3$) is the code of radical "日", i.e., the letter "R".

**步骤 3**  最后一个笔画"一"与倒数第二个笔画"一"跟其他两个笔画组成了键位表3.14里面的字根"日"——相当于表4.41当中"苹果"的 $B_2$ 部分,即第三个字形编码组分 $S_3$ 为字根"日",相应地,"春"的第三个形码就是字根"日"的代码R。

**Step 4**  Because "春" is read as /chūn/, its phonetic code-element is the letter "C".
**步骤 4**  由于"春"读作/chūn/,所以其字音码元就是字母"C"。

Table 4.41  The disassembly of the MCC "春" and its coding demon.
表4.41  杂合体字"春"的拆解及其编码示例

| Character example 例字 | Structure 汉字结构 | Phonetic code-element 字音码元 | | code-element of shape constituents 字形码元 | | | ECCode 汉易码 |
|---|---|---|---|---|---|---|---|
| | | Read as: 读作: | code-element 音码 | $S_1$ 形码1 | $S_2$ 形码2 | $S_3$ 形码3 | |
| 春 | (apple) | chūn | C | H | R | R | CHRR |
| | | Unknown 不知读音 | ? | (一一) | 大 | 日 | ? HRR |

157

**Conclusion** The Chinese code of "春" is "CHRR". Of course, its query code is "?HRR" if you do not know how to read "春".

结果:"春"的汉字代码是"CHRR"。当然,如果不会读这个字,其字典查询码就是"?HRR"。

**Example 4.36** For the MCC "表（read as /biǎo/）", according to the PRIORITY rule and the INTEGRITY rule as well as the SINGLE rule, its encoding process is shown as follows (Table 4.42).

例4.36 在杂合体字"表"(读作/biǎo/)中,根据优先律和完整律以及单一律,其编码过程如下(参见表4.42)。

**Step 1** The second stroke of "表" and the following two strokes compose the radical "土" in the KMT shown as Table 3.14 which cannot be separated into basic strokes, so its first encoded shape constituent is necessarily the first stroke (一), only one stroke, equivalently occupying the Part A in the "apple" (see Table 4.42). And its first shape code-element ($S_1$) of "表" is just the code of the first stroke of "表", namely the code "H" for the basic stroke (一).

步骤1 由于"表"的第二个笔画与其后面的两个笔画构成了键位表3.14中不能拆成基本笔画的字根"土",所以其第一个字形编码组分就只能是第一个笔画(一)了——相当于下面表4.42当中"苹果"的A部分,而其第一个形码($S_1$)就只能是"表"字的第一个笔画亦即基本笔画(一)的代码H了。

**Step 2** Obviously, the second shape code-element ($S_2$) of "表" is the code "T" for the radical "土" in the KMT shown as the Table 3.14 above, which equivalently occupies the Part $B_1$ in the "apple" (see Table 4.42). It is also the first shape code-element ($S_2$) of the rest part "衣" of "表" which has been taken the first stroke (一) away.

步骤2 很明显,第二个字形码元($S_2$)就是键位表3.14中字根"土"的代码T了,它也是"表"被取走第一个笔画(一)后所剩下部分"衣"的第一个字形组分的代码。这个字根"土"在"表"字当中的位置就相当于表4.42当中那个"苹果"的$B_1$位置。

**Step 3** None of the last two strokes in the part $B_2$ "ᄉ" of the character "表" don't form any radical in the KMT shown as Table 3.14 with any other strokes, so the last shape code-element ($S_3$) of "表" is the code "V" of the two stroke combination (丿、) because of the stroke "㇏" being taken as the stroke "、", and (丿、) = (、丿). And the place of the last two strokes is equivalent to the site $S_3$ or the part $B_2$ in the "apple" (see Table 4.42).

步骤3 由于"表"字最后两个笔画"ᄉ"中没有一个笔画是键位表3.14中某个字根的组分,即"ᄉ"中的最后两个笔画没有与其他任何笔画组成键位表3.14中的任何一个字根,所以,根据笔画约定,笔画捺"㇏"被视作"、",同时(丿、)=(、丿),"表"字的最后一个字形码元就是笔画组合(、丿)的代码 V。而这最后两个笔画的位置就相当于"苹果"中的 $S_3$ 或 $B_2$ 位置(参见表 4.42)。

**Step 4** "表" is read as /biǎo/, so its phonetic code-element is the letter "B".

**步骤4** 由于"表"读作/biǎo/,所以其字音码元就是字母 B。

**Conclusion** The Chinese code of "表" is "BHTV". Of course, its query code is "? HTV" if you do not know how to read "表" (see Table 4.42).

**结果** "表"字的代码就是 BHTV。当然,如果不会读这个字,其字典查询码就是"? HTV"(参见表 4.42)。

Table 4.42 The disassembly of the MCC "表" and its coding demon.
表 4.42 杂合体字"表"的拆解及其编码示例

| Character example 例字 | Structure 汉字结构 | Phonetic code-element 字音码元 | | code-element of shape constituents 字形码元 | | | ECCode 汉易码 |
|---|---|---|---|---|---|---|---|
| | | Read as: 读作: | code-element 音码 | $S_1$ 形码1 | $S_2$ 形码2 | $S_3$ 形码3 | |
| 表 | | biǎo | B | H | T | V | BHTV |
| | | Unknown 不知读音 | ? | 一 (一) | 土 | ㇏ (、丿) | ? HTV |

**Example 4.37** For the MCC "严 (read as /yán/)", according to the PRIORITY rule, the INTEGRITY rule, and the SINGLE rule, its encoding process is shown as follows (See Table 4.43).

**例 4.37** 对于杂合体字"严"(读作/yán/)而言,根据优先律、完整律和单一律,其编码过程如下(参见表 4.43)。

**Step 1** The first two strokes in "严" do not compose a radical included in the KMT shown as the Table 3.14, so the first shape code-element ($S_1$) of "严" is the code "I" for the combination (一丨). And correspondingly the first encoded object locates equivalently at the $S_1$ or the Part A in the "apple" of the Table 4.43.

**步骤1** 由于"严"中前两个笔画没有组成表 3.14 中的一个字根,所以"严"的第一个字形码元($S_1$)就是笔画组合(一丨)的代码。相应地,其第一个编码对象位于类似表 4.43

159

中那个"苹果"的 $S_1$ 处或 A 部分。

**Step 2** However, the second stroke "丶" of the rest part "产" of "严" composes a radical "㇌" in the KMT shown as the Table 3.14 with its both following strokes "丿" and "一", so the second shape code-element ($S_2$) of "严" is the code "I" for only the one stroke "丨" according to the INTEGRITY rule, and its place is located equivalently at the Site $S_2$ or the Part $B_1$ in the "apple" of Table 4.43.

**步骤 2** 不过,由于"严"被取走(一丨)之后剩余部分"产"的第二个笔画"丶"与紧随其后的两个笔画"丿"和"一"构成了键位表 3.14 中的字根"㇌"。所以,根据完整律,"严"的第二个形码($S_2$)就是单个笔画"丨"的代码了,其编码对象的位置大致相当于表 4.43 中"苹果"的 $S_2$ 或 $B_1$ 处。

**Step 3** The second-from-last stroke "一" and the other two strokes "丶" "丿" in front of it compose the radical "㇌", so the last shape code-element ($S_3$) of "严" is the code "P" for the only one stroke "丿" according to the PRIORITY rule and the INTEGRITY rule, which is a basic stroke, also the last stroke of 严, its place is located equivalently at the site $S_3$ or the Part $B_2$ in the "apple" in Table 4.43. For the character "严", even though the second-from-last stroke "一" and the last stroke "丿" compose the radical "厂" in the KMT shown as Table 3.14, i.e., the radical "㇌" and the radical "厂" share the same stroke "一", the stroke "一" should be given to the radical "㇌" according to the PRIORITY rule for the more strokes in radical "㇌".

**步骤 3** 由于"严"的倒数第二个笔画"一"与其前面的另两个笔画组成了键位表 3.14 当中的字根"㇌",所以,依据优先律和完整律,"严"的最后一个形码($S_3$)就只能是基本笔画"丿"的代码了——这个"丿"也是汉字"严"的最后一个笔画,其大致位置就相当于表 4.43 当中那个"苹果"的 $S_3$ 或 $B_2$ 处。虽然在"严"字中,倒数第二个笔画"一"与最后一个笔画"丿"组成了键位表 3.14 里面的字根"厂",即字根"㇌"与字根"厂"共享了笔画"一",但由于字根"㇌"比字根"厂"拥有更多的笔画,所以,根据优先律,笔画"一"应该划归给字根"㇌"。

**Step 4** "严" is read as /yán/, so its phonetic code-element is the letter "Y".

**步骤 4** 由于"严"读作/yán/,所以其字音码元就是字母 Y。

**Conclusion** The Chinese code of "严" is "YIIP". Of course, its query code is "?IIP" if you do not know how to read "严"。

**结果** 汉字"严"的代码就是 YIIP。当然,如果大家不会读这个"严"字,那么其字典查询码就是"?IIP"。

# Chapter 4  How to input a Chinese character without knowing its pronunciation
如何输入不知道读音的汉字

**Table 4.43**  The disassembly of the MCC "严" and its coding demon.
表4.43  杂合体字"严"的拆解及其编码示例

| Character example 例字 | Structure 汉字结构 | Phonetic code-element 字音码元 | | code-element of shape constituents 字形码元 | | | ECCode 汉易码 |
|---|---|---|---|---|---|---|---|
| | | Read as: 读作: | code-element 音码 | $S_1$ 形码1 | $S_2$ 形码2 | $S_3$ 形码3 | |
| 严 | (apple) | yán | Y | I | I | P | YIIP |
| | | Unknown 不知读音 | ? | 一 (一丨) | 丨 (丨) | 丿 (丿) | ? IIP |

**Example 4.38**  For the MCC "我 ( read as /wǒ/)", according to the four encoding rules, its encoding process is shown as follows (See Table 4.44).

例4.38  对于杂合体字"我"(读作/wǒ/),根据"四个编码规则",其编码过程如下(参见表4.44)。

**Step 1**  The second stroke "一" of "我" and the two following strokes "亅" and "丿" compose a radical "扌(扌)", so the first shape code-element ($S_1$) of "我" is the code "P" for the first stroke "丿" of "我" according to the PRIORITY rule and the INTEGRITY rule, and the first encoded shape object is located equivalently at the site $S_1$ or the Part A in the "apple" of the Table 4.44. (Here, it is suggested to look at the encoding flowchart of a MCC in order to strengthen the matters needing special attention when encoding rules are applied to MCCs.)

**步骤1**  由于"我"的第二个笔画"一"与紧随其后的两个笔画"亅"和"丿"组成了一个字根"扌(扌)",所以,根据优先律和完整律,"我"的第一个字形码元($S_1$)就是"我"的第一个笔画"丿"的代码P,其第一个字形编码对象的位置大致相当于表4.44当中那个"苹果"的$S_1$或A部分。(在此建议看看杂合体字编码流程图以便强化编码规则在杂合体字当中应用时需要特别关注的事项。)

**Step 2**  Obviously, the second shape code-element ($S_2$) of "我" is the code "T" for the radical "扌(扌)", its place is equivalently at the $S_2$ or the Part $B_1$ in the "apple" of Table 4.44.

**步骤2**  显然,"我"的第二个字形码元($S_2$)就是字根"扌(扌)"的代码T。其大致位置相当于表4.44中那个"苹果"的$S_2$或$B_1$处。

**Step 3**  The last and the second-from-last strokes of "我" are not constituents composing a radical in the KMT shown as Table 3.14, i.e., both of them are not included in a radical, the last shape code-element ($S_3$) of "我" is the code "V" for the stroke combination "丿、", and its place is located equivalently at the site $S_3$ or the Part $B_2$ in the "apple" in Table 4.44.

**步骤3**  由于"我"的最后一个笔画和倒数第二个笔画不是键位表3.14中任何一个字根的组成成分,即这两个笔画不是字根的一部分,所以,"我"的最后一个字形码元($S_3$)就是笔画组合(丿、)的代码V,其大致位置就相当于表4.44当中那个"苹果"的$S_3$或$B_2$处。

**Step 4**  "我" is read as /wǒ/, so its phonetic code-element is the letter "W".
**步骤4**  "我"读作/wǒ/,所以其字音码元就是字母W。

**Conclusion**  The Chinese code of "我" is "WPTV". Of course, its query code is "? PTV" if you do not know how to read "我".
**结果**  "我"的汉字代码就是WPTV。当然,如果大家不会读"我"字,其字典查询码是"? PTV"。

Table 4.44  The disassembly of the MCC "我" and its coding demon.
表4.44  杂合体字"我"的拆解及其编码示例

| Character example 例字 | Structure 汉字结构 | Phonetic code-element 字音码元 | | code-element of shape constituents 字形码元 | | | ECCode 汉易码 |
|---|---|---|---|---|---|---|---|
| | | Read as: 读作: | code-element 音码 | $S_1$ 形码1 | $S_2$ 形码2 | $S_3$ 形码3 | |
| 我 | | wǒ | W | P | T | V | WPTV |
| | | Unknown 不知读音 | ? | 一 (丿) | 扌 | 丶 (、丿) | ? PTV |

**Example 4.39**  For the MCC "在" (read as /zài/), according to the PRIORITY rule and the INTEGRITY rule, its encoding process is shown as follows (See Table 4.45 below).

例4.39  对于杂合体字"在"(读作/zài/)来说,依据优先律和完整律,其编码过程如下(参见表4.45)。

**Step 1**  The first two strokes are not constituents composing a radical in the KMT shown in Table 3.14, so the first encoded shape constituent is the stroke combination of (一丿)

which locate equivalently at the site $S_1$ or the Part A in the "apple" in Table 4.45, namely the first and the second strokes "ナ" of "在", therefore the first shape code-element ($S_1$) of "在" is the code "O" for the combination (一丿).

步骤1　由于"在"的第一个和第二个笔画不是键位表3.14中任何一个字根的组成部分,所以"在"的第一个字形编码组分就是这两个笔画的组合(一丿)了,即汉字"在"的第一个和第二个笔画"ナ"的组合,其编码对象的位置相当于表4.46中"苹果"的$S_1$处或A部分。所以,"在"字的第一个形码($S_1$)就是其第一个和第二个笔画"ナ"的组合(一丿)之代码O。

**Step 2**　The second stroke "一" of the rest part "䒑" of "在" and its following two strokes "丨" and "一" compose the radical "土", so the second encoded shape constituent is only one stroke "丨", namely the first stroke of the rest part "䒑" of "在", which locates equivalently at the $S_2$ or the Part $B_1$ in the "apple" in Table 4.45. And correspondingly the second shape code-element ($S_2$) of "在" is the code "I" for the first stroke "丨" of the rest part "䒑" of "在" according to the PRIORITY rule and the INTEGRITY rule.

步骤2　由于"在"字被取走"ナ"即笔画组合(一丿)后,所剩下部分"䒑"的第二个笔画"一"与紧随其后的两个笔画"丨"和"一"组成了字根"土",所以,"在"的第二个字形编码组分即编码对象就只能是一个单独的笔画"丨"了,就是汉字"在"被取走第一个编码对象即笔画组合(一丿)之后所剩下的"䒑"里面的第一个笔画"丨",其位置则相当于表4.45中"苹果"的$S_2$处或$B_1$部分。相应地,根据优先律和完整律,其第二个字形码元($S_2$)就只能是汉字"在"被取走第一个字形组分之后所剩部分"䒑"里面的第一个笔画"丨"的代码I了。

**Step 3**　The last stroke "一" and the second-from-last stroke "丨" are respectively a constituent composing the radical "土", so its last shape code-element ($S_3$) of "在" is the code "T" for the radical "土" according to the PRIORITY rule and the INTEGRITY rule, and its place is located equivalently at the site $S_3$ or the Part $B_2$ in the "apple" in Table 4.45.

步骤3　"在"的最后一个笔画和倒数第二个笔画都是字根"土"的组成部分,所以,依据优先律和完整律,它的最后一个字形码元($S_3$)就是字根"土"的代码T,其位置相当于表4.45当中那个"苹果"的$S_3$或$B_2$处。

**Step 4**　"在" is read as /zài/, so its phonetic code-element is the letter "Z".

步骤4　由于"在"读作/zài/,所以其字音码元就是字母Z。

**Conclusion**　The Chinese code of "在" is "ZOIT". Of course, its query code is "?OIT" if you do not know how to read "在".

结果　"在"的汉字代码就是ZOIT。当然,如果不知道这个汉字"在"如何读的话,其字典查询码就是"？OIT"。

Table 4.45   The disassembly of the MCC "在" and its coding demon.
表 4.45   杂合体字"在"的拆解及其编码示例

| Character example 例字 | Structure 汉字结构 | Phonetic code-element 字音码元 | | code-element of shape constituents 字形码元 | | | ECCode 汉易码 |
|---|---|---|---|---|---|---|---|
| | | Read as: 读作: | code-element 音码 | $S_1$ 形码1 | $S_2$ 形码2 | $S_3$ 形码3 | |
| 在 | | zài | Z | O | I | T | ZOIT |
| | | Unknown 不知读音 | ? | ナ (ノ 一) | 丨 (丨) | 土 土 | ? OIT |

**Example 4.40**   For the MCC "束"(read as /shù/), according to the PRIORITY rule and the INTEGRITY rule, its encoding process is shown as follows (See Table 4.46 below).

例 4.40   对于杂合体字"束"(读作/shù/)，依据优先律和完整律，其编码过程如下(参见表4.46)。

**Step 1**   The second stroke "丨" of "束" is a constituent composing the radical "冂" or the radical "口", so the first encoded shape constituent can only be the stroke (一) under the constraints of the four encoding rules, correspondingly, the first shape code-element ($S_1$) of "束" is the code "H" for the first stroke "一" of "束" according to the PRIORITY rule and the INTEGRITY rule.

步骤 1   由于"束"的第二个笔画"丨"是字根"冂"或字根"口"的一个组成部分，所以，在四个编码规则的约束下，编码对象只能是笔画"一"了。相应地，根据优先律和完整律，"束"的第一个字形码元($S_1$)就只能是第一个笔画"一"的代码 H 了。

**Step 2**   Attention, please. The fourth-from-last stroke "一" is shared by both of the front radical "口" and the latter radical "木"(here "front and latter" refers to the "front and latter" on the stroke order and in the following examples is also the same meaning), but due to the latter radical "木" with more strokes, so the fourth-from-last stroke "一" should be given to the latter radical "木" rather than the radical "口" according to the PRIORITY rule and the INTEGRITY rule, even though the radical "口" is written first in stroke order. Therefore, the second shape code-element ($S_2$) of "束" is the code "L" for the radical "冂" rather than the code "K" for the radical "口" according to the PRIORITY rule and the INTEGRITY rule.

Chapter 4　How to input a Chinese character without knowing its pronunciation
如何输入不知道读音的汉字

That is to say, the PRIORITY rule and the INTEGRITY rule are one level higher than the STROKE ORDER rule in the priority of rule execution—please remember this point.

**步骤 2**　这里需要注意一下,"束"的倒数第四个笔画"一"被前面的字根"口"和后面的字根"木"所共享了(这里的"前后"是指笔顺上的"前后",下面举例当中也是这个意思),但由于后面这个字根"木"比字根"口"拥有更多的笔画,所以,尽管前面那个字根"口"在书写时其笔顺比字根"木"的笔顺更靠前,但根据优先律和完整律,倒数第四个笔画"一"应该划归给后面那个字根"木"而不是"口"。因此,依据优先律和完整律,"束"字的第二个字形码元($S_2$)就是字根"冂"的代码 L 而不是字根"口"的代码 K。也就是说,优先律和完整律在规则执行的优先级别上要比笔顺规则高一个等级——请记住这一点。

**Step 3**　Here the last two strokes and the other two strokes are constituents composing the radical "木", so the last shape code-element ($S_3$) of "束" is the code "M" for the radical "木".

**步骤 3**　在此,"束"字的最后两个笔画与另外两个笔画一起组成了字根"木",所以,"束"的最后一个字形码元($S_3$)就是字根"木"的代码 M。

**Step 4**　"束" is read as ／shù／, so its phonetic code-element is the letter "S".

**步骤 4**　由于"束"读作/shù/,所以其字音码元就是字母 S.

**Conclusion**　The Chinese code of "束" is "SHLM". Of course, its query code is "? HLM" if you do not know how to read "束". And where every encoded shape object or encoded shape constituent locates is shown equivalently in the "apple" in Table 4.46.

**结果**　汉字"束"的代码就是 SHLM。当然,如果大家不会读"束",那么其字典查询码就是"? HLM"。而每个字形编码对象或字形编码组分的位置则在表 4.46 的"苹果"中标示了出来。

Table 4.46　The disassembly of the MCC "束" and its coding demon.
表 4.46　杂合体字"束"的拆解及其编码示例

| Character example 例字 | Structure 汉字结构 | Phonetic code-element 字音码元 | | code-element of shape constituents 字形码元 | | | ECCode 汉易码 |
|---|---|---|---|---|---|---|---|
| | | Read as: 读作: | code-element 音码 | $S_1$ 形码 1 | $S_2$ 形码 2 | $S_3$ 形码 3 | |
| | | shù | S | H | L | M | SHLM |
| | | Unknown 不知读音 | ? | 一 =(一) | 冂 | 木 | ? HLM |

**Example 4.41** For the MCC "夹" (read as ∕jiā∕), according to the PRIORITY rule and the INTEGRITY rule, its encoding process is shown as follows (See Table 4.47 below).

**例 4.41** 对于杂合体字"夹"(读作/jiā/),依据优先律和完整律,其编码过程如下(参见表4.47)。

**Step 1** The second stroke "丶" combined with the following strokes "丿" and "一" is a constituent composing the radical "龴" in the KMT shown as Table 3.14, so the first shape code-element ($S_1$) of "夹" can only be the code "H" for the first stroke "一" of "夹" according to the PRIORITY rule and the INTEGRITY rule.

**步骤1** 由于"夹"字的第二个笔画"丶"与紧随其后的两个笔画"丿"和"一"一起组成了键位表3.14中的字根"龴",所以,根据优先律和完整律,"夹"的第一个字形码元($S_1$)就只能是"夹"的第一个笔画"一"的代码H了。

**Step 2** Attention, please. The third-from-last stroke "一" in the character "夹" is shared by both of the front radical "龴" and the latter radical "大". Furthermore, both of these two radicals have the same number of strokes. However, the shared stroke "一" should be given priority to the front radical "龴" in light of the stroke order as well as the PRIORITY rule and the INTEGRITY rule. In other words, priority should be given to ensuring the integrity of the previous radical—the integrity of the radical in front of the stroke order is given priority when the number of the strokes is the same, so the second shape code-element ($S_2$) of "夹" is the code "V" for the radical "龴".

Please contrast this example with Example 4.40 above discussed just now—their similarity and difference can strengthen your understanding of the usage of the four encoding rules.

**步骤2** 这里也有一点需要注意,这就是"夹"的倒数第三个笔画"一"被前面的字根"龴"和后面的字根"大"所共有。更有甚者,这两个字根的笔画数量一样。但是,根据笔顺规则以及优先律和完整律,这个共享笔画"一"应该优先考虑划归给前面那个字根"龴",即要优先确保前面那个字根"龴"的完整性——当共享一个笔画的前后两个字根的笔画数相同时,要优先确保笔顺靠前的字根的完整性。所以,"夹"的第二个形码($S_2$)就是字根"龴"的代码V。

请与前面刚刚讲解过的例4.40对比一下——其异同点有助于强化对四个编码规则之用法的理解。

**Step 3** Obviously, after the first encoded shape object "一" and the second encoded shape object "龴" have been taken away, the third encoded shape constituent or encoded shape object can only be the radical "人". Correspondingly, the third shape code-element ($S_3$) of "夹" is the code "R" for the radical "人".

**步骤3** 很明显,在第一个编码对象"一"和第二个编码对象"龴"取码了之后,第三个编码对象就只能是字根"人"了。相应地,"夹"的第三个形码($S_3$)就是字根"人"的代

Chapter 4　How to input a Chinese character without knowing its pronunciation
如何输入不知道读音的汉字

码 R。

**Step 4**　"夹" is read as /jiā/, so its phonetic code-element is the letter "J".
**步骤 4**　由于"夹"读作/jiā/,所以其字音码元就是字母 L。

**Conclusion**　So the Chinese code of "夹" is "JHVR". Of course, its query code is "? HVR" if you do not know how to read "夹".
**结果**　"夹"的汉字代码是"JHVR"。当然,大家如果不知道怎么读"夹"字,那么其字典查询码就是"? HVR"。

Table 4.47 **The disassembly of the MCC "夹" and its coding demon.**
表 4.47　杂合体字"夹"的拆解及其编码示例

| Character example 例字 | Structure 汉字结构 | Phonetic code-element 字音码元 | | code-element of shape constituents 字形码元 | | | ECCode 汉易码 |
|---|---|---|---|---|---|---|---|
| | | Read as: 读作: | code-element 音码 | $S_1$ 形码1 | $S_2$ 形码2 | $S_3$ 形码3 | |
| 夹 | | jiā | J | H | V | R | JHVR |
| | | Unknown 不知读音 | ? | 一 =(一) | 丷 (丷) | 人 | ? HVR |

Here are some more examples of how to encode a Mixed Chinese Character by the ECCode™, simply through table illustration. Among these examples, the hollow strokes indicated as "⌒" also indicate that such strokes are not used in Chinese character encoding. In other words, they belong to the Chinese character writing information that are not collected by the Chinese character encoding ECCode™.

下面简单地用表格示例一些有关如何用"汉易码™"给杂合体字编码的例子。在这些示例当中,像"⌒"这样的空心笔画表示此类笔画在汉字编码时没有成为编码信息。即这些笔画所承载的汉字信息是"汉易码™"所不予考虑的汉字书写信息。

**Example 4.42**　The encoded shape objects or encoded shape constituents of the character "第" = (⺮) + (⊐) + (丿丨), and it is read as /dì/. Its phonetic code-element is "D" or "?". Its standard code is "DZEO" and its dictionary query code is "? ZEO" if you do not know how to read it (See Table 4.48 below).

**例 4.42**　汉字"第"的字形编码对象或字形编码组分 = (⺮)+(⊐)+(丿丨),读作

167

/dì/,其字音码元是"D"或者"?",其标准代码是"DZEO",如果大家不知道这个字怎么读,其字典查询码是"? ZEO"(参见表4.48)。

Table 4.48　The disassembly of "第" and its coding demon.
表4.48　杂合体字"第"的拆解及其编码示例

| Character example 例字 | Structure 汉字结构 | Phonetic code-element 字音码元 | | code-element of shape constituents 字形码元 | | | ECCode 汉易码 |
|---|---|---|---|---|---|---|---|
| | | Read as: 读作: | code-element 音码 | S₁ 形码1 | S₂ 形码2 | S₃ 形码3 | |
| 第 | | dì | D | Z | E | O | DZEO |
| | | Unknown 不知读音 | ? | ⺮ | ⼆ | 丿(丿丨) | ? ZEO |

**Example 4.43**　The encoded shape objects or encoded shape constituents of the character "承" = (子) + (一一) + (丶丿), and it is read as /chéng/. Its phonetic code-element is "C" or "?". Its standard code is "CZHV" and its dictionary query code is "? ZHV" if you do not know how to read it (See Table 4.49).

例4.43　汉字"承"的字形编码对象或字形编码组分=(子)+(一一)+(丶丿),该字读作/chéng/。所以其字音码元是字母"C"或者是"?"——如果大家不知道怎么读这个字的话,其标准代码是"CZHV",字典查询码是"? ZHV"(参见表4.49)。

Table 4.49　The disassembly of "承" and its coding demon.
表4.49　杂合体字"承"的拆解及其编码示例

| Character example 例字 | Structure 汉字结构 | Phonetic code-element 字音码元 | | code-element of shape constituents 字形码元 | | | ECCode 汉易码 |
|---|---|---|---|---|---|---|---|
| | | Read as: 读作: | code-element 音码 | S₁ 形码1 | S₂ 形码2 | S₃ 形码3 | |
| 承 | | chéng | C | Z | H | V | CZHV |
| | | Unknown 不知读音 | ? | 了(丨→) | 二(一一) | ㇏(丶丿) | ? HVR |

168

Chapter 4  How to input a Chinese character without knowing its pronunciation
如何输入不知道读音的汉字

**Example 4.44**  The encoded shape objects or encoded shape constituents of the character "爽" = (丿一) + (丶丿) + (人), and it is read as /shuǎng/. Its phonetic code-element is "S" or "?". Its standard code is "SOVR" and its dictionary query code is "? OVR" if you do not know how to read it (See Table 4.50).

例 4.44  汉字"爽"的字形编码对象或字形编码组分 = (丿一) + (丶丿) + (人), 读作 /shuǎng/, 所以其音码是"S"; 如果不知道怎么读这个字的话, 其音码也可以是"?"。汉字 "爽"的标准代码是"SOVR", 字典查询码是"? OVR"(参见表 4.50)。

Table 4.50  The disassembly of "爽" and its coding demon.
表 4.50  杂合体字"爽"的拆解及其编码示例

| Character example 例字 | Structure 汉字结构 | Phonetic code-element 字音码元 | | code-element of shape constituents 字形码元 | | | ECCode 汉易码 |
|---|---|---|---|---|---|---|---|
| | | Read as: 读作: | code-element 音码 | $S_1$ 形码1 | $S_2$ 形码2 | $S_3$ 形码3 | |
| 爽 | (B₂) | shuǎng | S | O | V | R | SOVR |
| | | Unknown 不知读音 | ? | ア (一丿) | ⁊ (丶丿) | 人 | ? OVR |

**Example 4.45**  The encoded shape objects or encoded shape constituents of the character "母" = (乛乛) + (丶一) + (丶), and it is read as /mǔ/. So, its phonetic code-element is "M" or "?". Its standard code is "MZAD" and its dictionary query code is "? ZAD" if you do not know how to read it (See Table 4.51 below).

例 4.45  汉字"母"的字形编码对象或字形编码组分 = (乛乛) + (丶一) + (丶), 读作 /mǔ/, 所以其字音码元是"M"或者"?"——如果不知道这个字怎么读的话, 其标准代码是 "MZAD", 字典查询码是"? ZAD"(参见表 4.51)。

**Table 4.51** The disassembly of "母" and its coding demon.
表 4.51　杂合体字"母"的拆解及其编码示例

| Character example 例字 | Structure 汉字结构 | Phonetic code-element 字音码元 | | code-element of shape constituents 字形码元 | | | ECCode 汉易码 |
|---|---|---|---|---|---|---|---|
| | | Read as: 读作: | code-element 音码 | S₁ 形码1 | S₂ 形码2 | S₃ 形码3 | |
| 母 | | mǔ | M | Z | A | D | MZAD |
| | | Unknown 不知读音 | ? | (⊃⊂) = (⊃) | (、一) | 、 | ? ZAD |

**Example 4.46**　The encoded shape objects or encoded shape constituents of the character "壹" = (士) + (冖) + (丷), and it is read as /yī/. Its phonetic code-element is "Y" or "?". Its standard code is "YTBV" and its dictionary query code is "? TBV" if you do not know how to read it (See Table 4.52 below).

例 4.46　汉字"壹"的字形编码对象或字形编码组分 = (士) + (冖) + (丷), 该字读作 /yī/, 所以其字音码元是"Y"; 如果不知道怎么读这个字, 字音码元就是"?"。汉字"壹"的标准代码是"YTBV", 字典查询码是"? TBV"(参见表 4.52)。

**Table 4.52** The disassembly of "壹" and its coding demon.
表 4.52　杂合体字"壹"的拆解及其编码示例

| Character example 例字 | Structure 汉字结构 | Phonetic code-element 字音码元 | | code-element of shape constituents 字形码元 | | | ECCode 汉易码 |
|---|---|---|---|---|---|---|---|
| | | Read as: 读作: | code-element 音码 | S₁ 形码1 | S₂ 形码2 | S₃ 形码3 | |
| 壹 | | yī | Y | T | B | V | YTBV |
| | | Unknown 不知读音 | ? | 士 | 冖 | 丷 | ? TBV |

Chapter 4 How to input a Chinese character without knowing its pronunciation
如何输入不知道读音的汉字

**Example 4.47** The encoded shape objects or encoded shape constituents of the character "聋" = (尢) + (丶丿) + (耳), and it is read as /lóng/. Its phonetic code-element is "L" or "?". Its standard code is "LUVE" and its dictionary query code is "? UVE" if you do not know how to read it (See Table 4.53 below).

**例 4.47** 汉字"聋"的字形编码对象或字形编码组分 = (尢)+(丶丿)+(耳),该字读作/lóng/,所以其字音码元是"L"或者是"?"。如果你不会读这个字,可用问号键代替字音码元。汉字"聋"的标准代码是"LUVE",字典查询码是"? UVE"(参见表 4.53)。

Table 4.53 The disassembly of "聋" and its coding demon.
表 4.53 杂合体字"聋"的拆解及其编码示例

| Character example 例字 | Structure 汉字结构 | Phonetic code-element 字音码元 | | code-element of shape constituents 字形码元 | | | ECCode 汉易码 |
|---|---|---|---|---|---|---|---|
| | | Read as: 读作: | code-element 音码 | $S_1$ 形码1 | $S_2$ 形码2 | $S_3$ 形码3 | |
| 聋 | | lóng | L | U | V | E | LUVE |
| 聋 | | Unknown 不知读音 | ? | 尢 | 丶丿 (ⅴ) | 耳 | ? UVE |

**Example 4.48** The encoded shape objects or encoded shape constituents of the character "病" = (疒) + (一) + (人), and it is read as /bìng/. Its phonetic code-element is "B" or "?". Its standard code is "BGHR" and its dictionary query code is "? GHR" if you do not know how to read it (See Table 4.54 below).

**例 4.48** 汉字"病"的字形编码对象或字形编码组分 = (疒)+(一)+(人),读作/bìng/,所以其字音码元是"B"或者是"?"(不会读这个字时用问号键代替字音码元)。其标准代码是"BGHR",字典查询码是"? GHR"(参见表 4.54)。

171

**Table 4.54** The disassembly of "病" and its coding demon.
表 4.54 杂合体字"病"的拆解及其编码示例

| Character example 例字 | Structure 汉字结构 | Phonetic code-element 字音码元 | | code-element of shape constituents 字形码元 | | | ECCode 汉易码 |
|---|---|---|---|---|---|---|---|
| | | Read as: 读作: | code-element 音码 | $S_1$ 形码1 | $S_2$ 形码2 | $S_3$ 形码3 | |
| 病 | | bìng | B | G | H | R | BGHR |
| | | Unknown 不知读音 | ? | 疒 | 一 (一) | 人 | ? GHR |

**Example 4.49** The encoded shape objects or encoded shape constituents of the character "包" = ( 丿 ㇇ ) + ( ⊐ ) + ( 乚 ), and it is read as /bāo/. Its phonetic code-element is "B" or "?". Its standard code is "BFEZ" and its dictionary query code is "? FEZ" if you do not know how to read it (See Table 4.55 below).

例 4.49 汉字"包"的字形编码对象或字形编码组分 = ( 丿 ㇇ ) + ( ⊐ ) + ( 乚 ), 该字读作 /bāo/, 其字音码元是"B"或者是"?"——如果不知道怎么读这个字的话。其标准代码是"BFEZ", 字典查询码是"? FEZ"(参见表 4.55)。

**Table 4.55** The disassembly of "包" and its coding demon.
表 4.55 杂合体字"包"的拆解及其编码示例

| Character example 例字 | Structure 汉字结构 | Phonetic code-element 字音码元 | | code-element of shape constituents 字形码元 | | | ECCode 汉易码 |
|---|---|---|---|---|---|---|---|
| | | Read as: 读作: | code-element 音码 | $S_1$ 形码1 | $S_2$ 形码2 | $S_3$ 形码3 | |
| 包 | | bāo | B | F | E | Z | BFEZ |
| | | Unknown 不知读音 | ? | 勹 (丿㇇) | ⊐ | 乚 (一) | ? FEZ |

Chapter 4  How to input a Chinese character without knowing its pronunciation
如何输入不知道读音的汉字

**Example 4.50**  The encoded shape objects or encoded shape constituents of the character "司" = (一㇆) + (口), and it is read as /sī/. Its phonetic code-element is "S" or "?". Its standard code is "SWK" and its dictionary query code is "? WK" if you do not know how to read it (See Table 4.56 below).

例 4.50  汉字"司"的字形编码对象或字形编码组分 = (一㇆) + (口),该字读作/sī/,所以其字音码元是"S"或者是"?"——如果不知道怎么读这个字的话。汉字"司"的标准代码是"SWK",字典查询码是"? WK"(参见表4.56)。

Table 4.56  The disassembly of "司" and its coding demon.
表 4.56  杂合体字"司"的拆解及其编码示例

| Character example 例字 | Structure 汉字结构 | Phonetic code-element 字音码元 | | code-element of shape constituents 字形码元 | | ECCode 汉易码 |
|---|---|---|---|---|---|---|
| | | Read as: 读作: | code-element 音码 | $S_1$ 形码1 | $S_2$ 形码2 | |
| 司 | | sī | S | W | K | SWK |
| | | Unknown 不知读音 | ? | ㇆ (一㇆) | 口 | ? WK |

**Example 4.51**  The encoded shape objects or encoded shape constituents of the character "国" = (囗) + (王) + (丶一), and it is read as /guó/. Its phonetic code-element is "G" or "?". Its standard code is "GLWA" and its dictionary query code is "? LWA" if you do not know how to read it (See Table 4.57 below).

例 4.51  汉字"国"的字形编码对象或字形编码组分 = (囗) + (王) + (丶一),该字读作/guó/,所以其字音码元是"G"或者是"?"——如果不知道这个字怎么读的话。汉字"国"的标准代码是"GLWA",字典查询码是"? LWA"(参见表4.57)。

Table 4.57  The disassembly of "国" and its coding demon.
表 4.57  杂合体字"国"的拆解及其编码示例

| Character example 例字 | Structure 汉字结构 | Phonetic code-element 字音码元 | | code-element of shape constituents 字形码元 | | | ECCode 汉易码 |
|---|---|---|---|---|---|---|---|
| | | Read as: 读作: | code-element 音码 | $S_1$ 形码1 | $S_2$ 形码2 | $S_3$ 形码3 | |
| 国 | | guó | G | L | W | A | GLWA |
| | | Unknown 不知读音 | ? | 冂 | 王 | 二 (、一) | ? LWA |

**Example 4.52**  The encoded shape objects or encoded shape constituents of the character "再" = (一) + (冂) + (一一), and it is read as /zài/. Its phonetic code-element is "Z" or "?". Its standard code is "ZHLH" and its dictionary query code is "? HLH" if you do not know how to read it (See Table 4.58 below).

例 4.52  汉字"再"的字形编码对象或字形编码组分 = (一) + (冂) + (一一),读作/zài/,所以其字音码元是"Z"或者是"?"——如果不知道怎么读这个字的话。这个汉字的标准代码是"ZHLH",字典查询码是"? HLH"(参见表 4.58)。

Table 4.58  The disassembly of "再" and its coding demon.
表 4.58  杂合体字"再"的拆解及其编码示例

| Character example 例字 | Structure 汉字结构 | Phonetic code-element 字音码元 | | code-element of shape constituents 字形码元 | | | ECCode 汉易码 |
|---|---|---|---|---|---|---|---|
| | | Read as: 读作: | code-element 音码 | $S_1$ 形码1 | $S_2$ 形码2 | $S_3$ 形码3 | |
| 再 | | zài | Z | H | L | H | ZHLH |
| | | Unknown 不知读音 | ? | 一 (一) | 冂 | 二 (一一) | ? HLH |

**Attention**  For the character "再", there are not three successive strokes composing the radical "土" according to stroke order (Note: here writing "the third-from-last stroke" first of the character "再", but in "土" the first stroke is the "一"). So, through this example, you

Chapter 4    How to input a Chinese character without knowing its pronunciation
如何输入不知道读音的汉字

can see that the inverted stroke order would affect the correctness of encoding a Chinese character in some situations. Of course, the ECCode™ provides some fault-tolerant codes for such characters.

注意:在"再"字当中,根据笔顺规则,没有三个连续的笔画组成一个字根"土"(注意,这里的"再"字当中,先写倒数第三个笔画,而"土"中第一个笔画则是"一")。所以,通过这个例字,大家应该看到,"倒笔画"会在有些时候影响到正确地给汉字编码。当然了,"汉易码™"在这种情况下往往提供了容错码。

**Example 4.53**    The encoded shape objects or encoded shape constituents of the character "画" = (一) + (冂) + (凵), and it is read as /huà/. Its phonetic code-element is "H" or "?". Its standard code is "HHLS" and its dictionary query code is "? HLS" if you do not know how to read it (See Table 4.59 below).

**例 4.53**    汉字"画"的字形编码对象或字形编码组分=(一)+(冂)+(凵),该字读作/huà/,所以其字音码元是"H"或者是"?"——如果不知道怎么读这个字的话。该字的标准代码是"HHLS",字典查询码是"? HLS"(参见表4.59)。

Table 4.59    The disassembly of "画" and its coding demon.
表4.59    杂合体字"画"的拆解及其编码示例

| Character example 例字 | Structure 汉字结构 | Phonetic code-element 字音码元 | | code-element of shape constituents 字形码元 | | | ECCode 汉易码 |
|---|---|---|---|---|---|---|---|
| | | Read as: 读作: | code-element 音码 | $S_1$ 形码1 | $S_2$ 形码2 | $S_3$ 形码3 | |
| 画 | | huà | H | H | L | S | HHLS |
| | | Unknown 不知读音 | ? | (一) | 冂 | 凵 | ? HLS |

**Example 4.54**    The encoded shape objects or encoded shape constituents of the character "笔" = (⺮) + (丿一) + (一㇏), and it is read as /bǐ/. Its phonetic code-element is "B" or "?". Its standard code is "BZOW" and its dictionary query code is "? ZOW" if you do not know how to read it (See Table 4.60 below).

**例 4.54**    汉字"笔"的字形编码对象或字形编码组分=(⺮)+(丿一)+(一㇏),该字读作/bǐ/,所以其字音码元是"B"或者是"?"——如果不知道怎么读这个字的话。该字的标准代码是"BZOW",字典查询码是"? ZOW"(参见表4.60)。

**Table 4.60** The disassembly of "笔" and its coding demon.

表 4.60 杂合体字"笔"的拆解及其编码示例

| Character example 例字 | Structure 汉字结构 | Phonetic code-element 字音码元 | | code-element of shape constituents 字形码元 | | | ECCode 汉易码 |
|---|---|---|---|---|---|---|---|
| | | Read as: 读作: | code-element 音码 | $S_1$ 形码1 | $S_2$ 形码2 | $S_3$ 形码3 | |
| 笔 | | bǐ | B | Z | O | W | BZOW |
| | | Unknown 不知读音 | ? | ⺮ (丿一) | = (一一) | 七 (一乛) | ? ZOW |

**Example 4.55** The encoded shape objects or encoded shape constituents of the character "戈" = (一乛) + (丶丿), and it is read as /gē/. Its phonetic code-element is "G" or "?". Its standard code is "GWV" and its dictionary query code is "? WV" if you do not know how to read it (See Table 4.61 below).

例 4.55 汉字"戈"的字形编码对象或字形编码组分 = (一乛) + (丶丿),该字读作 /gē/,所以其字音码元是"G"或者是"?"——如果不知道怎么读这个字的话。该字的标准代码是"GWV",字典查询码是"? WV"(参见表 4.61)。

**Table 4.61** The disassembly of "戈" and its coding demon.

表 4.61 杂合体字"戈"的拆解及其编码示例

| Character example 例字 | Structure 汉字结构 | Phonetic code-element 字音码元 | | code-element of shape constituents 字形码元 | | ECCode 汉易码 |
|---|---|---|---|---|---|---|
| | | Read as: 读作: | code-element 音码 | $S_1$ 形码1 | $S_2$ 形码2 | |
| 戈 | | gē | G | W | V | GWV |
| | | Unknown 不知读音 | ? | 七 (一乛) | 丿 (丶丿) | ? WV |

Chapter 4  How to input a Chinese character without knowing its pronunciation
如何输入不知道读音的汉字

**Example 4.56**  The encoded shape objects or encoded shape constituents of the character "必" = (、⁻) + (、丿) + (、), and it is read as /bì/. Its phonetic code-element is "B" or "?". Its standard code is "BAVD" and its dictionary query code is "? AVD" if you do not know how to read it.

**例 4.56**  汉字"必"的字形编码对象或字形编码组分 = (、⁻)+(、丿)+(、),该字读作 /bì/,所以其字音码元是"B"或者是"?"——如果不知道怎么读这个字的话。该字的标准代码是"BAVD",字典查询码是"? AVD"。

**Attention**  According to the stroke order, there is no radical "心" in "必" because the two strokes "、" are separated by the stroke "丿" (See Table 4.62 below).

**注意**:根据笔顺规则,这个"必"字当中没有字根"心",因为两个笔画"、"被笔画"丿"给分隔开了(参见表4.62)。

Table 4.62  The disassembly of "必" and its coding demon.
表 4.62  杂合体字"必"的拆解及其编码示例

| Character example 例字 | Structure 汉字结构 | Phonetic code-element 字音码元 | | code-element of shape constituents 字形码元 | | | ECCode 汉易码 |
|---|---|---|---|---|---|---|---|
| | | Read as: 读作: | code-element 音码 | $S_1$ 形码1 | $S_2$ 形码2 | $S_3$ 形码3 | |
| 必 | | bì | B | A | V | D | BAVD |
| | | Unknown 不知读音 | ? | 心 (、⁻) | 丿 (、丿) | 、 (、) | ? AVD |

## 4.5  The encoding method and examples of Chinese characters with unknown pronunciation
## 未知读音汉字的编码方法及其举例

It has been mentioned previously that the question mark key "?" can be used for any code-element that you don't know. That is to say, it can be used when the user does not know how to pronounce or write a Chinese character.

前面已经提及过问号键"?"可以用来代表任何一个读者所不知道的码元了,也就是说,当用户不知道汉字怎么发音或某个笔画怎么写时,可以用问号键"?"来代替字音码元或字形码元。

177

# A Crash Course on KEYLEARNING and KEYWRITING for Chinese
# 汉字键学与键写简明教程

**Example 4.57** If you do not know how to pronounce the character "浙" [ the encoded shape constituents of "浙" = ( 氵) + ( 扌) + ( 斤) = DTJ ], you can use "? DTJ" to look up "浙" ( See Table 4.63 below).

**例4.57** 如果用户不知道这个"浙"字怎么读,其中"浙"的字形组分是:"浙"=(氵) +(扌)+(斤)=DTJ,那么用户可以输入"? DTJ"来查字典(参见表4.63)。

Table 4.63  Code of the character "浙" while not knowing its pronunciation
表4.63  不知道读音时"浙"字的代码

| Chinese character 汉字 | Computer code 代码 | code-element 码元 | | | |
|---|---|---|---|---|---|
| | | Phonetic-code 音码 | Shape-code-1 ($S_1$)形码1 | Shape-code-2 ($S_2$)形码2 | Shape-code-3 ($S_3$)形码3 |
| 浙 | ? DTJ | ? | D(氵) | T(扌) | J(斤) |

When the code "? DTJ" is typed into the computer or the smartphone, there will be a window on the screen (Figure 4.7). Then the user can choose key 1 (No. 1) and input the character into a computer or an e-dictionary to look it up.

当用户输入"? DTJ"进电脑或智能手机后,屏幕上会弹出一个如图4.7所示的窗口。然后用户就可以点击数字键"1"来选择这个意欲查询的"浙"字了。

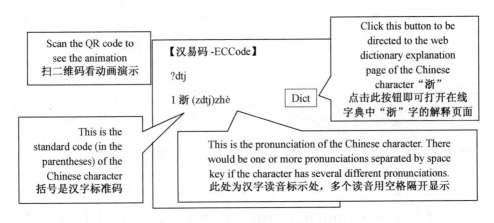

Figure 4.7  Character display box
图4.7  汉字显示框示例

In Figure 4.7, the button "Dict" links to the explanatory page of "浙" in the online dictionary provided by the ECCode™. The user can open the explanatory page of the word "浙" by clicking this button.

在图4.7中,按钮Dict链接到"汉易码™"提供的在线字典中"浙"的解释页面。用户点击这个按钮即可打开"浙"字的解释页面。

Chapter 4    How to input a Chinese character without knowing its pronunciation
如何输入不知道读音的汉字

If you know neither the pronunciation of "浙", nor how to write the encoded shape constituent or encoded shape object "扌", correspondingly not knowing the code of "扌", you can use two question mark keys "?" to replace its phonetic code and the shape code of "扌". That is to say, you only needs to type "? D? J" then there will be a window on the screen (Figure 4.8). Click the "◁▷" key to go to the up/next page until the character "浙" appears in the character list. Since the rate of coincident code in the ECCode™ is very low, usually the target character would be on the first page and there's no need to turn the page.

如果你既不知道怎么读这个"浙"字,也不知道第二个字形编码对象"扌"怎么写,相应地也就不知道第二个字形编码对象"扌"的形码了。那么你可以用两个问号键"?"来代替字音码元和有关的字形码元。即你只需输入"? D? J"即可在屏幕上弹出如图 4.8 所示的窗口。点击翻页键"◁▷"即可查找目标汉字"浙",直到找到位置。由于"汉易码™"的重码率极低,所以几乎不用翻页就可找到目标汉字。通常情况下,常用字会在第一页显示出来而无须翻页。

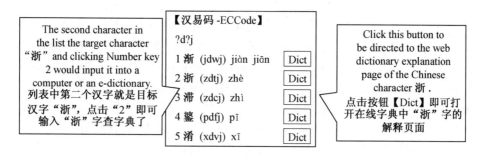

Figure 4.8    Illustration of a display box with more than one question mark key "?" while inputting a character
图 4.8    多个问号键"?"情况下的输入显示框示例

If type four question mark keys "????" in the ECCode™ software, the window will show the target character starting from the first page of the dictionary. And browse through all the pages until the target Chinese character appears.

如果你在"汉易码™"中输入汉字时,四个码元全部使用问号键"????",那么就相当于从字典的第一页一直翻下去,直到找到目标汉字为止。

## 4.6  Phrase input method
## 词组输入方法

For most people, after mastering Chinese language, using Chinese as the working language of paperless office may be a high probability demand. In this case, the speed of keywriting Chinese characters appears very important. At this point, it will be found that the speed of typing depends to a large extent not only on how many phrases people have mastered but also on whether the input method software provides powerful phrase functions.

对大多数人来说,学成汉语之后,想要把汉语作为无纸化办公的工作语言就是一项大概率的需求了。在这种情况下,键写汉字的速度就显得非常重要了。此时,人们将会发现,打字速度的快慢,在很大程度上不仅取决于大家的词组掌握了多少,也取决于输入法软件是否提供了强大的词组功能。

On this account, the ECCode™ provides phrases and associative functions for the need of future paperless office. That is, when a Chinese character is inputted, all phrases in the lexicon that begin with the character are automatically displayed. The display order is initially the default order in the lexicon, and then the order adjusted by its character frequency.

为此,"汉易码™"也为未来无纸化办公的需要提供了词组及联想功能。即当输入一个汉字后,词库中所有的以该汉字起头的词组都会自动显示出来,其显示顺序初始设计为词库内默认的顺序,以后会依据词频变化调整词组联想显示顺序。

Since foreign Chinese learners do not have the concept of Chinese phrases at the beginning of learning Chinese, they can only input one Chinese character at a time. So, the function of the phrase association can deepen foreign Chinese learners' understanding and cognition for Chinese phrases.

由于外国汉语学习者在开始学习汉语的初期还没有汉语的词组概念,只能一个字一个字地输入,所以,词组联想功能可以加深外国汉语学习者对汉语词组的体会和认知。

Now, let's look at the phrase function and its rules of ECCode™.
下面,介绍一下"汉易码™"的词组功能与规则。

(1) Phrase displayed after the characters in the window.
   词组都显示在字的后面

Chapter 4　How to input a Chinese character without knowing its pronunciation
　　　　　如何输入不知道读音的汉字

(2) Four letters rule: any phrase is simply entered in no more than 4 letters.

采用4码原则，即词组只需输入最多4个码即可。

(3) Phrase encoding formula.

词组取码公式。

In the ECCode™, there are different formulas according to the different character number in a phrase.

"汉易码™"词组根据词组汉字数量的不同而有不同的编码公式与之对应.

● The formula for a phrase including two characters
　双字词输入公式

　　　　　The code of a phrase including two characters
　　　　= Phonetic code-element of 1st character+
　　　　　1st shape code-element of 1st character+
　　　　　phonetic code-element of 2nd character+
　　　　　1st shape code-element of 2nd character
　　　　　　双字词编码=第一个字的音码+
　　　　　　　　　　　第一个字的形码 $S_1$+
　　　　　　　　　　　第二个字的音码+
　　　　　　　　　　　第二个字的形码 $S_1$

For example, the code of the phrase "组织" is shown in Figure 4.9 below.

例如，词组"组织"的编码如图4.9所示。

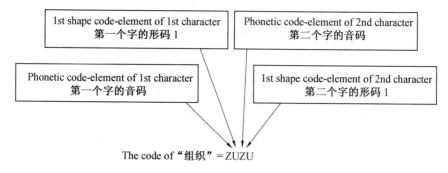

Figure 4.9　Illustration of the code for a phrase
including two characters
图4.9　双字词编码举例

● The phoneme-shape code formula for a phrase including three characters
　三字词输入公式

The code of a phrase including three characters
= Phonetic code-element of 1st character+
1st shape code-element of 1st character+
phonetic code-element of 2nd character+
phonetic code-element of 3rd character

三字词编码＝第一个字的音码＋
第一个字的形码1＋
第二个字的音码＋
第三个字的音码

For example, the code of the phrase "输入法" is shown in Figure 4.10 below.
例如,词组"输入法"的编码如图4.10所示。

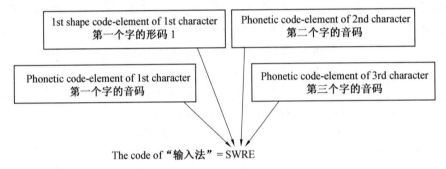

Figure 4.10　Illustration of the code for a phrase including three characters
图4.10　三字词编码举例

- The phoneme-shape code formula for a phrase including no less than four characters
  四字及以上词组的输入公式

The code of a phrase including no less four characters
= Phonetic code-element of 1st character+
Phonetic code-element of 2nd character+
Phonetic code-element of 3rd characte+
Phonetic code-element of 4th character

四字及以上词组的编码＝第一个字的音码＋
第二个字的音码＋
第三个字的音码＋
第四个字的音码

For example, the code of the phrase "规章制度" is shown in Figure 4.11.
例如,词组"规章制度"的编码如图4.11所示。

Chapter 4  How to input a Chinese character without knowing its pronunciation
如何输入不知道读音的汉字

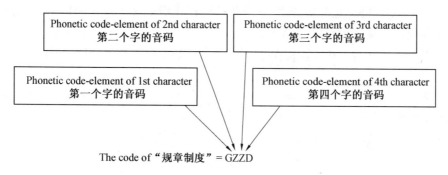

Figure 4.11　Illustration of the code for a phrase
including four characters

图 4.11　四字词编码举例

Another example, the code of the phrase "中华人民共和国" is shown in Figure 4.12.
再比如,词组"中华人民共和国"的编码如图 4.12 所示。

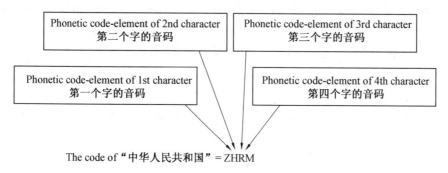

Figure 4.12　Illustration of the code for a phrase
including more than four characters

图 4.12　四个字以上词组编码举例

Besides, the ECCode™ also provides a phrase-making function. In the future, according to feedback from users, more optimization may be done on the method of phrase input. Please keep an eye on the updating information on the official website.

此外,"汉易码™"也提供造词功能。今后,根据用户的反馈,可能会在词组输入方法上做更多优化,请随时关注官方网站的更新提示信息。

# Review 4
# 复习题 4

Q1:"长" is a polyphone having two kinds of pronunciation which are respectively /cháng/ and /zhǎng/. Which one of the following answer group is the correct phonetic code-elements of the two voices?

183

思考题 1：汉字"长"是个多音字，它的两种读音分别是/cháng/和/zhǎng/。请问下面哪组答案是这两个读音的正确音码？

A.（ch, zh）     B.（áng, ǎng）     C.（c, z）     D.（ɑng）

Q2：Which of the following four answers is the first encoded shape constituent or object, namely $S_1$, of the character "我"?

思考题 2：下面哪一个选项是汉字"我"的第一个形码（$S_1$）？

A.（丿）     B.（丿一）     C.（丿丨）

Q3：In the character "两", which of the following choices is the first encoded shape constituent or object, namely $S_1$, of it?

思考题 3：下面哪一个选项是"两"字的第一个形码（$S_1$）？

A.（一丨）     B.（一）     C.（丿一）

Q4：Which of the following choices is the second encoded constituent or object, namely $S_2$, of the character "毯"?

思考题 4：下面哪一个选项是汉字"毯"的第二个形码（$S_2$）？

A.（一㇀）     B. 火

Q5：In the character "邀", which of the following choices is the second encoded constituent or object, namely $S_2$, of it?

思考题 5：下面哪一个选项是汉字"邀"的第二个形码（$S_2$）？

A. 方     B. 夂

Q6：In the character "赢", which of the following choices is the second encoded constituent or object, namely $S_2$, of it?

思考题 6：下面哪一个选项是汉字"赢"的第二个形码（$S_2$）？

A.（亠）     B.（口）     C.（月）     D.（丨一）

Q7：Please point out which of the following choices is the last encoded shape constituent or object, namely $S_3$, of the character "解".

思考题 7：下面哪一个选项是汉字"解"的最后一个形码（$S_3$）？

A.（一丨）     B. 牛

Q8：Which of the following choices is the last encoded shape constituent or object, namely $S_3$, of the character "夷"?

思考题 8：下面哪一个选项是汉字"夷"的最后一个形码（$S_3$）？

A.（丶丿）     B. 人

# Chapter 4  How to input a Chinese character without knowing its pronunciation
## 如何输入不知道读音的汉字

Q9: Which of the following choices is the last encoded shape constituent or object, namely $S_3$, of the character "我"?

思考题 9：下面哪一个选项是汉字"我"的最后一个形码($S_3$)？

A. (丶丿)        B. (丿一)

Q10: Which of the following choices is the last encoded shape constituent or object, namely $S_3$, of the three characters "冉""里", and "重"?

思考题 10：下面哪一个选项是汉字"冉""里"和"重"的末位形码($S_3$)？

A. (一)          B. 土

Q11: Which of the following choices is the last encoded shape constituent or object, namely $S_3$, of the two characters "谏" and "辣"?

思考题 11：下面哪一个选项是这两个汉字"谏"和"辣"的末位形码($S_3$)？

A. 木            B. 朩

Q12: Which of the following choices is the last encoded shape constituent or object, namely $S_3$, of the two characters "事" and "争"?

思考题 12：下面哪一个选项是这两个汉字"事"和"争"的末位形码($S_3$)？

A. (一丨)        B. (一亅)

Q13: Which of the following choices is the first encoded shape constituent or object, namely $S_1$, of the character "舜"?

思考题 13：下面哪一个选项是汉字"舜"的第一个形码($S_1$)？

A. (丿)          B. (丶丿)

Q14: Which of the following choices contains respectively the first and the second encoded shape constituents or objects, namely $S_1$ and $S_2$, of the character "米"?

思考题 14：下面哪一个选项分别包含了汉字"米"的第一个形码($S_1$)和第二个形码($S_2$)？

A. (丶丿),木     B. 丷,朩

Q15: Which of the following choices is the second encoded shape constituent or object, namely $S_2$, of the character "郑"?

思考题 15：下面哪一个选项是汉字"郑"的第二个形码($S_2$)？

A. (一)          B. 大          C. 阝

Q16: Which of the following choices is the second encoded shape constituent or object,

namely $S_2$, of the character "鹅"?
思考题16：下面哪一个选项是汉字"鹅"的第二个形码（$S_2$）？
A.（一丨）　　　　　B. 扌　　　　　C. 鸟

Q17：Please fill in the cells in Table 4.64 according to the template.
思考题17：请按照样板在表4.64空白格中填空。

**Table 4.64**
表 4.64

| Chinese characters 汉字 | code-elements of encoded shape constituents or encoded shape objects （字形编码组分或字形编码对象的）字形码元 | | |
|---|---|---|---|
| | $S_1$ | $S_2$ | $S_3$ |
| （Template 样板）将 | D | F | C |
| 就 | | | |
| 引 | | | |
| 张 | | | |
| 强 | | | |
| 些 | | | |
| 华 | | | |
| 器 | | | |
| 型 | | | |
| 众 | | | |
| 前 | | | |
| 命 | | | |
| 品 | | | |
| 花 | | | |
| 素 | | | |
| 置 | | | |
| 美 | | | |
| 老 | | | |
| 者 | | | |
| 道 | | | |
| 重 | | | |
| 表 | | | |

Q18：If you do not know how to read the character "谓" and the second encoded constituent or object (namely $S_2$), but know that its $S_1$ and $S_3$ are respectively (丶㇇) and

Chapter 4  How to input a Chinese character without knowing its pronunciation
如何输入不知道读音的汉字

"月", and you want to look it up in any e-dictionary of Chinese language. At this time, which characters should be entered in the prompt column of the ECCode™?

思考题 18:如果你不知道"谓"字的读音和第二个形码,仅知道第一个形码是(、一)和最后一个形码是"月"。此时,应该在汉易码提示栏输入哪几个字符?

Q19:Please fill in the codes of various phrases with the ECCode™ in Table 4.65 below.
思考题 19:请填写出表 4.65 中各类词组的"汉易码™"编码。

**Table 4.65**
表 4.65

| Categories<br>类型 | Phrases<br>词组 | Codes<br>编码 |
|---|---|---|
| Two character word<br>双字词 | gōng rén<br>工人 | |
| | rì yuè<br>日月 | |
| | nǚ shì<br>女士 | |
| | tǒng yī<br>统一 | |
| | shì guān<br>士官 | |
| | rì qī<br>日期 | |
| | zǔ zhī<br>组织 | |
| | kàn fǎ<br>看法 | |
| | tiān é<br>天鹅 | |
| | rú guǒ<br>如果 | |

Table4.65(Continued)　表4.65(续)

| Categories 类型 | Phrases 词组 | Codes 编码 |
|---|---|---|
| Three character word 三字词 | yí zhì xìng 一致性 | |
| | dòng tíng hú 洞庭湖 | |
| | gōng yè huà 工业化 | |
| | dà zhòng huà 大众化 | |
| | xiàn dài huà 现代化 | |
| | gòng chǎn dǎng 共产党 | |
| | yùn dòng yuán 运动员 | |
| | jiā ná dà 加拿大 | |
| | bó shì shēng 博士生 | |
| | lǐng dǎo rén 领导人 | |
| Word with more than four characters 四字以上词组 | zhōng huá rén mín gòng hé guó 中华人民共和国 | |
| | zhōng guó gòng chǎn dǎng 中国共产党 | |
| | qí tóu bìng jìn 齐头并进 | |
| | pái shān dǎo hǎi 排山倒海 | |
| | píng yì jìn rén 平易近人 | |
| | pò bù jí dài 迫不及待 | |
| | pǔ tiān tóng qìng 普天同庆 | |
| | qī shàng bā xià 七上八下 | |
| | qióng tú mò lù 穷途末路 | |
| | chī mèi wǎng liǎng 魑魅魍魉 | |

# Appendixes
# 附录

## Appendix 1  Encoding flow chart of ECCode™
## 附录1  "汉易码™"编码流程图

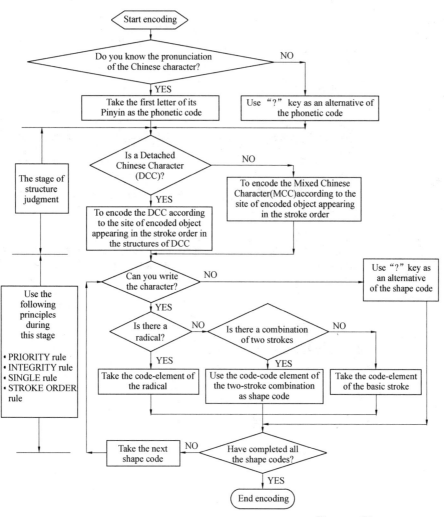

Encoding flow chart of the Easy Chinese Code™ (ECCode™)

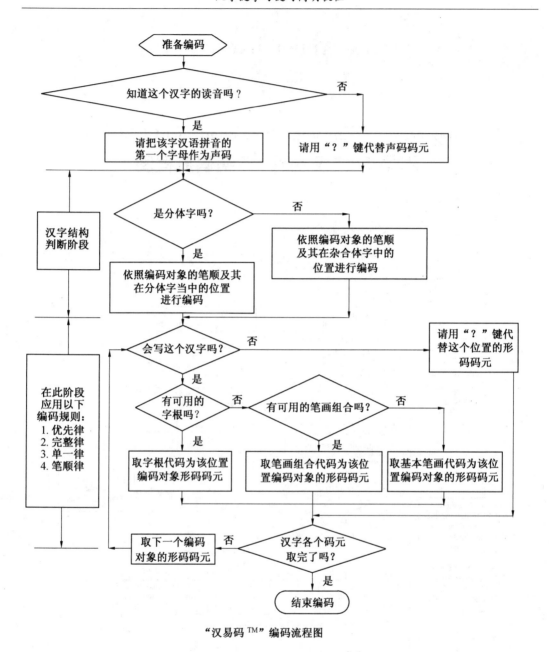

"汉易码™"编码流程图

# Appendix 2  Glossary
# 附录2  术语

Adjacent/ Noncontact Relation 分离关系 64
Computer Chinese Character (CCC for short), 计算机汉字, 8
Computer Chinese Character Code(CCCC for short), 计算机汉字编码, 11
Computer Chinese Character Theory (CCCT for short), 计算机汉字理论, 11
Chinese Character Encoding Method(CCEM for short), 汉字编码方法, 11
Chinese Character Keylearning (CCKL for short), 汉字键学, 7
Chinese Character Keywriting (CCKW for short), 汉字键写, 7
Component, 部件, 18
Connecting Relation, 相连关系, 65
Constituent, 组分, 7
Detached Chinese Character (DCC for short), 分体字, 99
Evaluation Index System(EIS for short), 评估指标体系, 13
Encoded Object or Encoded Constituent, 编码对象或编码组分, 122
Encoding Law, 编码规律, 122
Encoding Scheme (ES for short), 编码方案, 11
Encoding Theory (ET for short), 编码理论, 11
Final, 韵母, 30
Five-stroke, 五笔, 9
Initial, 声母, 20
THE INTEGRITY RULE, 完整律, 116
Intersection Relation, 交叉关系, 64
Key Mapping Table, KMT, (汉字字形组分)键位表, 86
Keywrite, (动词)键写, 65
Law of Visual Memory(LVM for short), 视觉记忆规律, 121
Logographic Language(LL for short), 语标性语言, 11
Macro Stroke Order(MaSO for short), 宏观笔顺, 105
Mixed Chinese Character (MCC for short), 杂合体字, 101
Micro Stroke Order(MiSO for short), 微观笔顺, 105
Phonetic Constituent(PC for short), 语音组分, 8
Phonetic Code(PC for short), 音码, 111
Phonetic Code-Element, 字音码元, 112
Position Relation(PR for short), 笔画位置关系, 63
THE PRIORITY RULE, 优先律, 114
Radical, 字根, 18
Rate of Coincidental Code(RCC for short), 重码率, 79
Shape Constituent (SC for short), 字形组分, 8
Shape Code-Element(SCE or SC for short), 字形码元, 87
Shape Code(SC for short), 形码, 111
THE SINGLE RULE, 单一律, 116
Stroke, 笔画, 18
Stroke Order(SO for short), 笔顺, 102
Tone, 声调, 54
Two Stroke Combination(TSC for short), 两笔画组合, 79

# References
# 参考文献

[1] LIU X. New practical Chinese reader[M]. 2nd Edition. Beijing: Beijing Language and Culture University Press, 2013.
    刘珣. 新实用汉语课本[M]. 2版. 北京:北京语言大学出版社,2013.

[2] KLAYMAN G S, ZHAO Y F. Urban Chinese[M]. Beijing: Beijing Language and Culture University Press, 2002.
    KLAYMAN G S, ZHAO Y F. 地道汉语[M]. 北京:北京语言大学出版社,2002.